The Theology of John

The Theology of John

by

W. Robert Cook, Th.D.
Academic Vice-President and Dean of Faculty
Professor of Biblical Theology
Western Conservative Baptist Seminary
Portland, Oregon

MOODY PRESS
CHICAGO

Library of Congress Cataloging in Publication Data

Cook, W. Robert.
The theology of John.

Bibliography: p. 252
Includes indexes.
1. Bible. N. T. Johannine literature—
Theology. 2. Bible. N. T. Revelation—Theology.
I. Title.
BS2601.C57 230 79–10261
ISBN 0–8024–8629–0

Printed in the United States of America

TO ELAINE,

a helper truly suited to me;
an excellent wife, whose worth is far more precious than jewels.
"Many daughters have done nobly,
but you excel them all" (Prov. 31:29).

Contents

Preface

At the outset, before this work is even well begun, an element of risk has already been introduced into this subject. In addition to making an attempt to give a serious treatment to a subject such as Johannine theology from a conservative vantage point (thus going against the preponderant tide of contemporary scholarship), I have designated the very first section as a preface. Who, in this age of instant everything, takes the time or cares enough to read a preface? Let it be said for the record, however, that just as every other author desires that his preface be read, so do I.

I write these words while on a sabbatical leave in Israel, where I am enjoying living, teaching, and learning. Just recently two incidents of a most refreshing nature have come to my attention; both augur well for theology in the middle of the seventh decade of the twentieth century. To hope that the two occurrences will have their potential salutary effects upon theological thinking in our day may be to look for more than may be reasonably expected, but hope we must.

The two things to which I refer above are as disparate as a prestigious gathering of American theologians in Hartford, Connecticut, and a professor in a class in the Hebrew University in Jerusalem. Recently, at the Hartford convocation of theologians (most of whom are of avowed liberal theological persuasion), there went forth a plea for a return of American theology to an emphasis upon the transcendent and the theological in contrast to the recent emphasis upon the immanent and the anthropological.[1] Certainly more than a shift in emphasis is

[1]The statement begins: "The renewal of Christian witness and mission requires constant examination of the assumptions shaping the Church's life. Today an apparent

necessary, but it is most interesting to hear liberals affirming what some conservatives have been saying for years. *The Theology of John* is premised upon the transcendence of the one true God, who is at the same time immanent in the universe. He has revealed Himself in propositional and verbally accurate form in the Scriptures. While His purposes include man in a prominent way, man's fulfillment is not in self-assertion or in realization of his ultimate humanity; rather, man's fulfillment is in submission to and demonstration of the glory of God. God, not man, is the standard by which all things are measured.

At about the same time as that of the Hartford convocation but many thousands of miles distant from it, a professor at the Hebrew University set forth an atypical but valid methodology for the teaching of a course titled "The Biblical Conception of Man." Despite much peer and student pressure to the contrary, he insisted in letting the text of the Bible *speak for itself.* When such questions as What do the rabbis say? or Don't you think it means such and such? were raised, he insisted on determining what the biblical record said and leaving it at that. Thus he was making an attempt to employ objectively an inductive approach to the study of Scripture, which approach has been all but forgotten by the majority of modern critical scholars. The inductive approach is the one taken in *The Theology of John.* I do not intend to overlook or minimize the need for and legitimacy of theological deduction (the exercise of the analogy of faith); rather, I want to emphasize the need to eliminate as much as possible the subjective element in theological study. I have rejected as a valid method of study the exercise of literary criticism in its speculative forms and have followed a straightforward approach to historico-grammatico-cultural hermeneutics.

But all objections to the kind of study I have employed will not come

---

loss of a sense of the transcendent is undermining the Church's ability to address with clarity and courage the urgent tasks to which God calls it in the world. This loss is manifest in a number of pervasive themes. Many are superficially attractive, but upon closer examination we find these themes false and debilitating to the Church's life and work." It then goes on to list thirteen themes of contemporary secularized theology together with brief answers to each. (This statement, originally set forth in mimeographed form, was later published as "An Appeal for Theological Affirmation" in *Against the World for the World: The Hartford Appeal and the Future of American Religion,* edited by Peter L. Berger and Richard John Neuhaus.)

from the theological left. There are conservatives who will object that biblical theology is at best a suspect discipline because of the recent association with it of names like Bultmann. On the other hand, there are those who, allowing the legitimacy of such study, challenge the approach implied by the title of this work: *The Theology of John.* To them the only legitimate approach to biblical theology is a unitary one, that is, an approach that considers the whole of the Old or the New Testament rather than a section according to period or human author. They object that the human-author approach, taken in this work, surrenders to the liberal theologian's naturalistic biases, which presuppose personal rather than propositional revelation, conceptual or dynamic rather than verbal inspiration, and evolutionary rather than revelational development of religious truth. Such objection is based upon the conviction that truth is ultimately only static and essential and not at all fluid or existential. According to some conservatives, then, truth is only to be received and not to be evaluated.

First of all, in answer to my fellow conservatives' misgivings, let it be said that Bultmann's approach, and even that of others in the neo-orthodox Biblical Theology school who are not as radical as he, is only biblical in that it takes the Bible as central to the study of theology. Scripture is prominent and is taken seriously, but it is not authoritative. It is the basic subject matter of theology but not the governor and judge of the theologian. Bultmann's following remarks reflect his approach to the Bible:

> The message of Jesus is a presupposition for the theology of the New Testament rather than a part of that theology itself. For New Testament theology consists in the unfolding of those ideas by means of which Christian faith makes sure of its own object, basis, and consequences. But Christian faith did not exist until there was a Christian kerygma; i.e., a kerygma proclaiming Jesus Christ—specifically Jesus Christ the Crucified and Risen One—to be God's eschatological act of salvation. He was first so proclaimed in the kerygma of the earliest Church, not in the message of the historical Jesus, even though that Church frequently introduced into its account of Jesus' message, motifs of its own proclamation. Thus, theological thinking—the theology of

> the New Testament—begins with the kerygma of the earliest Church and not before.[2]

My approach, on the other hand, is to see theology as a product of the Bible. The believer stands under the theological authority of Scripture. The early church, like the Old Testament prophets, was kerygmatic in the preeminently biblical sense of preaching the Word, the revelation of God given in written form through the apostles (see 2 Tim. 4:1-2).

Second, while biblical theology may certainly be studied with profit from a unitary standpoint, its study by human authors need not be inimical to a high view of revelation and inspiration. The fact that revelation is propositional does not demand that all theology be studied dogmatically and deductively, which method is the tendency of the unitary approach. Order and logical relationship do not necessarily require systemization in the traditional theological sense. (That is, an exercise in biblical theology need not be a modified exercise in systematic theology. There may be evidence of orderliness and logic in the organization and presentation of biblical theology without the full-blown systemization of doctrine necessary for a complete systematic theology. Among the prominent and particular ingredients of biblical theology are a close relationship with exegesis and a keen sense of the personal, historical, and cultural milieu of the writer. Systematic theology, by its nature, does not give prominence to those features, even though they must be presumed.)

Nor is the approach to biblical theology I have taken in this work a weakening of a verbal, plenary view of inspiration. In fact, if anything, the human-author approach serves to strengthen a properly conceived view of inspiration. One element of the doctrine of inspiration that is frequently overlooked or played down is the human element. A proper (biblical) doctrine of inspiration recognizes the confluent nature of inspiration: it involves both human and divine elements. An approach to biblical theology wherein each author is given his due allows for proper visibility to be given to both the Holy Spirit and the human writer. It allows for more than lip service to be paid to the contribution

[2] Rudolph Bultmann, *Theology of the New Testament,* 1:3.

given to biblical theology by divinely chosen and providentially prepared men.

The fear that the kind of study I have undertaken in this book gives support to an idea of evolutionary unfolding of religious truth is likewise unfounded. One of the basic premises of all biblical study, a premise no less true of theology than it is of any other discipline, is the doctrine of progressive revelation. The approach to biblical theology used in this book demonstrates that doctrine perhaps better than any other approach does. Revelation was not completed in one exhaustive act; rather, it was unfolded in a long series of successive acts. Biblical theology views the truths of Scripture in periods or, as in this book, as presented by a particular author of Scripture. Thus, progressive revelation views Scripture as it was written rather than as it stands written.

For the reasons listed above, I have undertaken this study with the following definition of biblical theology in mind: "Biblical Theology is that branch of theological science which deals systematically with the historically conditioned progress of the self-revelation of God as deposited in the Bible."[3]

Although I had done most of the research for this volume previously, I completed the final stages of study and wrote the manuscript during a sabbatical leave from Western Conservative Baptist Seminary, Portland, Oregon, during the winter and spring of 1975. I am profoundly grateful to the seminary for this opportunity to study and write, and I trust that the benefits thereof will not be limited to myself alone. I also want to thank *Bibliotheca Sacra* for its kind permission to print here the material in chapter 9, which is a revision of "Hamartiological Problems in 1st John," an article that was originally published in the July 1966 issue. And I gratefully acknowledge the assistance of Mrs. Teresa Amey, Mr. John Hutchison, and Mr. John Johnson, who compiled the indexes.

The Johannine literature, which is the focus of this study, is among the most sublime in all the world.[4] My prayer is that in some small way

[3]Charles C. Ryrie, *Biblical Theology of the New Testament,* p. 12.

[4]B. H. Streeter writes: "To John theology is the gateway to a temple; inside the temple is religion—the religion which in the rest of his Gospel he strives to unfold. . . . The point of the Gospel will be missed by a reader who approaches it primarily as a

this volume may aid Christ's church in reaching a more profound understanding of and a more ready obedience to the eternal truth contained in these portions of God's Word.

Jerusalem
Spring 1975

---

historical authority. It should be read as a book of devotion, as one would the *Imitatio Christi;* and the writer's attitude of mystic adoration may at times be better apprehended by a change of pronouns in the great discourses ascribed to Christ: '*Thou* art the vine, *we* are the branches'; or '*Thou* art the Resurrection and the Life' " (B. H. Streeter, "The Rise of Christianity," in *The Cambridge Ancient History,* ed. S. A. Cook, F. E. Adcock, and M. P.Charlesworth, 11:285).

Part One:
Introductory Considerations

I

Introduction to the Study of Johannine Thought

While certain biographical, historical, and ideological data are important to the understanding of Johannine thought, they are not the burden of this study. Rather, the following material is presented on the basis of certain presuppositions whose validity has been amply demonstrated elsewhere. I follow the classical view of the authorship and date of the Johannine literature set forth by B. F. Westcott in *The Gospel According to St. John: The Authorized Version with Introduction and Notes* and *The Epistles of St. John: The Greek Text with Notes and Essays* and more recently by Leon Morris in *Studies in the Fourth Gospel* and *The Gospel According to John: The English Text with Introduction, Exposition, and Notes.*[1]

In addition to the historical facts of the life, death, and resurrection of Jesus Christ, which form the primary backdrop of Johannine theology, there are three other sources that influenced John's thinking. The most important is the Old Testament, on which he repeatedly draws (see below, p. 22). It is clear that his way of thinking was greatly molded by the Hebrew Scriptures.[2] The second (Philonic thinking) and third (the Gnostic error) areas of influence were much less significant as determinative factors.

The Logos doctrine and its relation to Philo is discussed on pages

[1]For a more biographical approach to the author, see A. T. Robertson's *Epochs in the Life of the Apostle John.*

[2]In all, there are 766 quotations from or allusions to the Old Testament by John: 124 in the gospel, 13 in the epistles, and 629 in the Apocalypse. See *The Greek New Testament,* ed. Kurt Aland et al., pp. 897-918.

46-54), but a brief mention of Gnosticism is in order here. Gnosticism was a system of thought whose adherents sought salvation through occult knowledge. It became a major challenge to Christianity in the second and third centuries. During the last years of the first century, the time when John wrote, Gnosticism was merely in its incipient forms; yet some of its anti-Christian teachings are anticipated and dealt with forcefully and summarily in John's writings.

Contrary to earlier thinking, most scholars are now of the opinion that Gnosticism was probably of Jewish origin. This conclusion has been reached in light of the materials found near Nag Hammadi, Egypt, in 1945. It was discovered that the materials had many points of contact with orthodox Jewish interpretations of the Scriptures, although the theological position of the materials was thoroughly Gnostic.[3] The materials joined certain elements of Oriental dualism and Greek philosophy with Jewish concepts. The result was a syncretistic system based on an allegorical approach to Scripture. In the system, Scripture was closed to all but the initiated. One of the results of Gnosticism's encounter with Christianity was the idea of salvation through knowledge; another result was the association of evil with matter, which association led to denial of divine creation of the material universe, denial of the incarnation, and denial of the resurrection of the body. At the practical level, Gnosticism led to either antinomianism or asceticism. Paul dealt with the Gnostic errors related to salvation, creation, and resurrection (primarily in Colossians), and John dealt with the Gnostic errors related to the incarnation (John 1:14; 1 John 2:22; 4:2-3; 2 John 7) and with antinomianism (1 John 1:6, 8, 10; 4:20).[4]

A. The Distinguishing Characteristics.

1. *The relationship to the Old Testament.* Throughout his writing, John evidences a great love for the Old Testament. This is true despite

[3]Michael Stone, "Judaism in the Time of Christ," p. 1.

[4]For further discussion of this subject, see Donald Guthrie, *New Testament Introduction,* 1:250-52, 297-98; 3:191-94, 215-16, and Charles C. Ryrie, *Biblical Theology of the New Testament,* pp. 311-12.

an underlying hostility in the gospel toward a Judaism that rejected her Messiah. "There is much that bears on Jewish history. The Gospel shows that Jesus was a part of that history, and that the Jews, in rejecting Christ, were rejecting One who belonged to them (cf. Jn. 1:11)."[5] Both John's and the Lord's use of the Old Testament assume that it points to Christ.

The Apocalypse is saturated with Old Testament thought and imagery (although there is not one actual quotation from the Old Testament). The most evident influence is from Exodus, Psalms, Ezekiel, Daniel, Isaiah, Jeremiah, Joel, and Zechariah. Of the 404 verses in the Apocalypse, only 126 contain no allusion to the Old Testament. "The language of the Old Testament so moulded the author's thought that he cannot write without reflecting it."[6]

2. *The relationship to Pauline thought.* As Ryrie points out,[7] Paul was antecedent to John both in time and in thought. John worked in the same geographical areas in which Paul began works (especially in Ephesus). John built upon the foundations laid by Paul. Thus, although there are differences of emphasis, there is a kind of continuity that becomes complementary. But it should also be noted that most Pauline doctrine is latent in Jesus' upper room discourse, which was recorded by John (John 13-17).

Stevens gives a helpful comparison of Johannine and Pauline doctrine as summarized in the following chart:

Paul	*John*
Practiced analysis and argument.	Meditative and intuitive mind.
Argues out the truth.	Sees the truth.
Inductive: e.g., justification in Romans is proven by a series of arguments.	Deductive: e.g., salvation is presented as flowing naturally from God's loving nature.

[5]Guthrie, 1:212.
[6]Ibid., 3:285. See also, Ryrie, pp. 313–14.
[7]Ryrie, pp. 312–13.

Idea of God

Judge on throne of world.	The Being in whom all perfections are met.
Emphasis on the will of God.	Emphasis on the nature of God.

Person of Christ

Both emphasize pre-existence, exaltation to glory, relationship to the universe at large in revelation and redemption.

Contemplates the Savior chiefly in historic manifestation; note use of "Christ."	Emphasizes his essential, eternal nature; note use of "Logos."

Work of Christ

Both ascribe sacrificial significance to the saving work of Christ.

Christ's death is the ransom price by which men are redeemed.	Christ's death is an example of a universal law in operation (death must precede fuller life).

Sin

Both agree that it is universal and involves guilt. Both relate its beginning to the Genesis narrative of the fall.

Characteristically represents sin as a world-ruling power or personified principle controlling men.	Speaks in dualistic terminology of darkness in contrast to light; hate to love.

Method of Salvation

Great words are *justification* and *righteousness*.	Great words are *birth from God* and *life*.
Salvation is the result of divine declaration.	Salvation is the result of divine impartation of life.

Doctrine of Faith

For both it is more than mere belief. It involves personal relation and fellowship.

Both have a concept of life-union with Christ.

Paul's ideas are expressed by "in Christ," "dying with Christ," "newness of life."	John's ideas are "abiding in Christ," "living through Christ," etc.

Correlative with grace; the very opposite of merit; value of faith not in itself but in its object—Christ; not mere passive receptivity; faith works by love.[8]

3. *The relationship to the Scriptures as a whole.* Although it may be obvious, it needs to be said nonetheless that John's theology is climactic. The gospel of John is climactic to the synoptics, the epistles of John are climactic to the epistles of Paul and the others, and the Apocalypse is climactic to the whole of the Bible. This is true theologically as well as chronologically. While the synoptics are more nearly records of selected biographical data, the gospel of John is unabashedly a tract designed to convince its reader of the deity and saviorhood of Jesus Christ (John 20:30-31). While the other epistolary literature gives truth vital to the life of the church in Christ, the epistles of John give highly personal insights into the individual believer's fellowship with God, who is light and love (1 John 1:3, 5; 4:8, 16) and with his brother, who is in the same light and an object of the same love (1 John 1:7; 2:9-10; 4:7). While the rest of Scripture introduces us typically, prophetically, and historically to the person and work of our Lord Jesus Christ, the Apocalypse alone ties all the strands together and brings us to the climax of all things in time and eternity with *the* Revelation of Jesus Christ (Rev. 1:1).

4. *Distinctive features of Johannine thought.* Those features of Johannine thought that are distinctively Johannine are nowhere better stated than in Ryrie's analysis.[9]

a. It is ethical. One characteristic of John's thinking, especially seen in the first epistle, is that it is ethical. Proper ethical conduct is based upon the pattern of Christ's earthly life (1 John 2:6), is related to the incarnation (1 John 4:11 ff., which shows that the incarnation is

[8]G. B. Stevens, *The Johannine Theology: A Study of the Doctrinal Contents of the Gospel and Epistles of the Apostle John,* pp. 355 ff.

[9]Ryrie, pp. 314-16.

the only real basis for ethics), is primarily demonstrated by love for the brethren (1 John 2:7-11; 4:11-12), and will result in a life of habitual righteousness (1 John 3:4-18).[10]

b. It is antithetical.

> Antithesis is another characteristic of Johannine theology—not antithesis in the sense of contradictions but of contrasts.
>
> 1. *The antithesis of the Christian and the world.* Undoubtedly this is one of the most pronounced in John's thought. The world and the Christian stand apart from each other not in any metaphysical dualistic sense but more in an ethical sense. Such statements as those in John 3:16 and I John 2:2 guard against the idea that the world is intrinsically evil. Nevertheless, the cosmos hated Christ and His disciples, is under the headship of the Devil, is transient (John 7:7; 8:23; 14:17, 30; 15:19; 17:14; I John 3:13; 5:19); therefore, it must not receive the love of the Christian (I John 2:15-16).
>
> 2. *The antithesis of light and darkness.* John uses both light and darkness as symbols for knowledge, but these symbols are anthithetical in two areas. They are used to express the idea of God Himself (I John 1:5), and they represent spheres of life (I John 1:7). This latter idea is associated with love and hatred of the brethren (I John 2:10-11).
>
> 3. *The antithesis of death and life.* This is much the same as the preceding contrast, for John associated life with fullness of right ethical action and death with the lack of it (I John 3:14; John 8:51).[11]

c. It is contemplative. Like the prophets of the Old Testament, John is more a seer than a logician like Paul. "The Apostle John was an intuitionist and a mystic. He does not argue; he sees. . . . What men need is not more light, but an eye."[12]

> John is not an apologete or a polemicist; he is more of a mystic in the proper Christian sense. The truths of Christianity are set forth in their own beauties so that others may see and believe. Even in proving that Jesus is the Messiah he employs miracle-signs (2:11; 4:54), and throughout his use of symbols is graphic (10:1; 15:1).[13]

[10]Ibid., p. 314.
[11]Ibid., pp. 314-15.
[12]G. B. Stevens, *The Theology of the New Testament,* p. 566.
[13]Ryrie, p. 315.

B. The Approach to the Study.

1. *As to the critical problems and historical milieu.* Any serious student of the Johannine literature will soon discover that he must grapple with certain critical questions other than simply date and authorship. Whole schools of thought based upon certain literary assumptions illustrate the variety of attempts to answer such problems. The body of literature representing research in these areas grows each year. Much is helpful; some is so speculative that it is of little worth.[14] The aim of this study, to examine Johannine thought as set forth in the Bible, is closely related to certain convictions regarding the problems alluded to above. First, this study is based on the belief that one legitimate method of study is that which limits itself primarily to the internal statements of the documents and takes those statements at face value. It is no more an assumption that they are reliable and should be examined in that light than it is that they are not. Second, it is recognized that an examination of the problems together with proposed solutions is often included within such a study as this one.[15] Such work, dealing with questions of literary dependence, the relationship to the synoptics, the influence of the Qumran community on Johannine thought, and the relationship of theology and history in the Johannine writings, are of moment. The willingness and skill of conservative writers, such as Leon Morris *(Studies in the Fourth Gospel)* and Ladd *(A Theology of the New Testament),* in dealing with these issues is greatly appreciated. Third, it should be noted that this book is undertaken in light of such studies and does not attempt to cover the same ground again. It simply does not suit the purpose of this volume to repeat those men's work, although such work is very meaningful in Ladd's treatment, for example. He states as a part of his purpose in dealing with the fourth gospel that he intends "not only to set forth positively the Johannine thought but

[14]It is interesting to note the divergence of viewpoints in two such respected scholars as C. H. Dodd and Rudolf Bultmann (Robert Kysar, "Background of the Prologue of the Fourth Gospel: A Critique of Historical Methods"). At the least, this divergence of viewpoints should give us pause in making pronouncements about such matters as historical backgrounds.

[15]Cf. George Eldon Ladd, *A Theology of the New Testament,* pp. 213-22.

to attempt to discover to what degree it is similar or dissimilar to that of the Synoptics."[16]

A further word, although brief, regarding the historical milieu of John's writing is in order. It is interesting to note that some recent scholarship is returning to the traditionally conservative viewpoint, which says that John wrote in the later years of the first century. Among other things, the Dead Sea literature has shown that writing such as we find in the Johannine corpus is similar to other writing of the early Christian era (despite the marked differences between John and the Qumran writers.)[17] To place John's writings in the second century on the basis of distinctive Johannine language, thought patterns, themes, and reporting of incidents in Jesus' earthly life is purely gratuitous. As Albright has stated:

> There is no fundamental difference in teaching between John and the Synoptics; the contrast between them lies in the concentration of tradition along certain aspects of Christ's teachings, particularly those which seem to have resembled the teaching of the Essenes most closely.
>
> There is absolutely nothing to show that any of Jesus' teachings have been distorted or falsified, or that a vital new element has been added to them. That the needs of the early Church influenced the selection of items for inclusion in the Gospel we may readily admit, but there is no reason to suppose that the needs of that Church were responsible for any inventions or innovations of theological significance.
>
> One of the strangest assumptions of critical New Testament scholars and theologians is that the mind of Jesus was so limited that any apparent contrast between John and the Synoptics must be due to differences between early Christian theologians. Every great thinker and personality is going to be interpreted differently by different friends and hearers, who will select what seems most congenial or useful out of what they have seen and heard.[18]

[16]Ibid., p. 222.

[17]See Leon Morris, *Studies in the Fourth Gospel,* pp. 321-58. For another approach that demonstrates the first century character of John's thought, see Richard N. Longenecker, *The Christology of Early Jewish Christianity.*

[18]W. F. Albright, "Recent Discoveries in Palestine and the Gospel of St. John," pp. 170-71. Actually, a number of writers are suggesting dates for John's gospel (over against the epistles and the Apocalypse) that antedate traditional and conservative views. The tendency is to dissociate John's gospel from the synoptics to a greater or lesser degree and to date it as an independent tradition that developed prior to the fall

John was writing to a young but virile church, a church not yet separated by many years from the great events that had led to its creation. He was the last eyewitness and earthly companion of our Lord to die, and he was the most intimate of Jesus' apostolic appointees. The church had seen remarkable growth both numerically and geographically in his lifetime. It was facing a growing and invidious error that would be known as Gnosticism, and throughout the Roman Empire it was meeting with increasing pressure from the emperor cult. To this young church in this setting, the aging, spiritually alert saint wrote, displaying a loving and penetrating sensitivity to her need.

2. *As to sources.* There are two kinds of approaches to the study of Johannine thought. One kind considers all John's writings as a unit, as does Stevens in *The Johannine Theology,* while the other considers all but the gospel of John, which is viewed as part of the theology of Jesus, as does Stevens in *The Theology of the New Testament.* For reasons explained in the preface, the first of those two approaches is followed in this study.[19]

3. *As to analysis.* While it is entirely possible to analyze an individual's entire contribution to all the major divisions of theology, such study tends to be somewhat artificial and it certainly misses one of the basic emphases of biblical theology as a discipline. One aspect of the genius of biblical theology is that it enables one to see the distinctive contribution and emphasis of a given writer (or period) in the progress of revelation. Thus, the approach taken in this study is to emphasize what John emphasizes, to underscore the main areas of his thinking.

In John's thought, one all-pervasive and dominant note prevails. His thinking is predominantly theological, in the more restrictive sense of the term; and more particularly it is Christological. This theme is set forth in three major movements as they are seen in the three genres of

---

of Jerusalem in A.D. 70. See J. A. T. Robinson, *Twelve New Testament Studies,* pp. 98-99; Robert M. Grant, *A Historical Introduction to the New Testament,* p. 160; Albright, pp. 153-71; George Allen Turner, "The Date and Purpose of the Gospel by John," pp. 82-85; F. Lamar Cribbs, "A Reassessment of the Date of Origin and the Destination of the Gospel of John," pp. 38-55. It should be noted that proponents of this line of thinking need to grapple more adequately with the tradition of the early church, particularly as found in Eusebius.

[19]See also Ryrie, pp. 302-3.

his writings. In the gospel, the Johannine Christology is worked out along soteriological lines. In the epistles, it is worked out along the lines of the doctrine of the Christian life. In the Apocalypse, it is worked out along eschatological lines. Certainly there is soteriological truth in the epistles and the Apocalypse and eschatology in the gospel and the epistles, but the major emphases are as noted.

Furthermore, there are several minor movements, or doctrinal emphases, that appear in relationship to the major movements. (*Minor* is not used in the sense of "unimportant"; rather, it indicates that the movements are subservient to the enunciating of the three major movements.) These lesser emphases are in the areas of angelology, hamartiology, and ecclesiology. They will be considered as they relate to the major ideas rather than as independent doctrines.

Finally, it is to be noted that certain introductory items of a decidedly doctrinal nature are more implicit than explicit in John's writing. There are other introductory matters that, while explicit, are so fundamental to all that follows that they must appear as prolegomena. These introductory items are: first, some bibliological presuppositions; second, John's attitude, or understanding, about the nature of true (biblical) religion; and third, his fundamental theology proper.

4. *As to method of interpretation of the Apocalypse.* All readers will acknowledge that among the major subdivisions of theology, prophecy (eschatology) is in a special category of its own; and all readers will further acknowledge that among the genres of biblical literature, apocalyptic writing is in a class apart. The book of the Revelation is both prophetic and apocalyptic, and it is therefore unique in the New Testament. Consequently, it has produced a plethora of schools of interpretation, with the attendant theological peculiarities that have grown therefrom.

Both the Old Testament and the New Testament are replete with prophetic passages wherein God spoke of future events through human authors. The consistent pattern of the fulfillment of prophetic material, which fulfillment is now a matter of history, is one of literal and detailed exactness (e.g., prophecies regarding the first advent of Christ). Although certain schools of interpretation, especially those with postmillennial or amillennial systems of eschatology, have tended to demand a separate set of canons for prophecy relating to the second advent (e.g., the future of Israel, the rapture of the church), the biblical pattern does not support that approach.[20] The extensive use of an allegorical hermeneutic (often euphemistically referred to as "spiritualizing") by postmillennialists, amillennialists, and even some premillennialists is totally unwarranted, since a consistent application of the historico-grammatical system of hermeneutics yields perfectly understandable results that are harmonious with the analogy of faith. The presence of symbolic language in much prophetic literature is not to be denied, however; nor is it proper to claim that the interpretation of every passage is equally simple and obvious. What is proper, on the other hand, is to insist that symbols, just like all other language, yield to one normal, natural sense. They do not allow for "deeper," fanciful interpretation that is not testable by the usual laws of language.

In the case of the Revelation, the hermeneutical problem is compounded because this last book of the Bible is apocalyptic. *Apocalypse* simply means "revelation" and is a transliteration of the Greek ἀποκάλυψις (an unveiling). Since most apocalyptic literature extant from biblical times[21] uses esoteric language, is full of cryptic visions, is marked by certain dualistic tendencies, and tends to have an affinity for certain ancient mythological motifs, critics have tended to interpret biblical apocalyptic literature[22] as though it were no different.[23] While it must be granted that many of the typical phenomena of apocalyptic literature, such as cryptic visions, symbolic language, denouement, and final judgment, are evident in the biblical literature, there are also several striking differences between biblical and extrabiblical materials. There is in biblical apocalyptic literature an absence of excesses, dual-

[20]In addition, the majority of contemporary biblical literary critics, except for those of the conservative wing of Christendom, insist on disallowing the obviously supernatural demands of much Old Testament prophecy. This is particularly seen in their insistence on a late date for Daniel when all the evidence, apart from their a priori disposition against the supernatural, points to a date in the sixth century B.C.

[21]E.g., the pseudepigrapha, certain of the apocryphal books, and some of the Qumran literature.

[22]Daniel, Ezekiel, and Revelation.

[23]See, e.g., John Bright, *A History of Israel,* pp. 416, 458-60.

ism, dependence upon pagan mythology, and pseudonymity.[24] Other important differences are the biblical literature's overriding themes of sovereign monotheism, the purposeful fulfillment of a cohesive plan for the universe, the exercise of moral justice, and the evidence of a unification of thought in the general message of both the Old and the New Testament (without collaboration or artificially created continuity). The solution of the dilemma for both the literary critic and the allegorizer is a very simple one that has profound results: simply take the biblical apocalyptic, in this case the book of Revelation, at face value as it is written, allowing the text to speak for itself and using the normal canons of hermeneutics in its interpretation.

All interpretations of Revelation may be classified under one of four major categories or schools of thought: (1) the preterist view, which holds that the prophetic material of the book was all fulfilled in the early years of church history; (2) the historicist view, which claims a continuous fulfillment of the various prophecies throughout the church age; (3) the spiritualizing view, which considers the book to be an allegorical presentation of the eternal conflict between good and evil; and (4) the futurist view, which holds that the prophecies of Revelation 4:1—22:5 are to be fulfilled at the consummation of the present age. Only the fourth view follows to any degree at all the system of hermeneutics suggested above, and even some scholars who are generally futurists adhere to various aspects of other interpretive schools from passage to passage.[25] As Ryrie points out, one's approach to interpretation "casts the mold for the theology of the book."[26] Any allegorical approach, whether in whole or in part, leads one to a hopelessly indefinite and problematic eschatology. Either it will be inconsistent within the broader scope of theology, as is amillennialism, which sees the prophecies surrounding Christ's first com-

[24]While most critics would dispute this statement, it should not be overlooked that their assertions to the contrary are mere gratuitous assumptions. No critic can prove, for example, that Daniel or John was not the actual author of his writings as claimed.

[25]An example of this modified approach to the futurist view is George Ladd. He calls his view the "Moderate Futurist View" (Ladd, pp. 623-24). See also G. E. Ladd, *A Commentary on the Revelation of John,* pp. 12-14.

[26]Ryrie, p. 346.

ing as literal but those surrounding His second coming as allegorical, or it will be inconsistent within the narrower confines of eschatology, as is the futurism that is premillennial while holding to posttribulationism.

II

Theological Prolegomena: Implicit

A. Bibliological Presuppositions.

John's view of the written Word of God is not unique among the views held by the writers of Scripture. There are certain matters, however, that particularly mark his thinking.

1. *The integrity and authority of Scripture.* There are four lines of testimony adduced by John in affirmation of the integrity and authority of Scripture. He first appeals to Christ's own word and example. In His teaching, our Lord affirmed various items of history, such as the existence of Abraham (John 8:56; cf. Gen. 12:2-3), the manna in the wilderness (John 6:49; cf. Ex. 16:14-17), and the serpent-of-brass experience (John 3:14; Num. 21:6-9). He affirmed the Messianic, predictive character of Scripture in John 5:39, 45-47 and its fulfillment in Himself in John 7:37-39 (see Isa. 44:1-3; 55:1; 58:11), John 13:18 (see Psalm 41:9), John 15:25 (see Psalms 35:19; 69:4), and John 17:12 (see Psalm 41:9). As He taught, He appealed to verbal detail in such passages as John 8:17-18 (see Deut. 19:15), giving emphasis to the particular word "two," and John 10:33-36 (see Psalm 82:6), giving emphasis to the particular word "gods." Even more specific is His teaching in John 10:33-36 that "Scripture cannot be broken." It is one thing to make reference to Scripture in passing and quite another to make straightforward assertions such as this. Finally, in John 7:19-23 the Lord affirmed the Mosaic authorship of the Pentateuch.

The second line of testimony to which John appeals in support of the integrity of Scripture is fulfilled prophecy. Several examples may be noted, as follows: the claim of John the Baptist as given by Isaiah (John 1:23; cf. Isa. 40:3), recognition by the disciples of things fulfilled by Christ (John 2:17; cf. Psalm 69:9; John 2:22; cf. Psalm 16:10), the triumphal entry (John 12:12 ff.; cf. Zech. 9:9), Jewish unbelief (John 12:37-41; cf. Psalm 69:23; Isa. 6:9-10; 53:1), matters relating to the crucifixion (John 19:24; cf. Psalm 22:18; John 19:28; cf. Psalm 69:21; John 19:36; cf. Psalm 34:20 [see Ex. 12:46; Num. 9:12 for typological significance]; John 19:37; cf. Zech. 12:10; Rev. 1:7), and the resurrection of Christ (John 20:9; cf. Psalm 16:10).

Third, the integrity and authority of the written Word of God are tacitly implied by John through his widespread reference to the Old Testament.[1]

The fourth line of evidence to be noted is direct apostolic statement. John's emphasis upon the *written Word* and the clear implication of its authority cannot be missed in John 20:30-31 and 1 John 5:13 (cf. 1 John 1:4; 2:5, 7, 12, 13, 14, 21, 26). This emphasis is augmented by the promised blessing attached to the reading, hearing, and keeping of the *words* of the prophecy of Revelation (Rev. 1:3). Again, at the close of the book, the inviolable character of the prophecy is underscored (Rev. 22:18-19).

2. *The doctrine of illumination.* While a discussion of John 16:12-15 may well fit under consideration of the doctrine of the Holy Spirit and His role in the Christian life, the passage is also basic to John's whole theological outlook. A few observations on these verses will show that John teaches that the believer is provided with supernatural enlightenment on the biblical text.

It should be noted initially that this passage deals with the words, or sayings (λέγειν), of Christ. Since it is addressed to all the disciples, including the nonwriting ones, the promise it contains relates to all. The specific promise involves the Holy Spirit as a guide, or leader, in the way of truth (ὁδηγήσει...ἐν τῇ ἀληθείᾳ) for the disciple. Since the provision relates to an inability on the disciples' part, the guidance must be viewed as something that takes them beyond that which can be

[1]See comments in chap. 1, pp. 22-23, as well as H. B. Swete, *The Apocalypse of St. John,* pp. cxxxv-cliii, and M. C. Tenney, *Interpreting Revelation,* pp. 101-16.

perceived without divine aid. The scope of the assistance is indicated by the term "all" (v. 13). It is the truth (about spiritual matters, as the context shows) in its entirety into which the Holy Spirit will lead. This ministry of the Spirit is, indirectly at least, a self-effacing one. It consists of speaking of things not originated by Himself (ἀφ᾽ ἑαυτοῦ), but by others. By implication, the "others" are the members of the Godhead named in the passage; and by direct statement of the context the Spirit will particularly speak of Christ ("He shall glorify Me" [v. 14]).[2] As the text shows, when the Spirit takes of the things of Christ and discloses them to the believer, Christ is glorified. This gives clear indication of at least one major emphasis that any Christian ministry should take. Finally, it should be noted that the illuminating work of the Spirit has a particular relationship to future things.

3. *The doctrine of animation.* Underlying John's theology is the conviction that *God's* Word is living and therefore life-giving. In John 6:63 the Lord Himself indicates the relationship between His words and life. In one sense at least, that relationship is the key to the whole bread of life discourse (John 6:26-71).

To begin with, it is taught that God's Word has power to save its hearers: "He who hears [with obedient response] my word [i.e., my word about myself], and believes [the witness of] Him who sent Me [as recorded in the Old Testament scriptures], has eternal life" (John 5:24; cf. 5:38). This is true because the Word also has power to induce faith (John 17:20).

An expansion upon this concept is found in John 8:31-32, where the Word is seen to have power to set one free. Continuance in His Word leads to true discipleship, and this in turn brings knowledge of the truth. This truth will bring freedom.

At the same time, the freeing Word may be the judging Word. "He who rejects Me, and does not receive My sayings, has one who judges

[2]It should be noted that it is characteristic of John's gospel that the third person of the Godhead points to the second, and the second to the first (cf. John 14:9-10). The Spirit never glorifies Himself, and it is an indictment against certain movements in the contemporary church that they have overlooked this principle. It is certainly true that in the upper room discourse the second person says much about the third. That fact has to do with Christ's disclosure of basic information, however, whereas the point I am making involves a pattern of ministry.

him; the word I spoke is what will judge him at the last day" (John 12:48; cf. Rev. 1:16; 19:15).

Other functions of the animated and animating Word are that it is instrumental in fitting us for fellowship with God (John 14:23; cf. 17:6), it is related to our effectiveness in prayer (John 15:7), it has power to cleanse and sanctify (John 15:3; 17:17), and it has power to bring God's love to maturity in us (1 John 2:5).

This living quality of Scripture is not to be construed as an independent or magical property in any detached sense. It is because it is *God's* Word composed of God's *words* that it is thus effective (John 6:63).

B. The Nature of True Religion.

While John does not explicitly treat the subject of the nature of true religion, his views are quite evident as one reads through his writings. Since these concepts interpenetrate all John's thinking, it is important to consider them at the outset of this study. They will be presented as a series of propositions that may be expanded but that, nonetheless, capture the essence of his thinking about the nature of true religion.

1. *It involves a sovereign plan and purpose* (John 6:37-40). God's plan indicates that the saving process must be initiated by God (John 6:44, 65) and that His Son is pledged to honor it (John 6:37-40).

2. *It begins with an impartation of life from God Himself* (John 1:12-13).

3. *It involves faith in God and the one whom He sent* (John 5:24; 6:29). The specific means for provision of life through Christ is in His sacrificial death, the benefits of which in turn are appropriated through faith (John 6:47-51; 3:16).

4. *It recognizes that the Scriptures are God's ordained channel of life* (John 5:39-40; 6:63).

5. *It makes its appeal to the entire man.* Knowing God in the Johannine sense of the term involves obedience, trust, and love; mind, heart, and will; body, soul, and spirit.

> The mere intellectual possession of truth cannot suffice; truth is not merely something to be known but something to be done (iii. 21; I. i. 6).

> . . . Religion is life after the type which has been perfectly exemplified in Jesus Christ; but it is life in a full and rich, not in a narrow and limited, sense. It is life abundant, a life which embraces the fullest activity and best development of the entire man.[3]

6. *It involves personal fellowship with God and His family* (1 John 1:3, 6-7), *which in turn leads to likeness to God* (1 John 2:4-6; 3:1-9).

7. *It acknowledges that the sovereign God works in sovereign ways among the children of men* (John 9:1-34). God does not necessarily conform to patterns of practice preconceived by men or to hallowed forms and time-honored traditions of the establishment. His ways most frequently involve the *person* of Jesus Christ with a *person* in need through the medium of the *written* record of Scripture (see proposition 4, above).

8. *It understands that eternal life is a present possession as well as a future prospect* (John 5:24). This world is united with the world to come. To John, "the spiritual life is the heavenly life already begun."[4] Of this presently possessed eternal life it may be said that:

a. It involves the principle of multiplied life out of death (John 12:20-26). The servant whom the Father honors must have separated himself from a self-centered life and given himself to a Christ-centered life.

b. It involves a stance of active humility (John 13:1-17, esp. vv. 12-17). This particular passage may be interpreted as teaching that one reason for giving humble service is to help fellow believers overcome (cleanse) sin in their lives.

c. It involves the active and observable exercise of divinely originated *agapē* toward fellow believers (John 13:34-35; 15:10, 12-13).

d. It involves obedience to objectively revealed truth (i.e., God's commandments [John 15:10, 12, 14, 17]).

e. It involves the experience of divine fullness of joy (John 15:11).

f. It involves the experience of intimate friendship with the Godhead (John 15:14-15).

[3]G. B. Stevens, *The Johannine Theology: A Study of the Doctrinal Contents of the Gospel and Epistles of the Apostle John,* pp. 9-13.
[4]Ibid., p. 13.

g. It involves the production of lasting results (John 15:16).

h. It involves something so different from the satanic world-system that it will not merely evoke misunderstanding when evidenced, but hatred (John 15:18-21).

III

Theological Prolegomena: Explicit

A. John's Doctrine of God.

1. *The nature of God.* John gives a number of very important statements about God's essence that are foundational to the major movements of thought developed throughout his writings.

a. First, he teaches that "God is spirit" (John 4:24; cf. 1:18; 1 John 4:12). It should be noted that πνεῦμα (spirit) is anarthrous, emphasizing the nature or quality of "spirit" rather than the personal identity of "a spirit." This is not a statement to the effect that God is of that genre of beings known as spirits. It is not a reference, therefore, to the Holy Spirit. The word "spirit" is intended to be given prominence in the sentence, however, since it is in the emphatic position. When one worships, his worship will not be what it ought to be if he does not recognize that God is spirit. This is an affirmation that God is transcendent, pure person (in contrast to one who is a compound of matter and spirit or that which is only matter and therefore finite). He is unlimited by space and time and must be understood in spiritual terms. Therefore, we must worship Him personally (in spirit) and on the basis of truth.

b. Second, John teaches that "God is light" (1 John 1:5). This phrase has been understood by Stevens as meaning "God is holy love," based on 1 John 2:10; by Law as "God is self-revealed," based on a passage such as John 1:9; by Westcott as "God is redeemer," based on John 8:12; and by Weidner as "God is holy."[1] While each is most

[1]G. B. Stevens, *The Theology of the New Testament;* R. Law, *The Tests of Life: A Study of the First Epistle of St. John;* B. F. Westcott, *The Epistles of St. John: The Greek*

certainly a biblical as well as Johannine truth, the question that must be answered is, Does the context of 1 John 1:5 support the suggested interpretation? It seems that all but one of these views may be eliminated on the basis of the immediate and the broader context of 1 John. The concept of love is not introduced until late in 1 John 3, and it is not specifically related to God's nature until 1 John 4. The idea of self-revelation is at best a secondary or resultant teaching growing out of this phrase for two reasons: (1) The statement "God is light" is an affirmation about God's nature rather than about His activity, and (2) the context of 1 John 1 deals with sin and its antithesis (God) rather than with ignorance of the truth and its antithesis (the knowledge of God). To see this as a reference to God's economy of redemption is to miss the distinction between 1 John and the gospel of John. The emphasis in 1 John is upon the Christian life, while in the gospel it is upon redemption.

It would seem, then, that the context strongly supports the view that 1 John 1:5 is an affirmation of God's holiness. The emphasis of this first section of the epistle is upon fellowship and the sin that interrupts it. Fellowship is predicated upon a God who is light sharing common things with children who are walking in light. Since it is sin that mars and destroys this fellowship, the light that makes fellowship possible must be construed as the absence of sin (light is the absence of darkness [1 John 1:5*b*]). God's holiness represents among other things His absolute moral perfection. He is totally separated from sin in His essential being.[2] Figuratively speaking, the outstanding quality of light is its purity. This is especially apt here since light is used to picture a moral quality and the appropriate ethical relationship of man vis-a-vis God

---

Text with Notes and Essays; and R. F. Weidner, *Biblical Theology of the New Testament.*

[2]It may be asked why a figurative expression, *light,* was used here rather than a moral term like *holy.* Perhaps it is because God's holiness implies more than moral separation from sin. God is also holy in an ontological sense. That is, in His very being He transcends all His creation. Since John is here discussing the effect of sin in the Christian life as a condition of moral darkness, it is fitting that he use *light* as a figurative way of referring to God's moral perfection (holiness).

(1 John 1:7).[3] This interpretation is further supported by the broader New Testament doctrine of fellowship. In passages where this doctrine is set forth, holiness is given prominence (cf. 1 Cor. 10:14-22; 11:23-24; 2 Cor. 6:14—7:1).

Φῶς (light), like πνεῦμα (spirit) is anarthrous; so again the emphasis is upon God's essential being. He is not *a* light or even *the* light, but "God is light." He is holy; thus all He does and says is in holiness.

c. Third, "God is love" (1 John 4:8, 16). Once again, the Greek word (ἀγάπη [love]) is anarthrous, emphasizing a quality of His being. John is not saying that God is loving. God is loving, but John's aim here is to distinguish the activity of love from the attribute of love. The latter is the source from which the former arises. Love in God is that which moves Him to self-communication both within and outside the Godhead. Thus the affirmation that He is love asserts that God is, by nature, One who is wont to share Himself with others, especially His children. As the context shows, the primary ramifications of this are social. Consequently, further development will be left for the section on the theology of the Christian life (p. 107).

d. John makes a fourth essential statement about God in John 5:26: "The Father has life in Himself." This sets forth His aseity, or self-existence. It sets Him apart from every other being, all of whom are dependent in that they have life from a source outside themselves (a concept also implied in the Creator-creature relationship: "Thou didst create all things, and because of Thy will they existed, and were created" [Rev. 4:11]). Also, it gives the reason why He is the fountain of both physical and spiritual life.

It is most interesting to note that this truth about God's nature is set forth in a strongly eschatological passage (cf. references to eternal life, resurrection, and judgment in John 5:19-30). The ultimate questions and concerns of all animate moral beings relate to the eschaton (the ultimate dimension of life or death). God, who has life in Himself, is the only One who holds definitive answers to these questions.

e. Finally, God is, by nature, true (John 17:3; 1 John 5:20; cf. John

[3]It is instructive to notice the etymological relationships between *holy* (ἅγιος) and *pure* (ἁγνος) in Greek. Both terms derive from the same root, ἁγ—.

3:33; 8:40). The term used here is ἀληθινός, meaning true in the sense of "real" or "genuine." The God of Scripture, about whom John writes, is neither false nor counterfeit nor the figment of some man's or society's imagination. This God conforms to reality intrinsically; in fact, He is the source and standard for all that is genuine and real. Furthermore, this fact about His being forms the standard for His words and ways with men. It is most strategic to all theological thinking that John links this great fact with eternal life and the knowledge of God.

2. *The person of God.* John presents the first person of the Godhead primarily as Father. This term is used of God approximately 150 times in John's gospel and epistles. All the uses fall into one of two categories.

a. First, He is presented as the Father of our Lord Jesus Christ. Christ is said to be "the only begotten from the Father" (μονογενοῦς παρὰ πατρός [John 1:14; cf. 1:18; 3:16; 1 John 4:9]). Contrary to popular thinking, which has unfortunately been perpetuated by many English translations and overzealous defenders of the faith, the term μονογενής has nothing to do with begetting in the usual human sense of the term. It is poorly translated as "only begotten" in all but the most recent modern language translations, in which the term "only" has been substituted for "only begotten." Even this substitution is somewhat misleading, because the Greek word is literally "only of a kind," the equivalent of our "unique."[4] The point is that while God has many sons (πολλοὺς υἱούς) in the redeemed company of believers, He has only one Son who is full of grace and truth, who is in the bosom of the Father, and who has perfectly declared Him (John 1:14, 18).[5]

John also tells us that this special Son is loved by the Father (John 3:35; 5:20; 10:17). Both of the New Testament words for love (ἀγαπάω and φιλέω) are used of the Father's love for His Son. He

[4]"The [Old Latin] correctly translated [μονογενής] as *unicus,* 'only', and so did Jerome where it was not applied to Jesus. But to answer the Arian claim that Jesus was not begotten but made, Jerome translated it as *unigenitus,* 'only begotten' in passages like this one (also i 18, iii 16, 18). The influence of the Vulg. on the KJ made 'only begotten' the standard English rendition" (R. E. Brown, *The Gospel According to John,* 2:13). See also the excellent and extensive discussion by D. Moody, "God's Only Son: The Translation of John 3:16 in the Revised Standard Version," pp. 213-19.

[5]See also B. F. Westcott's excellent comments in *The Gospel According to St. John: The Authorized Version with Introduction and Notes,* p. 12.

loves Him both wisely and warmly, both deliberately and passionately, both with will and intellect as well as with heart. If μονογενής spoke of the Son's *unique* relationship with the Father, these words describe His *intimate* relationship with the Father. This in turn becomes the pattern of the intimate relationship that exists between Christ and the believer (John 15:9-10; 11:3, 36; 16:27; 20:2; Rev. 3:19).

The Son was sent by the Father, and His earthly life was sustained by the Father (John 6:57; cf. 5:36-37; 8:16, 18; 12:49; 1 John 4:14). The Son's being sent by the Father is related to the disciples' being sent by the Son (John 20:21), and His being nurtured by the Father is related to the disciples' being nurtured by the Son (John 6:57*b*). In both matters the divine-divine relationship provides the pattern for the divine-human relationship (καθὼς. . .καὶ [as . . . also] is used in both passages). Thus the Father-Son filial bond provides part of the cement that binds the believer to Christ.

In a variety of ways, John notes that the Son is the manifestation, or revealer, of the Father. Although the Father is invisible to human perception, the Son has "explained"[6] the meaning of the Father for men (John 1:18). To know the Son is to know the Father; and vice-versa, the Father is not known except through the Son (John 8:19; 14:7). He who has seen the Son has seen the Father (John 14:7-9). Herein lies the answer to the age-old question of child and adult alike: What is God like? He is like Christ. There is perfect family likeness. This is the glorious anticipation of the believer, too; one day our family likeness to Him will become evident (1 John 3:2). In light of 1 John 3:3-7, it would seem that a similar question, What is Christ like? should be able to be answered, He is like ________ (and the Christian should be able to fill in his own name).

As Son, Jesus Christ receives men as gifts from His Father (John 17:6, 12; cf. 6:37, 44; 10:29) and is the heir of all that is the Father's (John 5:22-23; 13:3; 16:15). In turn, that which He has received of the Father He makes available to the believer who asks in His name (John 14:13-14; cf. 16:24).

[6]The verb is ἐξηγέομαι and means "give a graphic and careful narration of specific information." (See other uses of the term in Luke 24:35; Acts 10:8; 15:12, 14; 21:19, which uses support this meaning.)

b. Second, as well as being the Father of the Lord Jesus Christ, God is the believer's Father, too. This relationship is posited upon the new birth (John 1:12-13; 3:1-8) and becomes the basis for intimate family fellowship (1 John). As Father, He desires and seeks true worshipers (John 4:21, 23), is the correct object of prayer (John 16:23), loves the believer because of his relationship to His Son and loves the believer as He loves the Son (John 14:23; 16:27; 17:23; 1 John 3:1), is concerned that the believer bear fruit and disciplines him to that end (John 15:1-2, 8), indwells the believer and desires to love through him (John 14:23; cf. 1 John 4:7; see also, in contrast, 1 John 2:15), gives those in this relationship the privilege of fellowship with Himself (1 John 1:3), and together with the Son provides for the believer's eternal safety (John 10:27-29).

B. John's Doctrine of Jesus Christ.

1. *Designations for the second person of the Godhead.* Designations used by John for Jesus Christ fall into three groupings.

a. First, His name, "Jesus," is used approximately 250 times by John in the gospel. This is the usual narrative name, as in the synoptics. "Jesus Christ" is not used as a name until the epistles and the Apocalypse.

b. There are at least seven titles for the second person recorded by John. He is referred to as "Christ," but not as frequently as in the synoptics. Messianic implications are not as prominent in John as in the other gospel writers. John the Baptist recognized that he was the forerunner of Messiah (John 1:20, 25; 3:28), and the disciples acknowledged that He was Messiah (John 1:41; 11:27; cf. John 1:49, 12:13, "King of Israel"). John also gives the important note that He Himself declared Himself to be Messiah (John 4:25-26). The title "Son of God" also has strong Messianic implications (John 1:49; 11:27; 20:31), as well as being an affirmation of deity. It was used by Christ with the implications of deity (John 5:25; 11:4) and was so understood by His hearers (John 10:33, 36). (See also the use of μονογενής [unique] with "Son" in this regard [John 3:16-18; cf. 1:18].) "Son of Man" seems to be the Lord's favorite designation for Himself. It is clearly used with soteriological implications, with particular emphasis upon His mediatorial functions and theanthropic character (John 1:51; 3:13-14; 5:27; 6:27, 53, 62; 8:28). He is called "Savior" only twice in John's writings (John 4:42; 1 John 4:14; cf. John 12:47).

The usual address used by His disciples was "Lord." Often it was merely a title of respect, but following the resurrection Thomas clearly used it in a different sense (John 20:28). It was used by Christ of Himself with the suggestion of authority beyond that of a merely human master (John 13:13-14). Along with "Lord," the common address of His followers as well as others was "Rabbi" (Teacher) (John 1:38, 49; 3:2; 4:31; 6:25; 9:2; 11:8, 28; 20:16).

One title that is peculiar to John is "Advocate" (1 John 2:1; cf. John 14:16). This is a judicial term that approaches the modern idea of "a friend in court." It is derived from the verb παρακαλέω, which originally meant "to call to one's side" or "to summon." As used of Christ, it pictures "a friend of the accused person, called to speak to his character, or otherwise enlist sympathy in his favor."[7]

c. The third grouping includes figurative and metaphorical designations. He is called "Logos" (Word) (John 1:1, 14; 1 John 1:1; Rev. 19:13), which will be discussed more fully below; "light" (John 1:4-9; 8:12; 9:5; 12:35-36, 46); "Lamb" (John 1:29, 36; Rev. 5:6, 8, 12-13; 13:8); "bread of life" (John 6:32-58); "door" (John 10:1-9); "good shepherd" (John 10:11-16); "true vine" (John 15:1-5); and "resurrection and . . . life" (John 11:25-26).

2. *The doctrine of the Logos.* The doctrine of the Logos has been much disputed and expounded. Only a summary of the doctrine will be attempted here. Much literature on the subject can be consulted with profit to the reader.[8]

a. The initial questions that must be answered are: Whence did John derive this term and what meaning is intended by it? Two views vie for prominence here. One view sees the root of John's Logos concept in Philo, the chief representative of Hellenic Judaism, and thus makes it primarily a philosophical idea. This view would say that John's prologue must be interpreted in the light of Philo. Certainly this influ-

[7]F. Field, *Notes on the Translation of the New Testament,* p. 102.

[8]See, e.g., Gordon H. Clark, *The Johannine Logos,* chaps. 1-3.

ence cannot be ignored; however, it must be borne in mind that more recently there has been a tendency to relate the Logos idea to Hebraic rather than Grecian thought.[9] There are certain other symbols (in addition to the Logos concept) that are common to both Philo and John, such as the description of God as light, as a fountain, and as a shepherd.

> As in the case of all the other elements in the non-Christian background the differences are more striking than the similarities. Whereas the differences belong to the essentials, the similarities are peripheral. The Logos of Philo becomes radically transformed in John's account. It becomes incarnate in Christ, an idea quite alien to Philo.[10]

The second view is represented by E. F. Harrison. He suggests that the Logos concept has Old Testament roots, including the ideas of "wisdom, power, and a special relation to God." He goes on to recognize that "it was widely used, too, by philosophers to express such ideas as reason and mediation between God and the world. In John's day all classes of readers would have understood its suitability here, where revelation is the keynote."[11] When notice is taken of such passages as Genesis 1:1-26, Psalm 33:6, and Psalm 107:20, it is quite evident that the Old Testament had its influence on John's thinking regarding the Logos (cf. also Prov. 8:22-31).

The word λόγος (logos) is a verbal noun from λέγω. It had two basic uses in the Greek of the day, with a third concept introduced in a technical sense by Greek philosophy, especially that of the Stoics. Liddell and Scott indicate that λόγος means "*the word or outward form by which inward thought is expressed and made known:* also *the inward thought or reason itself,* so that λόγος comprehends both the Lat. *ratio* and *oratio.*"[12] The third usage is actually an extension of the second

[9]For a discussion of the view that the Logos concept is more Oriental than Hellenistic see W. F. Albright, *From the Stone Age to Christianity: Monotheism and the Historical Process,* pp. 285-86.

[10]Donald Guthrie, *New Testament Introduction,* 1:297. It should be remembered, as Guthrie indicates, that parallels in thought do not necessarily involve literary dependence.

[11]E. F. Harrison, "The Gospel According to John," in *The Wycliffe Bible Commentary,* ed. C. F. Pfeiffer and E. F. Harrison, p. 1073.

[12]H. G. Liddell and R. Scott, *A Greek-English Lexicon,* pp. 862-63.

mentioned above. To the Stoics the word was used "to denote the controlling Reason of the universe, the all-pervasive Mind which ruled and gave meaning to all things."[13] Thus, the term λόγος may be seen to have had the meaning of (*a*) the intelligence behind an idea, (*b*) the idea itself, and (*c*) the expression of the idea. Jesus Christ as the ΛΟΓΟΣ of God was the intelligent, personal expression of God's loving heart to a needy world.

b. A further question related to John 1:1-18 and the λόγος concept is, How comprehensively is the term to be understood? It clearly relates to the truth of revelation—but how extensively? Vos suggests that it includes at least three parts: the mediation of the knowledge of God through nature (v. 3), the redemptive revelation given to the Old Testament people of God (v. 11), and the Word made flesh in the incarnation (v. 14).[14]

c. John's doctrine of the Logos revolves around John 1:1-5 and 1:14-18. These two portions deal with the preincarnate and the incarnate Word, respectively. Regarding the preincarnate Word, John tells us that the Word was God (v. 1), Creator (vv. 2-3), Life (v. 4), and Light (v. 5). As to the incarnate Word, he deals with the act (v. 14) and results (vv. 16-18) of incarnation.

John 1:1 is undoubtedly one of the most profound Christological verses in all Scripture.[15] It begins with a declaration regarding the eternality of the Word. "In the beginning," when the universe was created (see Gen. 1:1) the Word "was." This is clearly not a reference

[13]M. C. Tenney, *John: The Gospel of Belief,* p. 62.

[14]Geerhardus Vos, *Biblical Theology, Old and New Testaments,* pp. 368-72.

[15]"It has been noted that the prologue [of John's Gospel] reads like a hymn—it is written in the rythmical prose used in the hymns of the period—and that the same thing holds of Philippians ii, 6-11 [A. B. Macdonald, *Christian Worship in the Primitive Church,* pp. 119-20]. It is, perhaps, not accidental that the two passages in Paul and John which come nearest to being a theology of the Person of Christ have this almost lyric ring. Thomas Arnold said that the Creed should not be recited but sung as a hymn of praise; and, in the New Testament, theology is never found save as the impassionate expression of religion. John, a Christo-centric mystic of high intellectual power, had need of a thought-out religion; he knew that others had the same need; and there is more concentrated thought in the few verses of his prologue than in many whole treatises" (B. H. Streeter, "The Rise of Christianity," in *The Cambridge Ancient History,* ed. S. A. Cook, F. E. Adcock, and M. P. Charlesworth, 11:285).

to a point in time (as is true, for example, in vv. 3, 6, 10, 14, where the aorist verb ἐγένετο is used) but to an indefinite eternity that preceded all time and continued when time began. There is no given moment of which it may be said that then the Logos came into being. He always was (ἦν, imperfect tense). The Logos has had continuous existence, with the beginning of the space-time universe merely being a way-point in relation thereto.

Next, John sets forth the personality of the Word. Here was no impersonal life-force or emanation of divine power. He was an independent center of consciousness capable of individualizing Himself through the personal traits of intellect, sensibility, and will. In stating that "the Word was with God," John implies the Word's active intercourse and personal communion with God. The phrase πρὸς τὸν θεόν (with God) has the idea of "toward" or "face-to-face with," giving the picture of two personal beings facing one another and engaging in intelligent discourse. The use of the same verb that was used in the first clause of verse 1 (ἦν) indicates that ὁ λόγος and ὁ θεός have always been two separate centers of consciousness or individual persons. There should be no confusion of the two.

The third clause of verse 1 speaks of the nature of the Word. He is of the very essence of deity. The words θεὸς ἦν ὁ λόγος have been the target of various cultic and aberrant forms of pseudo-Christian theology since John first penned them. They have been variously translated as "God was the Word," "the Word was a god," "the Word was divine," and so forth. The only grammatically and exegetically correct translation, and therefore the only theologically correct translation, however, is "the Word was God."

While Colwell has demonstrated that in such a construction as this θεός does not need the article to be definite,[16] nonetheless it is to be

[16]"Loosely speaking, this study may be said to have increased the definiteness of a predicate nominative before the verb without the article, and to have decreased the definiteness of a predicate nominative after the verb without the article. The opening verses of John's Gospel contain one of the many passages where this rule suggests the translation of a predicate as a definite noun. καὶ θεὸς ἦν ὁ λόγος looks much more like 'And the Word was God' than 'And the Word was divine' when viewed with reference to this rule. The absence of the article does *not* make the predicate indefinite or qualitative when it precedes the verb; it is indefinite in this position only when the

construed as a predicate nominative rather than as the subject. This is not a convertible statement with either noun capable of being construed as subject. The article could have been used with θεός or it could have been omitted with λογός had there been the intent to have "God" as subject of the clause. "God" is in the first position in the clause for emphasis because this is the climactic statement of a series of remarkable statements. Not only was the Word in existence already at the beginning, and not only was He a personal being in fellowship with God, but He was Himself God. Furthermore, the statement "God was the Word" is in direct contradiction with everything else John teaches about God (to say nothing of the rest of the New Testament). He has already, in the second clause, distinguished God and the Word, and he will continue to do so throughout his writing. John was trinitarian and this translation would make him a unitarian. Where John mentions oneness regarding Father and Son, the context clearly shows that it is not oneness of person that is in view.[17]

The translation "the Word was a god" is openly intended to denigrate the obvious assertion of deity. This, too, does not stand the test of grammar or the test of the analogy of faith, and it totally ignores the development of the argument in the context. As has already been noted, θεός need not have an article to be definite in such constructions as this. Furthermore, if the sense of an anarthrous construction is to be captured in English, it is rarely best accomplished by the use of the indefinite article. Such constructions rather qualify than specify; so the sense is "the Word was of such a nature as God is."[18] As the Athanasian Creed puts it, "the Father is God; the Son is God; the Holy Spirit is God." Also, the translation "the Word was a god" teaches polytheism,

---

context demands it. The context makes no such demand in the Gospel of John, for this statement cannot be regarded as strange in the prologue of the Gospel which reaches its climax in the confession of Thomas [John 20:28]" (E. C. Colwell, "A Definite Rule for the Use of the Article in the Greek New Testament," pp. 20-21).

[17]See John 10:30, where "one" is ἕν, a neuter form rather than the expected masculine, thus setting forth oneness of essence. See also John 17:21.

[18]The New English Bible approaches this concept with the translation "what God was, the Word was." This is not too satisfactory, however, because it leaves things rather indefinite. In light of his putting θεός in the emphatic position, there is no question but that John is underscoring the *Godness* of the Word.

which is in direct conflict with John's teaching elsewhere (John 10:30) and with the rest of the New Testament (e.g., 1 Cor. 8:4-6). In addition, as John develops his argument throughout the prologue, climaxing it in verse 18 with a clear reference to Jesus Christ, the Word, as the unique God (μονογενὴς θεὸς), it becomes quite apparent that he did not have in mind a semidivine aeon or demigod.[19]

When one translates this third clause of John 1:1 as "the Word was divine," it is usually with the implication that divinity is something other and less than absolute deity.[20] If John had meant "divine" as the sense of the statement, he had access to the word θεῖος. Although θεῖος does express a biblical truth,[21] John was identifying person (λόγος) with person (θεός) here, not person with attributes.

The Word was God. Not only did He have a continuous existence from all eternity and a personal existence as a Fellow with God, but He also had an essential existence, being of one substance with God. The One who communed face-to-face with God in the second clause is seen to be equal with God in the third clause. Again, as the Athanasian Creed says, we must "neither confound the persons [of the Godhead] nor divide the essence."

In verses 2-3, John states that the Word was creator. The cosmic significance of the Word is seen in the fact and agency of creation—"all things came into being by Him." The change of verbs between verses 1 and 2 is striking. In verse 1 a continuous state of being (ἦν) was in view; here a crisis of creation (ἐγένετο [came into being]) is seen. The use of "by Him" (δὶ αὐτοῦ) indicates that the Word was the medium through which deity expressed itself in creation. This is such an important truth that John reinforces it with its negative opposite. "Apart from Him nothing came into being." Not only was He the agent of the

[19]An aeon is *"in Gnosticism esp as taught by the Valentinians:* one of the group of eternal beings that together form the fullness of the supreme being from whom they emanate and between whom and the world they are intermediaries" (*Webster's Third New International Dictionary,* s.v. "aeon").

A demigod is "a mythological divine or semidivine being (as the offspring of a deity and a mortal) thought to possess less power than a god" (Ibid., s.v. "demigod").

[20]E.g., J. A. T. Robinson, *Honest to God,* p. 71.

[21]It is "a summary term for the attributes of deity" (G. Abbott-Smith, *A Manual Greek Lexicon of the New Testament,* p. 204).

creation of all things (πάντα), but not even one thing (οὐδὲ ἕν) came into being without His involvement. The correspondence between the Word as Creator and the oft repeated "God said" of Genesis 1 is most significant. The divine fiat and the divine Word are to be understood in conjunction with one another (see also Heb. 11:3; Col. 1:16).

The Word as life and light are closely related concepts. Again there is a very suggestive relationship with Genesis 1. As God was the source of light and life in the physical creation, so is the Word for the spiritual re-creation of man. Life is located in Him, and the context shows that this life is to be understood in moral terms. The effect of this life is the illumination of mankind regarding the truth, because His was genuine light (v. 9). Thus the Word brings man to some sense of general accountability. This is focused more particularly in verse 5, where one specific activity of the light is noted. It shines in moral and spiritual darkness, and even there it maintains supremacy despite the sinister and blinding power of that darkness (cf. John 12:35).[22]

Verses 6-13 give a sort of parenthetical digression regarding the light and His witness (John the Baptist), and then in verse 14 the discourse concerning the Word resumes again. Here the incarnate Word is given continuity with the preincarnate Word. In verse 1 the picture given relates to what He was (ἦν), while here in verse 14 is a picture of what He became (ἐγένετο). The former describes an unbroken continuity of existence, while the latter indicates an act that can be pinpointed in history. The eternal Word steps into time; the personal Word enlarges the circle of fellowship beyond the Godhead to include man; the divine Word adds humanity to His deity.

In verse 14 John cites two lines of evidence to validate the incarnation of the Word: His presence in the midst of man as a man, and apostolic witness to His glory. In earlier days, God had manifested Himself in a tent in the wilderness or in the Temple in Jerusalem; in the present day, He dwells in the sanctuary of the believer's body; but in the days of His flesh, He set up His tent (σκηνόω) in our midst (ἐν ἡμῖν). Being there in plain view, so to speak, He was carefully scrutinized by those who looked on Him so as to understand (θεάομαι) the signifi-

[22]The verb κατέλαβεν in John 1:5 is best translated as "overtake" or "overcome." The translation "comprehend" given in many versions would be appropriate if the verb were in the middle voice.

cance of His being among men. In retrospect, John recognizes that they saw in Him a shining out of inner perfections such as a unique Son[23] from the Father would evidence. Specifically, they beheld a fullness of grace and truth in the Word. These two qualities are especially appropriate regarding λόγος. This full measure of grace assured that the Word always communicated that which was appropriate and fitting to men (cf. Col. 4:6), while the full measure of truth assured the accuracy and effectiveness of the communication (cf. John 17:17; Rev. 19:15*a*).

The results of the incarnation of the Word are next enumerated in verses 16-18. The experience of men with the Word was not limited to observation. Not only was His fullness beheld, it was also received. God's grace and truth were extended to men by the Word. More particularly, that portion of His fullness described as grace was given in repeated measure.[24]

If there is any question left in the reader's mind as to the identity of the divine incarnate Word, verse 17 settles it once and for all. Verse 14 states that the Word was full of χάριτος καὶ ἀληθείας (grace and truth), and verse 17 indicates that this same grace and truth came to pass (i.e., came into being) through Jesus Christ.[25] It is inescapable that John considered Jesus Christ to be the incarnate Word.

Finally, the incarnation of the Word resulted in a unique declaration of the person of God (John 1:18). God, with whom the Word has had eternal fellowship (John 1:1*b*), has never been seen by man. The Word, who is Himself God (John 1:1*c*) and is thus the unique God (μονογενὴς θεός), is in a position such as no other to interpret, or explain, this unseen God to men. The particular credential that John cites here as qualifying the Word for this holy task is that He "is in the bosom of the Father." Because of enjoying an intimacy of relationship

[23]The Greek text reads μονογενοῦς παρὰ πατρός (the only begotten from the Father). The masculine form of the adjective used in a substantival function implies "Son."

[24]Χάριν ἀντὶ χάριτος is best translated "grace in place of grace"; that is, as grace was appropriated and used, it was replaced with more. The Word supplied grace without limit to the believer.

[25]That v. 17 refers to the same "grace and truth" is clear by the use of the articular construction in the Greek. The addition of the article in v. 17 is anaphoric; that is, it is the article of previous reference. It is not that this is the first appearance of grace and truth in human experience, but that grace and truth in this form, as a system in contradistinction to "the Law" and in a personal manifestation, had never been known before.

with the Father that no other may have, He is best able to explain Him to others.[26]

3. *The person of Christ.* John makes three very distinct contributions to Christology. He affirms Christ's deity, strongly defends His humanity, and gives crucial instruction regarding the incarnation.

a. The deity of Christ is first of all supported by certain apostolic notes thereon. The most forthright and direct is contained in the prologue (John 1:1-18).[27] In addition, John identifies Jesus with Yahweh of the Old Testament (John 12:41; cf. 1:1; 5:18). In John 12:37-41 the apostle quotes from Isaiah 53:1 and 6:10, both of which clearly refer to Yahweh in their Old Testament contexts, and then says that in these passages the prophet saw Jesus' glory and spoke of Him.

Further Johannine testimony to Christ's deity is seen when the apostle ascribes to Him the works of God as creator (John 1:3), as life-giver (John 1:12; 20:31; cf. Rev. 2:7), and as baptizer with (in) the Holy Spirit (John 1:33) as well as giver-sender of the Holy Spirit (John 7:37-39; 14:16-17, 26; 15:26; 16:7). John also ascribes to Him the attributes of deity. These include omniscience (John 1:48-50; 4:29; 20:24-28; cf. Rev. 1:14; 2:18, 23; 19:12 for the practical implications of this as it relates to judgment), omnipotence (Rev. 1:8; cf. 4:8),[28] and omnipresence (John 1:48).[29]

[26]Note that the apparent anomaly of having God explain God is reconciled here. God is the Father, and the unique God (μονογενὴς θεός) is the Son (see John 1:14; 3:16). John, who was a Jew by birth, background, and training, indicated here that he recognizes that the unity of God is a complex rather than a simple unity. In other words, God is a Godhead.

[27]See pp. 46-54.

[28]The English "Almighty" is a translation of παντοκράτωρ, which, like its English counterpart, is a compound form. The Greek word's literal meaning is "He who holds onto [κράτωρ, from κρατέω] everything [παντο]," and it thus came to mean "the One who is Master of all things." It may be, therefore, that it is more sovereignty than omnipotence that is in view. This meaning is based on the recognition that the primary sense of κρατέω in the New Testament is "to seize" or "to hold." See W. F. Arndt and F. W. Gingrich, *A Greek-English Lexicon of the New Testament and Other Early Christian Literature,* p. 449; G. Kittel and G. Friedrich, eds., *Theological Dictionary of the New Testament,* 3:914-15. See also F. J. A. Hort (*The Apocalypse of St. John, I-III: The Greek Text with Introduction, Commentary, and Additional Notes,* p. 14), who states that "it means not One who can do anything but One who holds together and controls all things."

[29]John 3:13 in some texts would also fit here, but the reading that is probably preferable ends with ἀνθρώπου (Man), omitting ὁ ὢν ἐν τῷ οὐρανῷ (who is in heaven [*marg.*]).

One particular aspect of apostolic testimony to Christ's deity that deserves special notice is the witness of the signs (John 20:30-31; cf. 5:36). The unique thing about John's presentation of Jesus' miracles is that they are set forth as signs (σημεῖα) rather than merely as demonstrations of power (δυνάμεις) or producers of wonder (τέρατα). They are instructive of the character of Jesus Christ as divine. This is clearly stated in John 20:30-31, where John gives the general purpose of his writing of the gospel. "Many other signs therefore Jesus also performed in the presence of the disciples, which are not written in this book; but these have been written that you may believe that Jesus is the Christ, the Son of God; and that believing you may have life in His name." The particular signs John selected to include in his gospel were especially indicative that Jesus was "the Christ, the Son of God."[30]

John's use of the term "sign" throughout the gospel naturally falls into three groupings, and all of them attest to the deity of Jesus Christ. The miracle of the resurrection, recorded in John 20:1-29, is identified as a sign in John 2:18-22 and is one of the chief evidences that Jesus is God (see John 5:19-29). Christ's postresurrection miracle, recorded in John 21:1-14, although not specifically identified as a sign, seems to qualify as a sign since it is clearly an evidence of omniscience and omnipotence and gives testimony to His compassion for the physical and spiritual needs of the disciples in their lingering postcrucifixion confusions (see John 21:15-22).

The largest body of accumulated evidence to Christ's deity, however, is that of the seven signs of His earthly ministry (selected by John from among many more): He is seen to be (1) the master of quality when He changed water to wine (John 2:1-11) and compressed a natural process into a moment of time; (2) the master of space (distance) when He healed the nobleman's son (John 4:46-54), since the child was more than twenty miles away; (3) the master of time when He healed the impotent man (John 5:1-18), providing an instant cure of an affliction

[30]The term σημεῖον (sign), when used of a miracle, emphasizes that the important thing is the spiritual significance back of the miracle rather than the miracle itself. The miracle is a *means* unto the *end* of the meaning. John uses this term in his gospel in 2:11, 18, 23; 3:2; 4:48, 54; 6:2, 14, 26, 30; 7:31; 9:16; 10:41; 11:47; 12:18, 37; 20:30. See also Westcott, *The Gospel According to St. John,* pp. lxxv-lxxvii.

of thirty-eight years; (4) the master of quantity when He fed five thousand (John 6:1-15), for He provided for the physical needs of five thousand men, plus women and children, with five loaves and two fishes; (5) the master of natural law when He walked on the water (John 6:16-21), overcoming the law of gravity; (6) the master of misfortune when he healed the man born blind (John 9:1-41) by providing deliverance from a congenital condition for a man who in no way was responsible for that condition; and (7) the master of death when He raised Lazarus from the dead (John 11:1-47), thus overpowering man's greatest and most implacable enemy.[31]

The final category of support for Jesus' deity recorded by John is the Lord's own self-claims. He predicted His own resurrection (John 2: 19-22; 10:18), and when He had risen He made certain that the disciples understood its significance (see John 20:11-29). On various occasions He claimed heavenly origin and destination (John 3:13; 6:51, 62; 13:3; 16:28; 17:5, 24). He also claimed to have a special relationship to God that included such things as equality with God (John 5:16-18), the ability to raise the dead (including Himself) and give life (John 5:21 ff.; 10:10, 17, 18, 28), the responsibility to judge mankind (John 5:22 ff.), oneness with the Father (John 10:30-39), and being a special revelation of the Father (John 12:44-50; 14:7-11).

One group of self-claims worthy of particular note is the "I am" claims. Using ἐγώ εἰμι (I am), Jesus makes a series of seven claims to deity couched in figurative language, and each claim relates directly and practically to deep human needs. He says, "I am the bread of life" (John 6:22-71, but note especially verses 35, 47-51), claiming to be the divine provision for man's basic spiritual hunger; "I am the light of the world" (John 8:12; 9:5), claiming to be the divine illumination for man's spiritual darkness; "I am the door" (John 10:7, 9), claiming to be the divine entrance to God's sheepfold, the place of spiritual safety and abundant life; "I am the good shepherd" (John 10:11, 14), claiming to be the divine pastor, who lays down His life to secure the spiritual deliverance of the sheep from evil and who knows each sheep individu-

[31]See Tenney, p. 62.

ally; "I am the resurrection and the life" (John 11:25-26), claiming to be the divine overcomer of death on behalf of the believer; "I am the way, and the truth, and the life" (John 14:6), claiming to be the divine path to the Father for the one who is confused with bypaths, falsehood, and death; and "I am the true vine" (John 15:1, 5), claiming to be the divine source of an abundant spiritual harvest.

The deep significance of all the above is best seen in the most unusual of all the "I am" claims: the absolute claim (John 8:24, 28, 58; 13:19). In three occurrences of this construction, the omission in the Greek of the predicate nominative "He" may be explained in light of the contexts, since there are clearly identifiable antecedents (cf. 8:12, 23 with 24; cf. 8:28*a* with 28*b;* cf. 13:13 with 13:19). The supplying of the pronoun "He" in these cases is in order, since it is inferred from the context. This is not true in John 8:58. Here there is no antecedent in the context, and the obvious contrast intended between the two main statements ("before Abraham was born" and "I AM") is heightened by the fact that neither a predicate nominative nor a predicate adjective is used. By the use of πρίν (before), a word with unmistakable temporal meaning; by the reference to Abraham, a historical personage of paramount importance as the physical, natural, and spiritual progenitor of Israel; and by the use of the aorist infinitive γενέσθαι (was born),[32] which emphasizes the historical *fact* of Abraham's existence, or, better, entrance into existence, one half of the great contrast is set forth. Then by a dramatic change of verb (from γίνομαι to εἰμί) and *aktionsart* (from punctiliar to linear) the second half is stated. While γενέσθαι describes entrance into existence from a state of nonexistence, εἰμί describes timeless being and essential existence (cf. John 1:1). That Jesus was consciously identifying Himself with Yahweh of the Old Testament is beyond refutation. The parallels between this passage and Exodus 3:13-15 are too exact to be set aside. When Moses asked God

[32]The Lord's use of the nonfinite γενέσθαι rather than the finite ἐγένετο (came into being) underscores the aoristic *aktionsart* of the verb form. Two kinds of action or being rather than merely two points in time are contrasted here. The only important element of time is found in πρίν, which simply serves to separate one kind of being from another.

His name so that he could tell it to Israel, the answer was "I AM."[33] The text then goes on, "And God, furthermore, said to Moses, 'Thus you shall say to the sons of Israel, "The LORD [Yahweh],[34] the God of your fathers, the God of Abraham . . . has sent me to you." This is My name forever, and this is My memorial-name to all generations.' " As John 8:59 shows, Jesus' hearers recognized the relationship between Jesus' words and those of Exodus 3:13-15, and thus they reacted as it was customary to react to blasphemy: they picked up stones to stone Him.

This, then, is an open claim to deity. It is an affirmation of time-transcending, self-existent being. As Westcott points out:

> If the sentence had been a simple affirmation of the claim to Messiahship, it would have been welcomed. Comp. x.24. But it was the affirmation of a new interpretation of Messiah's nature and work. Comp. x.30 f.[35]

As with the signs, this statement was designed to demonstrate that "Jesus is the Christ, the Son of God" (John 20:31).

[33]The Hebrew אֶהְיֶה used here is the equivalent of the Greek ἐιμί used in John 8:58. See also the LXX, which reads ἐγώ ἐιμι.

[34] יְהוָה (Yahweh, which the NASB always translates as LORD) is derived from הָיָה (to be); so it becomes apparent that in making the claim "I am" Jesus was claiming to be Yahweh.

While it is not the purpose of this work to extend the current debate on the meaning of *Yahweh,* a brief note is in order. The three major views are as follows: 1. *Yahweh* is not a verb but a noun meaning "being" or "existence." Thus it means "The Existent One" when used of God (see R. K. Harrison, *Introduction to the Old Testament: With a Complete Review of Old Testament Studies and a Special Supplement on the Apocrypha,* pp. 400-401). 2. *Yahweh* is a verb form from the qal imperfect and means "He is" (or, if future, "He will be"). In an absolute sense, then, *Yahweh* would refer to God's being; and in a dynamic sense, it would refer to His presence (see J. Barton Payne, *The Theology of the Older Testament,* p. 147; G. Von Rad, *Old Testament Theology,* 1: 10-11; W. E. Eichrodt, *Theology of the Old Testament,* 1: 189-90). 3. *Yahweh* is a hiphil (causative) verb meaning "He who causes to be." This meaning is based to a large degree on Exodus 6:2-8 and is seen as a unique reminder to Israel, through this special name of God, that her existence as a nation is due to the gracious creative work of God (see Albright, pp. 259-60). Perhaps the solution lies in acknowledging that the name of God is fittingly complex. God is ineffable, and there is both mystery and inscrutability attached to His name. No one concept or use can adequately capture the complete nature of God.

[35]Westcott, *The Gospel According to St. John,* p. 140.

When all this is taken into consideration, the other "I am" claims take on new significance. Just as in the Old Testament a variety of descriptive titles for God are formed in association with the name *Yahweh* (e.g., "Yahweh of hosts," "Yahweh of lords," "Yahweh our righteousness," etc.), so in the New Testament a variety of epithets are built upon an association with the phrase "I am." The very name 'Ιησοῦς (Jesus) is the Greek equivalent of יְהוֹשׁוּעַ (Yah [abbreviated form of *Yahweh*] is Savior) (cf. Matt. 1:21). Thus, recognizing the divine significance of His name, when Jesus said "before Abraham was born, I AM" (John 8:58), He was saying, in effect, "Before Abraham was born, I existed as Yahweh." Similarly, when He said "I am the bread of life," He was saying "I am Yahweh, the bread of life"; when He said "I am the light of the world," He was saying "I am Yahweh, the light of the world"; and so on.

b. Equally as important as John's teaching regarding Jesus' deity is his teaching regarding the genuine humanity of Jesus. This is set forth in three ways. First, it is seen in the qualities of humanity He manifested. He had a human nature (John 19:31, 40; 11:33; 12:27; 13:21), He manifested human emotions (John 11:35; 12:27; 13:21), He experienced human limitations (John 4:6-7; 19:28-30), and He died (John 19:30, 32-34).

Second, His humanity is affirmed by direct apostolic witness. In 1 John 1:1-3, 4:2-3, and 2 John 7-11, John is apparently dealing with an error of his day similar to second century Gnosticism.[36] This error, because of its dualistic belief that all things spiritual are good and all things material are evil, denied the incarnation of Christ. While the approach to the subject varied, the net result was the same: the belief that Christ's humanity was only apparent and not real.[37]

John refutes this error, and thus confirms the genuine humanity of Jesus Christ by an appeal to empirical evidence (1 John 1:1-3). He

[36]See pp. 21-22.

[37]Hence the term *Docetism,* from the Greek word δοκέω (it seems to be). "Extreme Docetism held that Jesus was not human at all but was merely a prolonged theophany, while moderate Docetism considered Jesus the natural son of Joseph and Mary upon whom came the Christ at His baptism" (Charles C. Ryrie, *Biblical Theology of the New Testament,* p. 312).

appeals to the physical senses of hearing, sight, and touch, and then emphasizes the appeal by repetition to verify His humanness. Next he takes a theological tack: the prophet who confesses "that Jesus Christ has come in the flesh is from God" (1 John 4:2). (With this strong statement of humanity there is the inescapable implication of deity, too.) The phrase ἐν σαρκί (in the flesh) is to be understood as a reference to human nature.[38]

Many of the English translations miss the sense of 1 John 4:2 on this point.[39] The New American Standard Bible, for example, reads: "Every spirit that confesses that Jesus Christ has come in the flesh is from God." The Revised Standard Version, the New English Bible, and the New International Version give practically the same translation. The relative clause ὃ ὁμολογεῖ 'Ιησοῦν Χριστὸν ἐν σαρκὶ ἐληλυθότα would better read "who confesses Jesus Christ as having come in flesh." This allows "Jesus Christ" to be the direct object of the verb rather than a part of an objective clause; it also accounts for the anarthrous construction of the participle. It is not so much the *fact* that He has come as it is the *character,* or *nature,* of the One who came that is in view. It is the denial of *incarnate* deity that is of antichrist (1 John 4:3; 2 John 7). Notice in verse 3 that the spirit who is not of God is the one who does not confess τὸν 'Ιησοῦν (the anaphoric article τὸν refers to the particular Jesus who is characterized in verse 2 as having come in flesh).

Third, the Lord Himself testifies to His own humanity. In John 5:27, after having repeatedly referred to His divine sonship in the preceding verses, He describes Himself as υἱὸς ἀνθρώπου (Son of Man). One qualification to be Judge of mankind in the last day is to be the Son of God, that is, the One who, distinct from all other sons of God, is divine. But the judge also must be from among mankind. In John 1:51 He refers to Himself as τὸν υἱὸν τοῦ ανθρώπου (the Son of Man) because that is clearly a Messianic reference with emphasis upon the person. But the anarthrous construction in 5:27 emphasizes the nature of the judge (cf. Acts 17:30-31).

c. Finally, and as the climax of his teaching regarding the person

[38]See discussion in section c. below on the incarnation as set forth in John 1:14.

[39]Although the NASB, RSV, and NEB translate 2 John 7 more nearly as it should read.

of Christ, John teaches that Jesus Christ is the God-man through the incarnation. In addition to the truths noted earlier regarding John 1:14, the following should be observed as well. There is a continuity established between this verse and verses 1-5 (and especially vv. 1-2) by the phrase καὶ ὁ λόγος (and the Word), which begins the verse. The same subject is now reintroduced into the argument. The use of ἐγένετο (became) here in contrast to ἦν (was) in verses 1-2 emphasizes His becoming something He was not before. He is still the λόγος, with all the truth ascribed to Him in verses 1-2, but now He is the Word *in* the flesh. By this act the invisible God (cf. 1:1, 18) was enabled to dwell among us (in contrast to earlier Christophanies, which were transitory) and His glory was able to be beheld. The phrase σὰρξ ἐγένετο (became flesh) implies that He became *man,* not *a man;* that is, He was genuinely human while genuinely divine.[40] Westcott's excellent summary of John 1:14 is reproduced here in full, for it would be difficult to improve upon it.

> 1. The Lord's humanity was complete, as against various forms of Apollinarianism, according to which the divine Logos supplied the place of part of that which belongs to the perfection of Manhood. (The Word became *flesh,* not *a body* or the like.)
>
> 2. The Lord's humanity was real and permanent, as against various forms of Gnosticism, according to which He only assumed in appearance, or for a time, that which was and remained foreign to Himself. (The Word *became* flesh, and did not *clothe Himself* in flesh.
>
> 3. The Lord's human and divine natures remained without change, each fulfilling its part according to its proper laws, as against various forms of Eutychianism, according to which the result of the Incarnation is a third nature, if the humanity has any real existence. (The *Word* became *flesh,* both terms being preserved side by side.)
>
> 4. The Lord's humanity was universal and not individual, as including all that belongs to the essence of man, without regard to sex or race or time. (The Word became *flesh* and not *a man.*)
>
> 5. The Lord's human and divine natures were united in one Person, as against various forms of Nestorianism, according to which He has a human personality and a divine personality, to which the acts, etc.,

[40]Westcott, *The Gospel According to St. John,* pp. 10-11.

> belonging to the respective natures must be referred. (*The Word became flesh and dwelt,* etc., without any change of the subject to the verb.)
>
> 6. The Word did not acquire personality by the Incarnation. He is spoken of throughout, not as a principle or an energy, but . . . as a Person.[41]

C. John's Doctrine of the Holy Spirit.

At this juncture consideration will be given only to the *person* of the Holy Spirit. His *works* will be dealt with in chapters 6 and 8.

1. *The Holy Spirit is a person.* John's writings reveal two reasons for concluding that the Holy Spirit is a person, in addition to the proof of the various works that He performs. The first of the two reasons is quite substantial; the second is more speculative.

First, in several instances in the upper room discourse it may seem as if the Lord employed an ungrammatical use of the masculine gender to refer to the neuter word πνεῦμα (Spirit [John 14:26; 15:26; and 16:7-8 together with vv. 13-14]). Since τὸ πνεῦμα τὸ ἅγιον (the Holy Spirit), the primary title of the Holy Spirit, is built from a neuter word, it would be expected that all antecedential references thereto would likewise be neuter, in keeping with the laws of Greek grammar. The usual line of argument says that because Jesus used masculine instead of neuter pronouns to refer to τὸ πνεῦμα τὸ ἅγιον, the Holy Spirit is therefore a person.[42] A careful examination of the texts involved will show, however, that in fact normal grammatical laws are followed when pronouns are used to refer to τὸ πνεῦμα τὸ ἅγιον. The pronouns are neuter. It is true that the demonstrative pronoun ἐκεῖνος (that Person, *or* He) is used throughout these passages in the masculine gender, but its antecedent is not πνεῦμα but παράκλητος (Helper). When used of the Holy Spirit, παράκλητος is used as a substantive rather than as an adjective. As an adjective it would have no intrinsic gender. As a substantive, however, it could be expected to be in the

[41]Ibid., p. 11.

[42]See C. Hodge, *Systematic Theology,* 1:524; R. Pache, *The Person and Work of the Holy Spirit,* p. 13; Charles C. Ryrie, *The Holy Spirit,* pp. 14-15; and J.F. Walvoord, *The Holy Spirit,* pp. 6-7.

neuter gender to extend the sense of τὸ πνεῦμα (the Spirit) were it indeed true that the Spirit is an impersonal force or influence.[43] However, although Christ did not change the gender of πνεῦμα or of pronouns that refer to πνεῦμα (see John 14:17), He did express the fact of personality through παράκλητος by putting it in the masculine gender. Thus, when this title (παράκλητος) of the Holy Spirit is the antecedent of τὸ πνεῦμα τὸ ἅγιον, Christ repeatedly used the masculine gender; and when this title is referred to pronominally, He used the masculine form of the demonstrative pronoun, ἐκεῖνος.

The other, and less conclusive, support for the personality of the Holy Spirit is Christ's use of ἄλλος (another) in reference to the Spirit (John 14:16).[44] The Lord's statement is that He "will ask the Father, and He will give you another Helper [ἄλλον παράκλητον]." While some scholars would claim that the use of ἕτερος and ἄλλος is a matter of indifference in the New Testament, there does seem to be some evidence to the contrary. There is only one other passage in the New Testament, other than the upper room discourse, in which the term παράκλητος is used. In 1 John 2:1 it is used of Jesus Christ; hence the first, in relation to which the Holy Spirit is "another," is clearly a person. In classical Greek the distinction between ἄλλος and ἕτερος is "another of the same kind" as over against "another of a different kind."[45] That this difference, on occasion at least, holds in *koinē* Greek is maintained by many scholars,[46] although there is no

[43]In light of the extensive (and, in the New Testament, exclusive) use of παράκλητος as a masculine substantive from the fourth century B.C. on, it may well be questioned as to how significant the gender of the word actually is. It should not be overlooked, however, that this extensive use of the word provides weighty testimony to the personal *character* of a paraclete.

[44]Arndt and Gingrich (pp. 39, 315) dispute the line of argument given above by denying that ἄλλος and ἕτερος differ from one another in any substantial way in *koinē* Greek.

[45]These words have come into English as *else* (from ἄλλος) in a word like *elsewhere,* meaning "in another place," and *heterodox* (from ἕτερος), meaning "a different teaching" from the commonly accepted orthodoxy.

[46]See, e.g., J. B. Lightfoot, *Saint Paul's Epistle to the Galatians: A Revised Text with Introduction, Notes, and Dissertations;* R. C. Trench, *Synonyms of the New Testament;* H. Cremer, *Biblico-Theological Lexicon of New Testament Greek;* A. T. Robertson, *Word Pictures in the New Testament,* 5:292.

question that the sharp distinction was beginning to break down. It may be questioned whether the alternate use of these words in 1 Corinthians 12:8 and 10 and Hebrews 11:35-36 is didactic or merely a literary device, but the use in Galatians 1:6-7 seems to be purposeful and instructive. In fact, despite suggestions to the contrary,[47] the sense of the passage is vitiated if the distinction is not upheld. It would seem that while the hard distinction between the two words may have been fading during New Testament times, when a writer wanted to draw the quantitative-versus-qualitative difference he still was free to call upon the more classical meaning of the words. If this be the case in John 14:16, the Lord is saying that upon His departure He will request of the Father for believers another Paraclete like Himself, another of the same kind, who will give personal attention to their needs.

2. *The Holy Spirit is a distinct member of the Godhead.* The Holy Spirit is not merely another manifestation of Christ (John 14:26; 15:26). Like the Father and the Son, He indwells believers (John 14: 17, 20, 23), thus acting in concert with the triune God and giving indication that He, too, is divine. The relation of the Holy Spirit to the Father and Son is especially noteworthy in John 15:26. Whatever else the passage teaches, it most certainly indicates that the Holy Spirit will be sent by Jesus Christ (πέμψω [will send] probably refers to Pentecost), that He comes forth from the Father's side (παρὰ [from]), and that He will bear witness to Christ (cf. John 16:13-15). In contrast to the πέμψω, which refers to an act, ἐκπορεύεται (proceeds) is a present tense and may well refer to an eternal relationship (understanding this as a timeless present).[48] If this be so, the two future verbs of the verse refer to the Spirit's economical relationship to the Godhead, while the present verb refers to His ontological relationship.

[47]H.N. Ridderbos, *The Epistle of Paul to the Churches of Galatia,* p. 48.

[48]On good ground Westcott (*The Gospel According to St. John,* pp. 224-25) disputes this interpretation. If his thinking is correct, all three verbs in John 15:26 refer to intertrinitarian economical relationships.

Part Two:
Soteriology

IV

The Doctrine of Sin

This brief discussion of hamartiology is aimed at relating the doctrine of sin to salvation. In chapter 9, John's development of this doctrine as regards the Christian life will be considered.

A. The Character of Sin.

There are at least two ways to get a picture of the nature, or character, of sin as John sees it. First, it is revealed in the terminology he uses. It will be noted that the words he uses are familiar New Testament terms that are frequently used by other writers. They are ἁμαρτία, the general word for sin, used approximately thirty times (e.g., John 1:29; 1 John 1:9; Rev. 1:5); ἁμαρτάνω, another general word for sin, used approximately sixteen times (e.g., John 5:14; 1 John 1:10); πονηρός, meaning evil in its viciousness, used approximately ten times—six of which refer to Satan (e.g., John 3:19; 1 John 3:12); ἀδικία, describing sin as wrongdoing (John 7:18; 1 John 1:9, 5:17), and ἀδικέω, meaning the same thing as ἀδικία (Rev. 22:11); and ἀνομία, characterizing sin as rebellion, used only once by John—but in a very crucial way (1 John 3:4). Thus, a composite picture is painted of sin as a missing of God's standard, malicious evil, social evil, and willful rebellion.

The prime Johannine emphasis upon sin lies in two areas. Throughout the gospel it is epitomized as unbelief, the antithesis of belief, which is the theme of the book, as seen in 20:30-31 (see e.g., John 8:21, 24; 16:8-9). In his first epistle, John comes the nearest to defining his concept of sin. In 1 John 3:4 it is stated that ἡ ἁμαρτία ἐστιν ἡ ἀνομία. The statement is convertible[1] and therefore may read "sin is lawlessness" and "lawlessness is sin." It is

> both an exhaustive and definitive definition of sin. It is exhaustive because both words are preceded by the article, which means the phrase is convertible. . . . It is definitive because lawlessness is to be understood in the most absolute sense of the condition of being without law of any kind. It is contrariness to law, not simply violation of some specific in the Mosaic Law.[2]

Law represents, in the most absolute and basic sense, God's character. That is, it is the true standard for the universe because God is by nature righteous. Lawlessness is the antithesis of Law and is thus the antithesis of God. It is not only a missing of the mark (ἁμαρτία) set by God's character, but it is also overt rejection of that standard set by His character.

B. The Universality of Sin.

That sin pervades the whole of human experience, both quantitatively and qualitatively, is seen in that all have committed acts of sin (1 John 1:10); all, including believers, have a sin nature (1 John 1:8); all who are outside of Christ have God's judicial wrath resting upon them (John 3:16; 3:36); and all men need a Savior (John 1:29; 3:16-17; 4:42; 1 John 4:14).

C. The Consequences of Sin.

John has extensive teaching on the consequences of sin in the believer's life, but at this juncture it is the general doctrine that will be considered. For the unbeliever sin is viewed as moral bondage (John 8:34); culpable guilt (John 15:22, 24); spiritual death (John 3:16; 5:24; cf. 8:21, 24); and judgment, both present and future, with its consequent estrangement from God (John 3:18, 36).

[1]H. E. Dana and J. R. Mantey, *A Manual Grammar of the Greek New Testament*, p. 149.

[2]Charles C. Ryrie, *Biblical Theology of the New Testament*, pp. 333-34.

V

The Savior

As was noted in chapter 1 (pp. 23-25), in contrast to Paul, whose theology is a theology of the passion of our Lord and thus focuses on His death, John's is a theology of the incarnation and focuses on the revelation of God in Christ (see John 1:14; 12:44-47; 14:9). Certainly Paul's teaching is not limited to the death of Christ any more than John's is limited to the incarnation, but we may expect that John's teaching regarding the Savior will find its emphasis at this point. Note, however, that despite the observable emphasis he does not fail to deal with Jesus as the suffering, sacrificial Savior.

A. The Witness of John the Baptist (John 1:29, 36).

Since there is some debate as to the significance of this passage, it will be good to notice the various components item by item.

First, a suggestion may be made regarding punctuation. In John 1:29, the New American Standard Bible is right in placing a comma after "Behold" (ἴδε), with the remaining words considered as a unit unto themselves. Thus, since "Behold" is a separate grammatical unit the statement cannot read, "Behold the Lamb of God, that is the one who takes away the sin of the world." Ἴδε is an exclamation rather than a true imperative. This is proved by the fact that ἀμνός (Lamb) is in the nominative case. The proper reading, then, is, "Behold! The Lamb of God who takes away the sin of the world." This is an occasion for excitement and wonder. One can almost hear the animation in John's voice as he cries out this good news.

Next, it should be noticed that this is *God's* lamb. In contrast to the man-provided lambs of the Old Testament sacrifices, this is one of God's own provision (cf. Gen. 22:8). This is certainly one signal of some change in God's economy.

Another vexing question is, What did John have in view in this reference? What was it that triggered this unusual description of Jesus Christ on this occasion? Since John and Jesus were kin, it is most likely that they had known one another prior to this; but John had never assessed Jesus in this way before. It is true that God had instructed John as to how he might identify the Messiah from among all those whom he would baptize (John 1:32-33), but the instructions had apparently not given any intimation that this one was to be viewed as a sacrificial lamb. This was a spontaneous assessment made by John himself.

Did he have in mind the morning and evening sacrifice offered daily in the Temple (Exod. 29:38 ff.)? Was it the Paschal lamb (Exod. 12)?[1] Was it the lamb of Isaiah 53? In light of John's use of and quotation from Isaiah the day before (v. 23), it would seem that he may well have had the Messianic passage of Isaiah 53 in mind.[2] Nonetheless, the other truths that are so prominent in Jewish experience cannot be excluded, especially the Passover experience (cf. John 19:36). Surely the description brought (and probably was intended to bring) a combination of thoughts to the Jewish mind, including the image of vicarious suffering and patient submission from Isaiah 53, sacrificial worship (burnt offering) from the morning and evening sacrifice, and substitution and redemption from the Paschal offering. (Note that the sacrificial lamb concept is further seen in John's writings in Rev. 5:12; 7:14; etc., as well.)

[1]Actually, the Passover sacrifice was not necessarily a lamb, nor was it designated as "the Paschal lamb." The term used to refer to the Paschal sacrifice was τὸ πάσχα (the Passover [see 1 Cor. 5:7]).

[2]John Bright, for all practical purposes, denies that "Jews expected a suffering redeemer" (*A History of Israel,* p. 457), and Leon Morris questions whether Isaiah 53 was understood Messianically in pre-Christian times (*The Gospel According to John: The English Text with Introduction, Exposition, and Notes,* p. 145). While it may be that Judaism in general did not so view this passage, it is quite apparent that this was a view held *early* in the history of the church (cf. Acts 8:30-35), and it is inconceivable that this view did not have roots in the early decades of the first century, at the very least.

The next question revolves around the meaning of ὁ αἴρων. Should it be understood in the sense of "He who takes away" or "He who takes upon"? That is, is it deliverance from the power of sin—the abolition of sin—that is in view,[3] or is it the penal endurance of guilt? It must be admitted that a strong case may be made for "takes away." By the witness of Westcott, Septuagint usage favors this meaning;[4] and certainly John's usage in the gospel and epistles favors it. (See John 11:48; 17:15; 19:31, 38; 1 John 3:5. In John 15:2 "takes away" is better translated "lifts up.") The last passage, 1 John 3:5, is especially significant since it speaks of taking away sins. In its context, it almost certainly refers to the power rather than the penalty of sin, "since the point of the argument lies in the antagonism between the Christian life and sin."[5]

In light of this weighty evidence, what can be offered in favor of the second view? Note that all the other uses of αἴρω (other than John 1:29) in the gospel do *not* relate to the matter of sin. Also, note that in 1 John 3:5 the apostle refers to "sins," while in John 1:29 it is "sin" that is taken away. Perhaps we have here an intended distinction between the sinful acts of believers (1 John 3:5; cf. 1:9) and the sin principle with its attendant guilt. While it may be true that "of the two aspects of the Atonement, as 1) The removal of the punishment of sin, and 2) The removal of sin, St. John dwells habitually on the latter,"[6] we cannot overlook passages like John 3:36 and 1 John 2:2. Perhaps the solution to this problem lies in the possibility that the two thoughts are combined in the one term.

Related to the preceding question is the significance of the present tense of the participle αἴρων. In a reference to Christ's death, one would normally expect an aorist rather than a present tense. Hendriksen suggests that it means Christ has already at this point begun His sin-bearing work.[7] This hardly seems acceptable, however, in light

[3]As held by G. B. Stevens, *The Johannine Theology: A Study of the Doctrinal Contents of the Gospel and Epistles of the Apostle John,* pp. 167-70, 186.

[4]B. F. Westcott, *The Gospel According to St. John: The Authorized Version with Introduction and Notes,* p. 20.

[5]Stevens, p. 168.

[6]Westcott, p. 20.

[7]W. Hendriksen, *Exposition of the Gospel According to John,* 1:99.

of the consistent New Testament emphasis that His death rather than His life provided atonement for sin (Rom. 3:24-26; Gal. 3:13; Eph. 1:7; 1 Pet. 2:24). If the force of the present participle is to be pressed, it is perhaps better to see it as viewing Christ's life-mission as characterized by the taking of sin. Probably, however, Westcott's suggestion is more acceptable. He remarks that the present tense "marks the future result as assured in the beginning of the work and also as continuous."[8]

Finally, it is to be noticed that this work of Christ's has some kind of a comprehensive significance and consequence. It is the sin of the *world* that is taken away. But in what sense is the term "world" to be taken? And, when that question has been decided, what is the theological truth that is intended by the assertion that the world's sin is removed? The obvious meaning of "world" is all mankind; but since at first glance such an interpretation points in the direction of universalism, other interpreters have qualified the term to mean the world of the elect. It is true that sometimes apparently universal terms such as *all* and *world* are in certain contexts limited to the entirety of a particular group rather than all men without limitation. It is equally true, however, that at other times such terms are intended to be taken in an unrestricted way. John's statements (John 1:29; 3:16-17; 1 John 2:2) do not lend themselves to the restrictions suggested above. This is especially apparent in the other two passages noted. In John 3:16-17 there is a clear distinction drawn between a larger group, "the world," and a smaller group, "whoever believes." Also, in 1 John 2:1-2 a contrast between two groups is seen. On the one hand, there are the believers, "my little children," for whose sins Christ is propitiation; and on the other hand is "the whole world," for whom He is likewise the propitiation. It is quite apparent that the interpretation of the term "world" by those who relate it to the elect only is determined by theological rather than hermeneutical considerations.

If "world" is taken in the unrestricted sense, three possible theological views present themselves. Some scholars hold that this verse teaches that all men have been reconciled to God by His elective love and merely wait to be told this news. Men are not really eternally lost apart from personal faith in Jesus Christ; they are simply ignorant of their

[8]Westcott, p. 20.

real condition and need to be told so that they may enjoy the reconciliation that is already theirs in Christ. This neouniversalism finds no support whatsoever in the New Testament when it is literally interpreted (see, e.g., John 3:18-21, 36).

Another, more evangelical, form of universalism would teach that Christ's death released man from the penalty, or guilt, of sin and that the *only* reason a man today is lost is because he refuses (or fails) to believe in Jesus Christ. That is, in His death Christ secured a redemption sufficient for all men by actually canceling out all the claims of God against man due to sin. Men choose their own condemnation by willful rejection of Christ and the grace of God.[9] While this is *one* of the reasons for man's condemnation (see John 16:8-9; cf. 3:36), it is not the only one (see John 5:28-29; Rev. 13:8; 17:8; cf. Rom. 5:12-21; Eph. 2:1-3).

The third option is to recognize that the Scriptures teach that both for judicial reasons (having to do with imputed sin) and for natural reasons (having to do with imparted sin) all men are lost even prior to any decision about Christ, that it is not in God's eternal design and purpose that all be saved, and that the death of Christ was intended to involve the condemnation of the lost as well as the salvation of the elect. That is, Christ died for the sin of the world (all men) and in so doing provided a basis for the redemption of the elect and the condemnation of the nonelect. Thus, the Lord's death made salvation *possible* for every man, although the *actualization* of this potential is only realized by the exercise of the gift of faith on the part of the elect (John 6:29, 44). This avoids the two common errors of "evangelical" soteriology: (1) that man assists in his redemption by exercising his will in an independent sense,[10] and (2) that the elect are actually redeemed by a limited atonement (death for only the "world" of the elect).[11]

[9]This teaching ignores, or attempts to redefine, the New Testament doctrines of *total* depravity and divine election. Since these doctrines are basically Pauline and Petrine, they are not dealt with here.

[10]Man's will *is* involved, but only as it is a will quickened by God (John 6:44).

[11]This understanding of "limited atonement" affirms the doctrines of the total depravity of man and his inability to exercise faith on his own and attempts to avoid the danger of a kind of universalism that allegedly arises from a belief in general atonement. The problem is that "limited atonement" thus defined leads to theological overkill: it sees men as being saved *only* on the basis of the death of Christ—rather than on the

According to John, there is a limited reception of the gift of God (see John 1:12, "as many as received Him;" John 3:16, "whoever believes"); and that limited reception accounts for the salvation of elect men only. By the same token, rejection of Christ (John 3:18) combined with God's eternal purpose (Rev. 13:8; 17:8), not a limited atonement, accounts for the condemnation of men.[12]

B. The Witness of John the Apostle.

Any attempt to separate the Savior Himself from His work of salvation is nearly impossible. If John makes any distinction, it is in terminology and imagery rather than in essence.

Actually, John intends his *whole gospel* to be a testimony to the Saviorhood of Jesus Christ, as is seen in John 20:31: "These [signs] have been written that you may believe that Jesus is the Christ, the Son of God; and that believing you may have life in His name." Note also John 4:42, where John records the words of the Samaritans as they acknowledge Jesus to be the "Savior of the world."[13]

In 1 John 3:5 and 8 the apostle speaks of two purposes of the *manifestation* of Jesus Christ that are related to His saviorhood. They are not so much related to initial salvation, however, as to daily salvation—the Christian life. In 1 John 4:14 he bears personal witness again to the fact that the Father sent the Son to be Savior of the world.

C. The Witness of Jesus Christ.

Jesus made several statements that show His personal anticipation of the fulfillment of His saving work. He spoke of His being "lifted up"

---

basis of personal faith in the crucified and risen Christ, as well. Careful distinction must be maintained between *(a)* the provision of redemption and *(b)* its personal application and realization.

[12]The mysterious and beautiful combination of human responsibility and divine purpose is thus maintained in perfect balance. Neither can be overemphasized or underemphasized without disturbing the biblical symphony of salvation.

[13]Vv. 20-22 should be compared with v. 41. It is apparent that the Samaritans recognized that Jesus was not merely the Jews' Savior: He was their Savior, too. Salvation is "from" (ἐκ) the Jews not "for" (ὑπέρ) the Jews exclusively.

(John 3:14-15; 8:28; 12:32), which John interprets for us in John 12:33 as a reference to His death.[14] The Lord clearly viewed His death as being in line with the purpose of God as foreshadowed in the Old Testament, wherein the sacrifice for sin takes on the character of sin and thereby provides the antidote to the death-bearing malady (cf. John 3:14 and Num. 21:6-9).[15]

Christ also made frequent reference to "My hour" and "My time" (John 2:4; 7:6; 12:23; 13:1; John used the phrase "His hour" in 7:30; 8:20). As the statement in John 13:1 shows, it was not just His passion but the completion of the purpose of the incarnation in toto that was in view. Christ viewed the arrival of His hour as the occasion for the supreme glorification of Himself and His Father (John 13:31-32; cf. 12:23). In Christ's death, burial, resurrection, and return to the Father, the splendor of God's character was manifested in a way it could not have been otherwise.[16]

Christ's role as Savior is also alluded to by the figure of the cup that He was to drink (John 18:11). It portrays Christ's submissiveness to the Father's will despite the fact that the cup He was to drink was repulsive to Him since it involved sin and death.[17]

[14]In light of the use of ἐκ τῆς γῆς from the earth in John 12:32, Christ's being "lifted up" probably goes beyond His death and includes His exaltation as well.

[15]The same principle is seen elsewhere in the Old Testament in the use of the scapegoat on the Day of Atonement (Lev. 16:21-22) and in the New Testament in Paul's writings (2 Cor. 5:21; Gal. 3:13; cf. Deut. 21:22-23). In fact, it is entirely possible that the concept set forth in the last two references was in our Lord's mind when He used the phrase "lifted up."

[16]The glory of God, whether relating to Jesus Christ or to the Father, is the display of His nature in His various perfections. John indicates that the righteousness (John 16:10), love (John 3:16; 1 John 3:16), life (John 17:3), faithfulness (John 17:11-12), and unity (John 17:21-23) of God were evidenced by the arrival of His hour and the subsequent glorification of Father and Son. The theme of "glory" is quite prominent in John (see, e.g., John 7:39; 8:50, 54).

[17]This figure is found much more frequently in the synoptics (Matt. 20:22-23; 26:39; Mark 10:38-39; 14:36; Luke 22:42).

VI

The Holy Spirit

John sets forth the place of the Holy Spirit in the work of salvation under two primary headings. The first, His work as convictor, is a presalvation work; the second, His work as regenerator, relates directly to salvation itself.

A. The Holy Spirit as Convictor.

The aspect of the Spirit's work set forth in John 16:7-11 is directly related to the finished work of Christ. "It is to your advantage that I go away; for if I do not go away, the Helper shall not come to you; but if I go, I will send Him to you" (John 16:7). This is underscored by noting that the three areas of conviction presuppose the completed work of Christ, too.

As Westcott notes:

> The idea of "conviction" is complex. It involves the conceptions of authoritative examination, of unquestionable proof, of decisive judgment, of punitive power. Whatever the final issue may be, he who "convicts" another places the truth of the case in dispute in a clear light before him, so that it must be seen and acknowledged as truth. He who then rejects the conclusion which this exposition involves, rejects it with his eyes open and at his peril.[1]

[1]B. F. Westcott, *The Gospel According to St. John: The Authorized Version with Introduction and Notes,* p. 228.

This is reinforced by Trench, who says:

> But ἐλέγχειν [convict] is . . . so to rebuke another, with such effectual wielding of the victorious arms of the truth, as to bring him, if not to a confession, yet at least to a conviction, of his sin, just as in juristic Greek ἐλέγχειν is not merely to reply to, but to refute, an opponent.[2]

The work of conviction, then, may be considered as a work of common grace.

The specific matters of conviction are identified by the threefold repetition of περί (concerning, *or* in the matter of). They are sin, man's problem; righteousness, God's provision; and judgment, the rejector's punishment. Likewise, the threefold use of ὅτι (because) marks the causes of the conviction in the three areas just noted. In each case the work of the Holy Spirit to the world, which is the object of the conviction, centers in the person and work of Christ rather than in peripheral things. There are many things concerning which one's conscience may bring an uneasy feeling, but the Holy Spirit's ministry of conviction relates to faith in Christ, His righteousness, and His judgment of Satan.

It is important to notice the subjects of each causal clause in verses 9-11 if the significance of this passage is to be properly grasped. Conviction of sin comes because *"they"* (citizens of the world-system) do not believe in Christ, conviction of righteousness comes because *"I"* (Christ) go to the Father, and conviction of judgment comes because *"the ruler" of this world-system* (Satan) stands judged.

Now notice the three major elements of the Spirit's convicting work. First, He convicts men of *the* sin of unbelief in Christ. Here we get right at the central theme of John's gospel, for he builds his case around the antithesis between belief and unbelief. To believe in Christ reveals the very essence of salvation, for such belief reveals an attitude of obedience to God's Word. The believer assumes the posture of submissiveness to, or dependence upon, God's provision. To disbelieve Christ (that is, to reject Him) is of the very essence of sin, for to disbelieve is to judge God's Word and assert personal independence of God Himself. The disbeliever trusts in himself or in some other pseudosavior rather than in God. This is where everything of spiritual significance begins and

[2]R. C. Trench, *Synonyms of the New Testament,* pp. 12-13.

ends; so it is no wonder that the Spirit's convicting work begins here.

Second, the Spirit convicts men of Christ's righteousness. The cause for this conviction, which is given in John 16:10, is twofold, and the force of the statement, although expressed by a different construction, is similar to that of Paul's statement about Christ in Romans. Even as justification is proved by the resurrection (Rom. 4:25)[3], so Christ's righteousness is demonstrated by the ascension, "because I go to the Father" (John 16:10). Christ's statement is the theological explanation of the historical confirmation, in His resurrection and ascension, that "it is finished!" (John 19:30). Both the person and work of Christ are vindicated. The Spirit convicts men that Jesus Christ is who He claimed to be and that He did what He claimed to do. Going to the Father and being seen no more are indications that the righteous work of the righteous Son is completed.

Third, the Spirit convicts men of Satan's judgment. If you do not submit to the God of the universe, you must submit, knowingly or unknowingly, to the ruler of this cosmos. He, however, stands under sentence of judgment.[4] To be identified with him is to be identified with a condemned master. His judgment assures the judgment of those who persist in unbelief in Christ.

B. The Holy Spirit as Regenerator.

The doctrine of regeneration as set forth by John will be considered in the next chapter (pp. 84-101), but a few observations regarding the Holy Spirit as regenerator are in order here.

The birth that is identified in John 1:12-13 as being of God is specifically identified in John 3:6 with the Holy Spirit. As a human being (and

[3]The construction in Romans 4:25 is διά with the accusative, ἠγέρθη διὰ τὴν δικαίωσιν ἡμῶν, rather than διά with the genitive. The justification was the cause of the resurrection; the resurrection was not the agency of the justification. In raising His Son the Father was giving visible witness to His satisfaction with Jesus' death for sin.

[4]The verb translated "has been judged" (v.11) is a perfect passive form, κέκριται. In the eternal counsels of God, Satan stands condemned. The death of Christ secured the sentence historically, and the punishment will be administered in the end times when Satan is thrown into the lake of fire to experience eternal torment (Rev. 20:10).

any human effort) begets after its kind—and, the implication is, *always* does so—likewise the Spirit, and He alone, brings forth after His kind. His work of conviction is a general work of grace, since many will be faced with their sin but not all will accede to the evidence. This work, on the other hand, is a special work of grace, for all who are born of the Spirit are spirit. John 3:8 shows by illustration that His regenerating work is both sovereign and inscrutable. The evidence of the new birth is unmistakable; but, as with the wind, the Spirit's course of action, His time of action, and His methodology are of His own choosing.

VII

The Work of Salvation

A. The Death of Christ.

1. *It is antitypical.* As the Lord indicates in John 3:14, His death corresponds to the Old Testament type of the serpent of brass raised up on a pole (Num. 21:8-9). As in the incident in Israel's early history, so in the death of Christ: it is as He assumes the character of the cause of the affliction that He meets the need.

2. *It is necessary.* Again in John 3:14 it is seen that it was an obligation "arising out of the laws of the divine nature"[1] that His death should be such as it was. Sin being what it is, man's need being what it is, and God's grace, mercy, love, righteousness, and holiness being what they are, the Son of Man had to be lifted up.

3. *It is voluntary.* In John 10:17-18 Jesus emphasized the voluntariness of His death. Notice the repetition of the pronoun ἐγὼ (I) and the use of the phrase ἀπ᾽ ἐμαυτοῦ (on My own initiative). The first verb in verse 18 is ἦρεν (has taken, *or* took) rather than αἴρει (takes).[2] No one, even in the pretemporal counsels of the Godhead, forced this decision upon Him. It was His choice. The use of the aorist tense indicates that His death was so certain that it was seen as already accomplished. The great significance of this fact is underscored in that "here only does Christ claim to do anything 'of Him-

[1] B. F. Westcott, *The Gospel According to St. John: The Authorized Version with Introduction and Notes,* p. 53. Δεῖ is an impersonal verb expressing logical necessity.

[2] K. Aland et al. *(The Greek New Testament)* give αἴρει as the preferred reading, although with a "C" rating, which reflects a "considerable degree of doubt whether the text contains the superior reading." There is good manuscript evidence for ἦρεν and it is clearly a more difficult reading, hence it is followed here.

self' (ἀπ' ἐμαυτοῦ)."[3] As a sequel to this statement by Christ, John records in John 19:30 that His prophecy "I lay [My life] down on My own initiative. I have authority to lay it down, and I have authority to take it up again" (John 10:18) was fulfilled, for He "gave up His spirit."

4. *It is substitutionary.* There is much debate over whether ὑπέρ (for [John 10:11, 15; 11:50-51; 1 John 3:16]) may ever be understood as similar in force to ἀντι. John used the former preposition but not the latter in connection with Christ's death. Undoubtedly ὑπέρ usually means "on behalf of" or "for the benefit of" rather than "in the place of" or "instead of" ἀντι. Thus, ὑπέρ normally emphasizes the blessings of the atonement rather than the truth of substitution as clearly set forth in ἀντι.[4]

Of the various pertinent passages, 1 John 3:16 cannot be understood as referring to substitution because of the second half of the statement. John 10:11 and 15, however, as found in the overall context of the chapter, seem to point to a combination of the two ideas. Note especially verse 10, which speaks of the good shepherd's desire to see that *(a)* the sheep have life (in contrast to false shepherds, who would take life), which suggests His willingness to make their life possible by dying in their place, and *(b)* they have this life abundantly, which points to the benefit (blessings) of the death. John 11:50-51 makes little sense if ὑπέρ is not understood as referring to substitution. Caiaphas (like Balaam's ass) did not understand the full significance of his statement, but he certainly meant that it was better for Jesus to die "for [instead of, ὑπέρ] the people" than for all the nation to be slaughtered by the Roman legions. It was not merely a question of benefit; it was also a question of one instead of many (substitution).

5. *It is propitiatory.* The concept of propitiation, which John refers to twice (1 John 2:2; 4:10), is inseparably linked with the fact of divine

[3]Westcott, p. 156.

[4]There are several non-Johannine passages in which ὑπέρ either very nearly approximates ἀντι or seems to be the exact equivalent. For example, Galatians 3:13 reads "having become a curse for us"; Colossians 1:7 has "a faithful servant of Christ for us" (author's translation); and Philemon 13 has "that he might minister for you to me" (author's translation). The last reference is especially strong since Paul is speaking of a *personal* debt Philemon owed him. See also L. Morris, *The Apostolic Preaching of the Cross,* pp. 62-64.

wrath. This association, however, does not have to do with appeasement, as with heathen deities who are not favorably disposed toward men. It is not that God is unwilling to accept men; it is that He is *unable* to accept them apart from propitiation. Thus the idea is that of satisfaction of the demands of His holy and righteous character so that in loving He may also be just.

> He does not have to be made willing by expiations[5] to forgive sin. He is, and always has been, willing. The Biblical idea is that the obstacle to forgiveness lies in his essential righteousness which so conditions his grace that without its satisfaction God cannot, in self-consistency, forgive. In the heathen view expiation renders the gods willing to forgive; in the Biblical view expiation enables God, consistently with his holiness, actually to do what he was never unwilling to do. In the former view sacrifice changes the sentiment of the gods toward men; in the latter it affects the consistency of his procedure in relation to sin. The divine character is in no way changed. . . . God cannot forgive as if he were mere good nature. He can forgive only in accord with his changeless, essential righteousness, which must be vindicated and satisfied. To effect this vindication and satisfaction is the function of sacrifice or expiation in the Bible.[6]

6. *It is a demonstration of love.* First John 3:16 reads, "We know love by this, that He laid down His life for us; and we ought to lay down our lives for the brethren." In light of the moral obligation, expressed by ὀφείλω (ought), that arises from the love demonstrated in Christ's death, it is clear that there is an element of truth in the example, or moral-influence, theory of the atonement. A certain kind of life is incumbent upon us by virtue of our entering into the benefits of His death. As the apostle states in 1 John 2:6, "the one who says he abides

[5]There is some question as to the appropriate translation of ἱλασμός into English. Should it be translated as *expiation* or as *propitiation? Expiation* seems to emphasize the idea of the paying of a penalty and the consequent cancellation of sin, while *propitiation* refers to the satisfaction of God's righteous demands and the consequent turning away of His wrath. See the discussion by Leon Morris in *Baker's Dictionary of Theology,* ed. E. F. Harrison, p. 425.

[6]G. B. Stevens, *The Johannine Theology: A Study of the Doctrinal Contents of the Gospel and Epistles of the Apostle John,* p. 184. See also Morris, *The Apostolic Preaching of the Cross,* chaps. 4-5.

in Him ought [ὀφείλει] himself to walk in the same manner as He walked." "We love, because He first loved us" (1 John 4:19). The errors of the above-mentioned theories of atonement were anticipated by John, as well. The words of 1 John 3:16 are addressed to believers rather than to the lost, and 1 John 4:10 shows that Christ's death was more than a demonstration of love. The subjective love of God for us took objective form in that He provided His Son as "the propitiation for our sins" (1 John 4:10).[7]

7. *It is complete, finished.* In John 19:30, the sixth of the Lord's seven utterances from the cross is recorded. It is a cry[8] of triumph rather than a whimper of despair and defeat. His statement may be translated, "It stands finished," or "It has come to a state of completion." The use of the third person singular perfect passive form τετέλεσται is most remarkable. There seems to be a purposeful ambiguity on our Lord's part in this statement. The subject is left unidentified as to particulars, although there is no question that the general sense is clear. He is not merely saying, "My life is over"; rather, He is affirming the completion of the work of redemption.[9] "The absence of a definite subject forces the reader to call up each work which was now brought to an end."[10] Every facet of the redemptive work is done. The perfect tense of the verb views the work as consummated, with its results enduring from the point of consummation onward. This particular verb (τελέω) was sometimes used to refer to the payment of debts (Matt. 17:24; Rom. 13:6),[11] and in classical literature when a debt was paid it was marked τετέλεσται (paid in full).[12]

[7]It should be noted that items four, five, and six view Christ's death as meeting our need, God's need, and our brother's need, respectively.

[8]Although John simply uses εἶπεν (He said), all three of the synoptists use verbs that indicate something much more than a conversational tone (κράζω [cried out], ἀφίημι [uttered], φωνέω [crying out]) and all supplement the verb with the phrase φωνῇ μεγάλῃ (a loud voice, *or* a loud cry) (Matt. 27:50; Mark 15:37; Luke 23:46).

[9]Leon Morris, *The Gospel According to John: The English Text with Introduction, Exposition, and Notes,* p. 815.

[10]Westcott, pp. 277-78.

[11]Also, the related word τέλος, which basically means "end," was used to refer to "customs" or "revenue" (Matt. 17:25; Rom. 13:7).

[12]Note: John 6:47-58 is frequently interpreted as teaching that the death of Christ takes away sin and imparts eternal life (see, for example, Charles C. Ryrie, *Biblical*

B. The Doctrine of Regeneration.

1. *The new birth.* When approaching the subject of the new birth, it is good to keep in mind that the discourse on the new birth given in John 3 is based upon the death of Christ (vv. 14-15). Although Nicodemus's coming to Jesus by night occurred during our Lord's earthly ministry, the Lord ties His words to this "ruler of the Jews" who was "the teacher of Israel" to His anticipated passion. The new birth cannot be separated from the finished work of Christ.

a. It should be noted, first, that the new birth involves *relationship* rather than position (John 1:12). When John talks in this passage of our place in the family of God, he uses terms relating to birth, and thus relationship, in contrast to Paul, who uses terms relating to legal standing and privilege, and thus position.[13] John's emphasis, then, is upon personal intimacy in the family rather than upon legal rights. The wonder of this privileged place as children of God is beautifully communicated by the apostle in 1 John 3:1. Something of the awe of this truth is captured in *The Living Bible*'s paraphrase of the verse: "See how very much our heavenly Father loves us, for he allows us to be called his children—think of it—and we really *are!*"[14]

From a negative standpoint, this teaching implies a natural condition wherein men are not children of God.

b. No question is left by John regarding the means for appropriation of the new birth. It is conditioned upon faith in Jesus Christ (John

---

Theology of the New Testament, p. 338). It appears, however, to be more in keeping with the context, both grammatical and historical, to see the passage as teaching our spiritual appropriation of Christ (Stevens, pp. 159-64). Consequently, John 6:47-58 will be treated in the section on the Christian life (pp. 113-15).

[13]John's terms are τέκνον, meaning "one who is born," "a child" (from τίκτω [to bring forth or give birth to]), and γεννάω, meaning "beget" when used of the father and "bear" when used of the mother. Paul's favorite terms, on the other hand, are υἱός, meaning "son" and having the connotation of "heir," and υἱοθεσία, meaning "son-placing" or "adoption," a verbal noun that indicates the act of being made a son (or daughter) in God's family.

[14]The abrupt καὶ ἐσμέν (and such we are) in 1 John 3:1 cannot be adequately translated in written form. It needs to be vocalized to capture something of the breathless amazement of the apostle as he seeks to impress this upon our consciousness indelibly.

1:12). Receiving Him is equated with believing in His name.[15]

c. The new birth is a passive experience. By this it is meant that the recipient is passive, since this birth is received, not self-performed. This is emphasized both by the use of ἔλαβον (received) and ἔδωκεν (gave) in John 1:12 and by the use of the passive voice of ἐγεννήθησαν (were born) in John 1:13. The source of life or point of origin for this birth is indicated by the phrase ἐκ θεοῦ (of God [John 1:13]), which is placed in sharp contrast (ἀλλά [but]) with the other three suggested possible sources.[16] By negating those three possible sources, John stresses the completely divine character of this birth. It is nonbiological ("not of bloods")[17] and nonvolitional, both as to humankind in general ("nor of the will of the flesh") and of man in particular ("nor of the will of man").

Related to this is the use of ἄνωθεν (John 3:3, 7) and its proper translation. Does it mean "again" or "anew"; or does it mean "from above" (as in John 3:31; 19:11; James 1:17; 3:15, 17)? Westcott argues convincingly for "anew,"[18] and the context seems to support his translation, for it best accounts for Nicodemus's perplexity. The context does not, however, allow for the meaning "again," since, as Morris points out, "it is a new thing, not the repetition of an old one, of which Jesus speaks."[19] At the same time, Jesus' reference to "heavenly things" in John 3:12 and the fact that every other use of ἄνωθεν in the gospel (3:31; 19:11, 23) has the meaning "from above" provides strong evidence for the translation "from above" in verses 3 and 7, too.[20] In light

[15]A full discussion of the doctrine of faith is given below (pp. 97-101), so no further comments will be made at this juncture.

[16]Note the repeated use of ἐκ (of) in v. 13.

[17]The NASB has "blood." The use of the plural form suggests the mingling of the maternal and paternal strains in procreation (E. F. Harrison, "The Gospel According to John," in *The Wycliffe Bible Commentary,* ed. C. F. Pfeiffer and E. F. Harrison, p. 1073; see also Morris, *The Gospel According to John,* p. 101).

[18]Westcott, p. 63.

[19]Morris, *The Gospel According to John,* p. 213.

[20]Although they follow different lines of argument, both E. A. Abbott *(Johannine Grammar)* and H. L. Strack and P. Billerbeck *(Kommentar zum Neuen Testament aus Talmud und Midrasch)* argue for this meaning as well. If Jesus spoke Hebrew rather than Aramaic, as some scholars now believe, or if He spoke Greek on this occasion, the argument of Strack and Billerbeck that there is no Aramaic adverb with the meaning "again" becomes irrelevant.

of the balance of evidence for both "anew" and "from above," Morris's suggestion may be the best solution: "Both senses are true, and in the Johannine manner it is likely that we should understand both here (as Barclay does; he gets the best of both worlds with his 'unless a man is reborn from above')."[21] At any rate, the term clearly describes a supernatural act that is beyond the ability of man to perform.

d. Next, it is to be noted that the new birth is necessary (John 3:3, 5, 7). Negatively, without it one *cannot* see or enter the Kingdom of God. Positively, the new birth makes both possible. By the use of δεῖ (must) in verse 7 the Lord shows that the new birth is not an option: it is a necessity.

e. Whatever else the new birth may be, it is most certainly spiritual (John 3:5-6). It involves spiritual renewal, that is, birth of spirit. This is not to imply that prior to regeneration man has no spirit, but only that it is dead in the sense that it is separated from God's Spirit.[22] Likewise, the new birth is a spiritual operation; that is, it involves birth from the Holy Spirit. The spirit of man is vivified by the Spirit of God.

The phrase "unless one is born of water and spirit" (author's translation)—"unless one is born of water and the Spirit" (NASB)—has been the occasion of much sharp disagreement throughout the history of the church. Is "water" to be taken sacramentally, metaphorically, biologically, or materially? Does "spirit" refer to the human or the divine realm? An examination of the historical and grammatical contexts in which the statement was made will probably yield the most accurate conclusions to these questions.

When the Lord's words in verse 3 are compared with those in verse 5 it will be seen that there is exact correspondence, with two notable exceptions: ἀμὴν ἀμὴν λέγω σοι, ἐὰν μή τις γεννηθῇ (truly, truly, I say to you, unless one is born) are common words. Whereas in verse 3 Jesus followed the verb with the adverb ἄνωθεν (again, *or*

[21]Morris, *The Gospel According to John,* p. 213.

[22]This doctrine is substantiated by 1 Corinthians 2:11. Both lost and saved men are spiritual beings in that both kinds of men function at the spiritual level as they exercise cognitive powers. Also, the spirits of both sorts of men are under the influence of one superhuman spirit or another (Eph. 2:2; Rom. 8:9). Man would cease to be human if he ceased to be a spiritual entity.

anew), in verse 5 He used the adverbial phrase ἐξ ὕδατος καὶ πνεύματος (of water and spirit). Again there are common words—οὐ δύναται (he cannot) . . . τὴν βασιλείαν τοῦ θεοῦ (the kingdom of God)—with different complementary infinitives: ἰδεῖν (see) and εἰσελθεῖν (enter). Although exact equivalence is certainly not intended, the distinctive terms seem able to provide an epexegesis upon one another. Ἄνωθεν (anew) should give us some insight into the meaning of ἐξ ὕδατος καὶ πνεύματος (of water and spirit), and vice versa, while ἰδεῖν (see) should help interpret εἰσελθεὶν (enter), and vice versa.

Taking the second item first, it seems apparent that Jesus is saying that the Kingdom of God involves an ideological and spiritual realm, for entering it involves mental perception. At the same time, the Kingdom is more than a concept, for its perception involves entering into.

The more problematic area is the relationship between "anew" and "of water and spirit." If being "born of water and spirit" is being born "anew," it must be an experience not hitherto experienced in any sense. Since being born "anew" involves birth "of water and spirit," it is clearly a complex rather than simple experience. It has at least two dimensions, as indicated by the two nouns. That the phrase is governed by just one preposition (ἐξ [of]) strongly identifies the two objects, "water" and "spirit." That is to say, although they are distinct they may not be separated. This last consideration rules out the interpretation that "water" refers to natural birth and "spirit" to spiritual birth. Some see "water" as a metaphor of the Spirit and thus must translate the καί (and) in an epexegetic sense. While this is a grammatical possibility, such use of καί is relatively infrequent. Also, as Westcott points out, the term "water" in this context seems to symbolize purification (John 1:25-26) if it symbolizes anything. "Hence all interpretations which treat the term *water* here as simply figurative and descriptive of the cleansing power of the Spirit are essentially defective, as they are also opposed to all ancient tradition."[23]

In light of the historical context (see John 1:19-34; 3:22-26; as well as parallel passages in the synoptics), it seems nearly certain that Jesus'

[23]Westcott, p. 49.

words would have brought John's baptism to Nicodemus's mind.[24] Mark 1:4 describes John's baptism as a "baptism of repentance," which may have been an abbreviated or interpretive way of referring to John's ministry. Certainly the rite itself is not efficacious.[25] Neither Jesus' nor John the Baptist's ministry was in any sense instrumental, mechanical, or ritualistic. John's message was "Repent, for the kingdom of heaven is at hand" (Matt. 3:1-2). This repentance was in preparation for the coming of the Lord (Matt. 3:3), and the baptism that followed was on the basis of (ἐις)[26] repentance (Matt. 3:11; cf. Acts 2:38). Thus, John's baptism symbolized purification (John 3:25-26) and signified outward as well as inward repentance. Repentance (μετάνοια) means "mind-change." In its most external sense it refers to a change of opinion (see Heb. 12:17), while at its deepest level it refers to transformation of character.[27] In Jesus' statement, "water" probably emphasizes the outward, demonstrative aspect of the new birth, while "spirit" refers to the inward, transformational side of the same thing. That is, He is saying there must be both external and internal change if one can claim to be born anew.[28]

f. The new birth is sovereignly bestowed. Just as the wind blows where it wishes, so the Spirit gives birth where, when, and as He wills (John 3:8).

[24]Some scholars even see a reference to Christian baptism here, but such reference would be anachronistic, since at this time there was no Christian baptism.

[25]Nor was the Lord suggesting that water is efficacious for the removal of sin. Baptismal regeneration is a concept foreign to Jesus' teaching, to John's gospel, and to the entire New Testament. John's message throughout the gospel is keyed on faith, not ritual, and "the whole passage [John 3] emphasizes the work of the Spirit, not the permanence of any rite" (Morris, *The Gospel According to John,* p. 217).

[26]For this usage of ἐις see Matthew 10:41; 12:41. Also, see A.T. Robertson (*Word Pictures in the New Testament,* 3:35-36).

[27]See 2 Corinthians 7:9-10 and Revelation 2:5. In the first passage, the noun is used, and unbelievers and their salvation are referred to. The passage in Revelation, as well as many others there, uses the verb and refers to believers.

[28]Many commentators understand πνεύματος in John 3:5 to be a reference to the Holy Spirit. That interpretation, which is possible in light of the clear reference to the Holy Spirit in vv. 6 and 8, would not substantially alter the interpretation suggested above. Two things, however, seem to militate against seeing πνεύματος as referring to the Holy Spirit here. 1. The phrase "of water and spirit" is so tightly knit that it is unduly ruptured if the two nouns are seen as referring to two entirely separate things. 2. In vv. 6 and 8, where the Holy Spirit is in view, πνεῦμα is articular, while here it is anarthrous.

But regeneration is not only sovereignly bestowed; it also involves the believer's entering a sphere of sovereignty, the Kingdom of God (John 3:3, 5).[29] The phrase "kingdom of God" is a difficult one to interpret in John's writing, since it is basically a non-Johannine concept. It is used here alone in all of John's literature,[30] although the sense that seems to be required for the phrase on this occasion is found in John 6:15 and 18:33-37. From John 3:3 and 5 it is clear that the Kingdom of God is entered only through regeneration by the Holy Spirit. John 18:36-37 shows that the Kingdom is not of this world system and therefore it is neither entered nor defended by violence; 6:15 indicates that it involves spiritual matters rather than material; and 6:28-29 tells us that it is entered by the work of faith rather than by the works of men.[31]

The attempt by some scholars to categorize the term "kingdom" as having either a static or a dynamic sense seems unduly restrictive of the depth of meaning of the word.[32] It refers to both a realm and a reign. Hence, the phrase "sphere of sovereignty," which encompasses both concepts, is used. From the beginning of history God has related to His creatures on the basis of covenant promises. Every age has been administered under one dispensation of the Kingdom or another. That is to say, all men of all time have related to some sphere of God's sovereignty. That sphere of which Jesus spoke in John's gospel may be

[29]As Morris notes, " 'The Kingdom of God' is the most common topic of Jesus' teaching in the Synoptic Gospels. As such it has attracted a great deal of attention, and the literature on the subject is enormous" (*The Gospel According to John,* p. 213). In addition to his helpful bibliography, note should also be made of J. F. Walvoord, *The Millennial Kingdom;* G. N. H. Peters, *The Theocractic Kingdom of Our Lord Jesus, the Christ: As Convenanted in the Old Testament and Presented in the New Testament;* and A. J. McClain, *The Greatness of the Kingdom.*

[30]The other uses of *βασιλέια* (kingdom) by John are eschatological and are found in the Apocalypse. See pp. 234-41 for further discussion.

[31]Some scholars have construed from these passages that Jesus was abrogating completely any political or earthly aspect of the Kingdom. As will be seen in the section on eschatology (especially pp. 234-37), that is not what He was doing at all. In John 6 His objection was to the atempt by misguided zealots to make Him a bread-king. His words to Pilate (18:36-37) fit into the same historical and cultural framework. God will yet fulfill His covenant promises to Israel, and her kingdom will be natural, political, and earthly *as well as spiritual;* but the phase of God's eternal Kingdom that was ushered in at Christ's first advent was not of this character (see Acts 1:6-8).

[32]See Morris, *The Gospel According to John,* pp. 212-13.

distinguished from others by the characteristics noted above (as well as by others given in other parts of the New Testament), but it is still only one facet of the larger and more comprehensive, eternal, and universal Kingdom whereby God rules the universe for time and eternity.

Another related question is, What, if any, is the relationship between the phrases "kingdom of God" and "kingdom of heaven"? The answers given have tended to create much unfortunate friction between various schools of thought. It would appear that on occasion, at least, the differences are created more by blind devotion to a partisan theology than by an attempt to assess the facts carefully. It is not germane to the purpose of this volume to examine this question extensively, but a few observations are unavoidable.[33] There seems to be little question that "heaven" in the phrase "kingdom of heaven" is a euphemism for "God." Thus, to press for sharp distinctions between "kingdom of heaven" and "Kingdom of God" seems unwarranted. On the other hand, the fact that Matthew is the only evangelist who uses "kingdom of heaven" cannot be dismissed simply by saying it is because his is the particularly Jewish gospel. As Ryrie notes, "if that is all that is involved then why do not Mark and Luke use kingdom of heaven at least occasionally as a synonymous phrase to kingdom of God?"[34] To lump the various uses of "kingdom" together under the somewhat nebulous concept of a "spiritual" kingdom is to evidence a form of spiritual myopia. As suggested earlier, God's Kingdom takes various forms and no one form is sufficient to exhaust the larger concept.[35]

[33]See Ryrie's helpful discussion (pp. 73-77). His observation that "the essential distinction is between the eternal kingdom, the Messianic, millennial kingdom, and the mystery form of the kingdom (whichever phrase is used in any instance)" is most insightful.

[34]Ibid., p. 75.

[35]Those dispensationalists who object to considering Jesus Christ as King today suffer from the same problem (a wrong view of dispensationalism) as do the antidispensationalists who refuse to recognize Israel and the church as distinct entities. Such a dispensationalist tends to compartmentalize his theology to such a degree that he does not admit any relationship of saints from one dispensation with those of another. Although he may affirm, and rightly so, that the cohesiveness of his theological system is a doxological theocentricity (rather than the redemptocentric theme of the covenant theologian), rarely is his affirmation demonstrated in practice. He often fails to remember that his theocentricity must have as its vehicle of expression a form of theocracy. The glory of God must be the dominant note of all theology and practice, but He is supremely

g. Finally, the new birth is self-confirming (John 3:8). There are unmistakable, although not always fully explainable, evidences of the new birth in the life of the believer. Just as there are identifiable evidences when the wind blows, so there should be notable results in an individual's life when the Spirit gives him life in Christ.

2. *Eternal life.* There are at least seventeen different verses in the gospel of John in which the words ζωὴ αἰώνιος (eternal life) occur and fifteen more that speak of ζωή (life) as eternally conceived. Consequently, a brief consideration of the terminology used is important before the doctrine itself is outlined. The word αἰώνιος (age-long, *or* eternal) is derived from αἰών, which in turn is connected to the root ἀεί.[36] A consultation of the major lexicographers, both classical and *koinē,* will show that all agree that αἰώνιος may, and usually does, mean "eternal."

It is important to keep in mind that in biblical usage the idea of time is generally minimized or excluded. Westcott writes that "it is necessary to premise that in spiritual things we must guard against all conclusions which rest upon the notions of succession and duration."[37] Sauer reinforces this with his note that

---

glorified only when the sovereign King of the universe is allowed to extend His rule within every sphere of reality, including the church, of which Christ is Head *and* King (Eph. 1:22-23; 1 Tim. 6:13-16).

Conversely, the antidispensationalist unnecessarily lumps all saints into one amorphous group. He fails to see that the one grand theme of the universe, the glory of God, may be served by several lesser purposes. When a historico-grammatical hermeneutic is consistently applied to Scripture, the future of Israel as a separate entity from the church is substantiated without sacrificing either the concept of covenant or the concept of Kingdom.

[36]Ἀεί means "always," or "ever," and was combined with the present participle of εἰμί to form αἰών, which means "always being," literally, and came to mean "a long or indefinite period of time." Αἰώνιος, which is the adjectival form of αἰών, may be used in a restricted sense to refer to that which is measurable in very general terms (see Rom. 16:25; Titus 1:2—χρόνος αἰώνιος); or it may be used in an unrestricted sense, having either qualitative (e.g., Matt. 18:8; 2 Thess. 2:16; Heb. 9:12, 15) or quantitative (e.g. Rom. 16:26; Heb. 9:14) emphasis.

[37]B. F. Westcott, *The Epistles of St. John: The Greek Text with Notes and Essays,* p. 215.

> eternity is more than merely unending time. Not only as to continuance but also as to content it is different in *essence* from everything temporal. It is something other, something higher, therefore not only a "before" and an "after." Eternal is no bare notion of quantity, but above all of quality. One must guard against introducing the idea of time into that of eternity. "We do not arrive at the idea of eternity by any sort of adding together of time."[38]

There is ample evidence to prove that in biblical usage ἀιώνιος is usually nontemporal. The Johannine treatment of the subject is presented below.[39]

The term ζωή had gone through a significant transformation of meaning by the time it was used in the New Testament.[40] It had replaced βίος as the higher word for "life." Jesus' statement concerning Himself, ἐγώ εἰμι . . . ἡ ζωή (I am . . . the life) (John 11:25; 14:6) amply demonstrates this, especially when it is compared with a passage like 1 John 3:17, where βίος has the sense of "livelihood," or "provisions of life." Thus, ζωή is the appropriate term to describe the gift of God to man, the gift that is the antithesis of sin and death. The triune God is the only being in the universe who has "life in Himself" (John 5:26). Being thus the fountain of life, He provides eternal life for His own without cost (Rev. 21:6; δωρεάν [without cost, *or* as a gift])

[38]Erich Sauer, *The Triumph of the Crucified,* p. 99.

[39]Examination of every New Testament usage of ἀιώνιος in its context will show that in nearly every case time is *not* in view in any way. In some cases, such as Romans 16:26, the passage would be reduced to nonsense if any meaning other than "eternal" were understood. Even the phrase ἐις τὸν ἀιώνα frequently means more than "for the extent of the age." See Hebrews 7:24, where the contrast set up with v. 23 requires "forever" as the proper translation.

The view that ἀιώνιος is usually nontemporal is disputed by O. Cullmann (*Christ and Time: The Primitive Christian Conception of Time and History,* pp. 45 ff.). He contends that eternity is merely unlimited time. The fallacies of Cullmann's position are pointed out by J. Barr (*Biblical Words for Time,* pp. 67-85).

[40]In classical literature, βίος evidently had a qualitative, ethical meaning that ζωή did not possess. Whereas the true antithesis of ζωή was θάνατος (death) when life was physically contemplated, when the moral element was introduced the antithesis was between βίος and θάνατος. See R. C. Trench, *Synonyms of the New Testament,* pp. 91-95; E. W. Bullinger, *A Critical Lexicon and Concordance to the English and Greek Testament,* p. 453.

through the medium of faith (John 3:16). Certainly " 'eternal life' is indeed endless life (comp. Matt. 25:46), but at the same time more than deathlessness. It is *divine* life."[41]

a. The cause of eternal life is entirely divine. It may be traced to God's love as demonstrated in the incarnation (John 1:4) and in the cross (John 3:16; 17:1-2). The only source of eternal life for man is God manifest in the flesh and dying for his sin (1 John 4:9). Since it is a gift of God, eternal life is also an evidence of God's grace (John 6:32-33; 10:28); and since it is according to His wise purpose, it is an expression of His will (John 6:40). Because it comes to us via the preached Word, "His commandment is eternal life" (John 12:49-50).

b. Eternal life has but one condition, from a human standpoint, and that is faith (John 3:16, 36; 1 John 5:20).[42] This faith must be directed toward Christ as its proper object (John 5:40), and it is found *only* in Him, as can be seen from the use of ἐγώ εἰμι (I am) in John 6:35, 41, 48, 51; 11:25; and 14:6. "Christ *is* the life which He *brings,* and which is realized by believers *in* Him."[43] (See further discussion in section c, immediately below.)

c. As suggested above, eternal life has a dual character. It is both quantitative and qualitative. Quantitatively, it is unaffected by physical death (John 6:51, 58; 11:25) and may be more or less enjoyed experientially (John 10:10). Qualitatively, Jesus taught that to assimilate Him is to assimilate life (John 6:52-54). Thus to receive eternal life is to receive the life of God in Christ.

[41]Sauer, p. 99.

[42]John 3:36 gives a most enlightening insight into the meaning of faith by juxtaposing ὁ ἀπειθῶν (he who does not obey) with ὁ πιστεύων (he who believes) rather than the expected ὁ μὴ πιστεύων (he who does not believe). If the antithesis of believing is disobedience, then it follows that faith involves obedience to something. That "something" is the testimony of God to His Son as found in the gospel (John 5:24; cf. 14:23-24; 15:10, 14; 1 John 3:23). Also, it should be noticed that belief in the Son brings "eternal life," but disobedience to the Son even obscures one's vision of "life" in its ordinary dimension. It may be argued that the adjective is not repeated with "life" because the context makes it clear what life is in view. If that were the case, however, we would normally expect the anaphoric article.

[43]Westcott, *The Epistles of St. John,* p. 8.

The content of this life is identified in John 17:3.[44] Eternal life[45] is that we may continually know (γινώσκομεν) the Father (the only genuine [ἀληθινός][46] God) and Jesus Christ, whom He sent. That is, the *personal* element is strongly emphasized in our Lord's definition of eternal life. Knowledge here is seen to be an appropriation of these persons, not merely an acquaintance with them (cf. 1 John 1:2). Eternal life is a dynamic relationship rather than a static one, but it is based upon static (fixed) truth that endures forever (John 17:17).[47]

Life thus defined involves the following elements: *consciousness,* for there must be knowledge; *contact* with the only true God; *continuity,* or duration, for such a knowledge "presupposes co-existence with Him"; *development,* for knowledge of God must be growing not static.[48]

> The knowledge spoken of is no mere head or heart knowledge,—the mere information of the mind, or the excitation of the feelings,—but that living reality of knowledge and personal realization,—that oneness in will with God, and partaking of His nature, which IS itself life eternal.[49]

The significance of this truth cannot be overemphasized. Herein lies a fundamental tenet of the Christian faith. "Really to know God means more than knowing the way to life. It *is* life."[50]

[44]Is the ἵνα (that) purposive or objective? It could very well be the near equivalent of ὅτι (that) here in light of the fact that it is sometimes used to introduce appositional statements (e.g., John 13:34; 1 John 5:3) and in light of the declarative nature of the main clause. Westcott, on the other hand, says that it "expresses an aim, an end, and not only a fact" (*The Gospel According to St. John,* p. 239).

[45]This is the only place in John's writings where the adjective precedes the noun in the combination αἰώνιος ζωή. The word order seems to be more than just a literary nicety for variety (Morris, *The Gospel According to John,* p. 719). Rather, this definitive statement places *emphasis* on the quality of the life (see also Acts 13:46; 1 Tim. 6:12).

[46]As with αἰώνιος ζωή (see footnote 44), John here uses the emphatic order, contrary to his usual practice (Morris, *The Gospel According to John,* p. 720).

[47]Here in John 17 we see the true biblical tension between existential and essential, personal and propositional truth. There is no knowing of Jesus Christ apart from the Truth (God's written Word), but a knowledge of the Truth without personal relationship with Jesus Christ is merely an academic exercise.

[48]M. C. Tenney, *John: The Gospel of Belief,* p. 32.

[49]Henry Alford, *The Greek Testament,* 1:875.

[50]Morris, *The Gospel According to John,* p. 719. He goes on in a footnote to give a quotation from William Temple's *Readings in St. John's Gospel* that is worth reproduc-

Following this matchless prayer on down through John 17, one finds eternal life defined in practical as well as abstract terms. In its functional aspects, life is best understood by its privileges and effects. A few of these are enlightenment (v. 8), preservation (vv. 11-12), joy (v. 13), sanctification (v. 19), commission (v. 18), unity (v. 22), and fellowship (v. 24).[51]

One final note regarding the character of eternal life relates to its preclusions. Eternal life, by its very nature, makes spiritual death impossible (John 11:26), is the opposite of perishing (John 3:16), precludes being under God's wrath (John 3:36), and delivers from judgment and death (John 5:24).

d. The chronology of eternal life may also be viewed from two standpoints. Experientially, it is to be possessed *now* (John 3:15-16, 36; 5:24—note the use of the present tense of the verb ἔχω [has]). Westcott says of the expression "have eternal life" that the use of the auxiliary verb ("have") marks life more as a realization of present blessing than as the act of living.[52] But it has a future aspect as well (John 12:25). In John 17:24 Jesus prays that believers may "be with Me where I am, in order that they may behold My glory." When this request is placed in the context of verses 1-3, which initially introduce the topic of eternal life, it becomes apparent that we do not now realize certain aspects of our eternal life.

> For if future ζωή is established by the event of salvation already enacted in the death and resurrection of Christ, the decisive thing has already taken place and the future resurrection of the dead is simply the

---

ing here. "At one time I was much troubled that the climax of the *Veni Creator* should be

> Teach us to know the Father, Son,
> And Thee, of Both, to be but One.

It seemed to suggest that the ultimate purpose of the coming of the Holy Spirit was to persuade us of the truth of an orthodox formula. But that is mere thoughtlessness. If a man once knows the Spirit within him, the source of all his aspiration after holiness, as indeed the Spirit of Jesus Christ, and if he knows this Spirit of Jesus Christ within himself as none other than the Spirit of the Eternal and Almighty God, what more can he want? *This is the eternal life.*"

[51]Tenney, pp. 246-49.

[52]Westcott, *The Gospel According to St. John,* p. 54.

consummation of the event of the replacement of the old aeon by the new which has already commenced in Christ.[53]

A second approach to the chronology of eternal life is to consider its duration (John 10:27; cf. 4:14; 11:26).[54] The affirmations of John 10:27 are statements of fact rather than conditions leading to the truth of verse 28. Those who are His sheep characteristically hear and follow. He characteristically knows them and gives them eternal life.[55] Then, suddenly, there is a change from present-tense verb forms to an aorist (ἀπόλωνται [shall . . . perish]). To this is added the emphatic negative (οὐ μή) and εἰς τὸν αἰῶνα, which phrases the New American Standard Bible translates together as "never." Here is a *very strong* statement, covering all exigencies, without exception. "No one" (*lit.,* not anyone [τις]), including ourselves, can snatch us out of Christ's hand. Especially the last clause of verse 28 focuses upon external enemies. Likewise, the πάντων μεῖζόν ἐστιν (is greater than all) of verse 29 coupled with οὐδείς (no one) verifies the all-inclusive (as well as all-exclusive) security of the believer. God's hand is an impregnable fortress where the sheep who possess eternal life may rest in absolute safety.

e. As a climax, along with safety there comes the certainty of eternal life. Because of God's promises regarding this life (e.g., John 10:27-29; 1 John 5:11-12), the believer may have assurance of life (1 John 5:13). Note well that the ultimate basis of assurance is not a restless striving, the ecstatic experiences of an uncontrolled spirit, or a comfortable feeling (although that may be the result). Rather, it is simply the straightforward statements of God's Word (ταῦτα ἔγραψα ὑμῖν ἵνα . . . εἰδῆτε [these things I have written to you . . . that you may know]).

The following words of Bishop Westcott are difficult to improve upon and provide a fitting summary for this section.

[53]R. Bultmann, "ζωή," in *Theological Dictionary of the New Testament,* ed. G. Kittel and G. Friedrich, 2:865.

[54]Some scholars would cite John 17:11-12 as an exception to the principle of the perseverance of the saints. It should be noted, however, that the εἰ μή here is adversative rather than exceptive and should read "but" (as does the NASB) rather than "except." See John 18:9 for the completed explanation of Judas's defection.

[55]The series of present-tense verbs have in view the ongoing provision and sustenance.

> If now we endeavor to bring together the different traits of "the eternal life" we see that it is a life which with all its fulness and all its potencies is *now:* a life which extends beyond the limits of the individual, and preserves, completes, crowns, individuality by placing the part in connexion with the whole: a life which satisfies while it quickens aspiration: a life which is seen, as we regard it patiently, to be capable of conquering, reconciling, uniting the rebellious, discordant, broken elements of being on which we look and which we bear about with us: a life which gives unity to the constituent parts and to the complex whole, which brings together heaven and earth, which offers the sum of existence in one thought.[56]

C. The Doctrine of Faith.

John presents faith, in an active sense, as *the* condition for salvation.[57] The nearest synonym he uses is *repentance,* which word is not found in its noun form in his writings and is used in its verb form only a few times in the Apocalypse. This is not to imply that John sets forth a different condition for salvation from other New Testament writers, for faith, as directed toward Christ, does not exclude repentance. There may be repentance of a certain kind without faith, but there is no genuine faith without repentance (in the sense of μετάνοια [mind-change]).

John uses πίστις (faith) only five times (none in the gospel; once in 1 John 5:4; four times in Rev. 2:13, 19; 13:10; 14:12), while the verb form, πιστεύω, occurs ninety-eight times in the gospel and nine times in 1 John. As will be seen from the predominance of the verb rather than the noun, "John dwells on the active exercise of the power, not on the abstract idea."[58]

[56]Westcott, *The Epistles of St. John,* p. 218.

[57]Faith is not merely an *act,* although that is John's emphasis. It is also a *life,* as may be seen in 1 John 5:4-5. Faith as a life will be considered in Part Three of this book (The Christian Life), especially pp. 147-54.

[58]Westcott, *The Gospel According to St. John,* p. 239. Tenney writes: "The underlying Greek word *pisteuo,* is used no less than ninety-eight times in the Gospel and is customarily translated *believe,* though in a few instances it is rendered *trust* or *commit.* Never does it mean a mere assent to a proposition. It usually means acknowledgment of some personal claim, or even a complete personal commitment to some ideal or person" (p. 32).

One further introductory note is that, in the gospel, with each example of belief (or unbelief) there is instruction about salvation and Christ Himself.

1. *Faith is the work of God.* In John 6:29 is found a beautiful balance of divine initiative and human responsibility in the saving work of God. It is "the work of God," but it involves the action of "you believe." Therefore, while it is a work, the work does not bring earned merit. Although it is the believer's faith, it may be traced ultimately to God; so all suggestion of synergism is ruled out.

2. *The proper object of faith.*

a. The proper object of faith may be seen from a study of the two common grammatical expressions in which the verb πιστεύω is used. The most frequent combination is πιστεύειν ἐις (believe in), which is characteristically Johannine.[59] It is found elsewhere, but only infrequently. Westcott suggests that this expression conveys the idea of absolute transference of trust from oneself to another,[60] while Dana and Mantey write:

> Deissmann in *Light From the Ancient East* gives several convincing quotations from the papyri to prove that πιστεύειν ἐις αὐτόν meant *surrender* or *submission to.* A slave was sold *into the name of the god of a temple;* i.e., to be a temple servant. G. Milligan agrees with Deissmann that this papyri usage of ἐις αὐτόν, is also found regularly in the New Testament. Thus to believe on or to be baptized into the name of Jesus means to renounce self and to consider oneself the lifetime servant of Jesus.[61]

It seems too categorical to assume this meaning without exception. Perhaps it is better taken as a general truth as opposed to the usage of πιστεύειν with the dative (see below). For example, John 2:23-24 seems to be an exception (cf. John 6:64-66). Harrison says of this passage that this faith is a "miracle-faith" and likens it to John 8:30-59 and 12:42-43. He suggests that there was a lack of genuine trust, in

[59]Πιστεύειν ἐις occurs approximately thirty-eight times in the gospel and epistles. E.g., John 2:11; 3:16, 18, 36; 4:39; 6:29, 35, 40, 47; 7:5, 31, 38-39, 48; 8:30; etc.

[60]Westcott, *The Gospel According to St. John,* p. 39. J. H. Moulton (*A Grammar of New Testament Greek,* 1:67) substantially agrees.

[61]H. E. Dana and J. R. Mantey, *A Manual Grammar of the Greek New Testament,* p. 105.

contrast to the full confidence in Christ attributed to the disciples.[62] "This faith, resting on miracles, is in this Gospel never commended as the highest kind of faith, although it is by no means despised. It is what Luther calls 'milk-faith' and may grow into something more trustworthy."[63] When this passage is compared with John 1:50 and 20:29, it may safely be said that there is a distinction made in men's faith. This does not imply that some are more saved or less saved than others, for salvation depends upon the object of faith, not the amount (John 20: 30-31; cf. Mark 9:22-23). The difference is in that which moves one to faith: the person Himself, His word, or His miraculous works (which of course point to His person [John 10:38]).[64] The other frequent combination in John of πιστεύειν with the dative (used eighteen times) is illustrated in John 8:31, 45-46. See also John 2:22; 4:21, 50; 5:24, 38, 46-47; 14:11. This usage relates to the acceptance of a person's statements as true and is a phase of believing that grows naturally out of trust in the person. On the other hand, failure to believe one's words precludes trust in the person. See John 6:29-30 for a contrast between these usages.

b. The proper object of faith may also be seen in figurative expression in John. A comparison of John 6:47 with 6:54 (which in turn is explained by v. 63) suggests that believing is symbolized by eating, that is, by *appropriating,* Christ.[65]

[62]Harrison, p. 1077.

[63]M. Dods, "The Gospel According to John," in *The Expositor's Greek Testament,* ed. W. Robertson Nicoll, 1:710-11.

[64]Another passage that should be noted is John 3:15. That verse allows the textual variant ἐν αὐτῷ (in Him) for εἰς αὐτόν (in Him). The ASV and NASB follow the former reading, while the KJV and RSV follow the latter. The NEB includes both in translation, although it follows ἐν αὐτῷ in its Greek text. The former reading has somewhat stronger manuscript evidence, and it is the harder reading, although it seems to be doctrinally out of place at this point, since the believer's union with Christ seems to be a Pauline revelation. Perhaps it is an anticipation of Paul's ἐν χριστῷ (in Christ) doctrine (just as the upper room discourse anticipates much Pauline doctrine). There is a similar construction in John 5:39, and the occurrence of "believe" in an absolute sense is not uncommon (see John 3:12; 4:42, 53). That is, perhaps the ἐν αὐτῷ should be construed with "have" rather than with "believes," and thus "believes" has no expressed object.

[65]A comparison of the Greek text shows the following:

V. 47. ὁ πιστεύων . . . ἔχει ζωὴν αἰώνιον (he who believes . . . has eternal life).

c. The significance of faith's having a proper object cannot be overemphasized. John 1:4; 5:26, 39-40; 6:35; 11:25; 14:6; and 1 John 5:20 all show that Christ is life. Thus He must be appropriated if one is to receive life.

d. Certain specifics concerning the object of faith need to be distinguished. "Faith in His person involves belief in His deity" (see John 8:24; 20:31; 1 John 5:1; cf. 1 John 2:23; 4:15), while "faith in His work involves belief in the efficacy of His death to effect deliverance from sin"[66] (see John 3:14-18).

3. *The subjects of faith.* The subjects of faith are stated very simply, yet profoundly. In John 1:12 the apostle uses ὅσοι (as many as), while in John 3:16 the phrase is πάς ὁ(whoever, *or* everyone who). From a human standpoint, faith may be exercised by every man. The divine dimension is seen in John 6:35-37, 44, and 64-65, where it is stated that all whom the Father gives to Christ, and only those whom He draws, will come.[67] John 6:65 makes it clear that even the coming is a gift.

4. *The synonyms for* faith. John also gives several synonyms for *faith.* Believing is equated with *receiving* Jesus Christ in John 1:12. This implies a gift. It is equated with *obeying* Him in John 3:36 (cf. Rom. 2:8; Eph. 2:2). This implies a revelation of truth. In John 6:35-37, 64-65 (cf. 14:6) believing is equated with *coming to* Christ. This implies a way to follow.

5. *The media of faith.* The media of faith are word, work, and witness. One may come to faith in Jesus Christ through Jesus' and the Father's word (John 5:24; 1 John 5:10 ff.; cf. John 5:39-40);[68] through Jesus' works, including His resurrection (John 11:45; 20:29, 30-31); and through a believer's witness to Jesus Christ (John 17:20; cf. 1:7; 4:39-42).

V. 54 ὁ τρώγων . . . κὰι πίνων . . . ἔχει ζωὴν ἀιώνιον (he who eats . . . and drinks . . . has eternal life). The statement of v. 54 is further explained in v. 57. The eating (ὁ τρώγων με [he who eats Me]) causes (δὶ ἐμέ [because of me]) the eater to have life. As Morris points out, this is another indication that the eating and drinking may not be taken sacramentally here (*The Gospel According to John,* p. 381).

[66]Ryrie, p. 340.

[67]John 6:44 is a clear statement of the truth of efficacious grace.

[68]Life is not *in* the Scriptures, as the Jews superstitiously thought, but *through* them.

Finally, by way of summary, these words from Stevens will suffice:

> Faith rests upon objective grounds; it appeals to historic facts for its justification. But it is not mere opinion respecting these facts. John never conceives of faith as consisting in a mere intellectual possession of the truths of the gospel. The whole nature embraces them, or, more exactly, faith embraces him in whom all these truths centre. Faith is neither a subjective play of feeling nor a speculative conviction or assent; it is a personal relation. It carries man out of himself, and commits him to another. It is self-renouncing trust, repose of soul in Jesus Christ. It involves, therefore, an experience which tests and proves the external grounds on which it reposes, and gives to the soul an assured certainty of their validity. Then faith and knowledge are seen to be, to John's mind, essentially one. Either may be called the condition of salvation (I. iv. 16, vi. 47; xvii. 3). The true knowledge of divine things is an ethical and spiritual knowledge; it is the certitude which faith begets.[69]

D. The Attendant Blessings.

It is doubtless a risky task to attempt to delineate the blessings that attend faith, for almost certainly something of significance will be omitted. This is almost as impossible a task as an attempt to define the infinite, for ultimately the blessings of God are numberless. The following, then, is merely a suggestive list to which more may and should be added. It will, however, serve the purpose of introducing the richness of the believer's relationship with God through Jesus Christ.

1. *We are "released [loosed] . . . from our sins"* (Rev. 1:5).
2. *We enjoy His ongoing love* (present participle, ἀγαπῶντι [loves] [Rev. 1:5]).
3. *We are released from eternal judgment* (John 5:24; cf. 3:18).
4. *We receive the gift of the Holy Spirit* (John 7:37-39).
5. *We enjoy the care of the good shepherd* (John 10:1-28).
6. *We are enabled to know the Father* (John 14:7-11).
7. *We are given the privilege of prayer in the name of Jesus Christ* (John 14:13-14; 15:16; 16:23-24, 26).

[69]Stevens, p. 239.

8. *We are enabled to perform greater works than our Lord* (John 14:12-14).[70]

9. *We receive the bequest of peace* (John 14:27; 16:33).

10. *We receive a new sanctification, especially as related to our mission in the world* (John 17:17-19).

11. *We are made one with the Father and His children* (John 17:21-23).

12. *The Christian life is made possible* (John 6:30-58; 8:12; 12:46; 15:1-16; 1 John).

[70]This is made possible, according to the context, because of Christ's intercessory ministry and is related to prayer in His name. Verse 13 makes it clear that even these greater works are His works, too. That is, we share, not inherit, His ministry. "Greater" is probably not to be limited merely to "more in number," and certainly not to "more miraculous." Possibly, it means "greater in magnitude" as believers of this age become instruments of salvation on the basis of His finished work ("I go to the Father"; cf. John 16:10) and the subsequent sending of the Holy Spirit (John 14:16). An example of a work "greater in magnitude" is Pentecost's ingathering of believers, an experience for which there is no parallel in our Lord's earthly ministry.

Part Three:
The Christian Life

VIII

The Theology of the Christian Life

A. God's Nature.

In chapter 3 consideration was given to John's theology proper. Here it is our task to relate this truth to the believer's life in Christ.

1. *God is spirit.* The occasion for Jesus' statement that God is spirit was His discussion with the Samaritan woman regarding worship (John 4:7-26).[1] A number of things Jesus said in answer to her give insight into worship. First, notice the *oughtness* of true worship (cf. John 4:20, 24). He says that true worship *must* be conducted in a certain way.[2]

Next, the *nature* of true worship is specified. True worshipers worship in spirit and truth (John 4:23-24).[3] Therefore, true worship must likewise be in spirit and truth. This relates not so much to form devoid

[1]The word "worship" is derived from an Anglo-Saxon term denoting the quality of worth. The principal biblical terms translated as "worship" are שָׁחָה and προσκυνέω. שָׁחָה in the hithpael means "to bow down" or "to prostrate." Πρόσκυνέω originally meant "to kiss the hand (or earth) toward." Emphasizing the physical act of falling down and worshiping, sometimes kissing the feet of the object of adoration (see, e.g., Job 31:26-28; Psalm 2:12), both words came to mean "to do obeisance to." The second commandment (Exod. 20:4-5) is to be understood in light of this concept. One ought not to bow down to any graven image, because in so doing one acknowledges its worth by an act of adoration and honor. As Isaiah notes, Yahweh is a jealous God. "I am the LORD [Yahweh]; . . . I will not give My glory to another, nor My praise to graven images" (Isa. 42:8; see also 45:5-6). "No injury to God compares with the denial of His uniqueness and the transfer to another of the recognition due to Him" (E. F. Harrison, "Worship," in *Baker's Dictionary of Theology,* ed. E. F. Harrison, p. 561).

[2]Δεῖ (must), expressing logical necessity, is from δέω (to bind).

[3]Ἀληθινός (truth) refers to that which is genuine or real as opposed to the counterfeit or spurious.

of substance ("you do not know" [John 4:22]) as to that which is according to the essential nature of things, that which agrees with reality (truth). According to verse 22, this truth is something that can be and is known: namely, salvation. Because one is rightly related to God in Christ,[4] he can worship God. This worship is not "in spirit and in truth" but "in spirit-and-truth." That is, the two concepts hang together and are not to be separated. True worship involves both at the same time, not one and then the other.[5]

The *object* of true worship is God,[6] who is spirit; that is, He is transcendent, pure person. Therefore, to worship this person one must worship personally (in spirit) and on the basis of truth. One of the most striking statements that Jesus makes in this whole dialogue is that the Father "seeks" such worshipers.[7] Not only is man to be active in the worship experience; God, too, is active.

[4]The salvation that is "of [ἐκ] the Jews" (John 4:22, KJV) is the Savior, as the following verses of John 4 show.

[5]In both v. 23 and v. 24 only one preposition governs the two nouns (ἐν πνεύματι καὶ ἀλήθεια [in spirit and truth]).

[6]This concept is developed in the synoptics, also, but by the recording of an incident to which John does not make reference. In Matthew 4:1-11 and Luke 4:1-13 (cf. Mark 1:12-13), in the temptation narrative, Satan offers the kingdoms of the world to Jesus if He will fall down and worship (προσκυνέω) him. In answer, the Lord quotes Deuteronomy 6:13—with an interpretative variation. Instead of "you shall fear only the LORD your God," He says "YOU SHALL WORSHIP [προσκυνήσεις] THE LORD YOUR GOD" (Matt. 4:10; Luke 4:8). Also, instead of "and you shall worship Him, and swear by His name" (Deut. 6:13), Jesus says "AND SERVE [λατρεύσεις] HIM ONLY" (Matt. 4:10; Luke 4:8). (Λατρεύω, from λάτρον [reward or wages], meant "to work or serve for reward," then "to render services" or "to serve" with no thought of reward and irrespective of whether one is bond or free. It then came to be used to describe the cultic aspects of worship service, especially by sacrifice. θυσία [sacrifice] is from θύω [to sacrifice by slaying]; thus, it describes an offering to God that implies loss on the part of the offerer and gain on the part of the one so honored. (See, e.g., Heb. 13:15-16.) Jesus' interpretation of Deuteronomy 6:13 as well as His association of worship and service in Matthew and Luke shows that worship involves reverence for *God* and that in the act of worship one commits himself to serve *God.* The concept of sacrifice, as it relates to worship, is retained; but it is transformed from the purely external to the internal (λογικὴν λατρείαν [spiritual service of worship]) in Romans 12:1. This, however, is to be manifested in a physical way, namely, by presentation of one's body.

[7]The term ζητεῖ (seeks) is pregnant with meaning. It implies not only God's vital interest but also man's lack of it. The present tense suggests that continual seeking is a characteristic of God, as is also implied in passages like Genesis 3:9 and Luke 19:10 (see also Rev. 22:17).

2. *God is light.* The statement that God is light (1 John 1:5) has strongly ethical connotations. The truths to which it is related in context make it clear that only through moral likeness to Himself may one truly know God and truly live the eternal life He has given. It is God's holiness, as illustrated positively by "light" and negatively by "in Him there is no darkness at all," that is in view. This is not redundancy; it is, rather, a practical heightening of the basic statement. The statement as a whole "brings out 1) the idea of God's nature, and 2) the perfect realisation of the idea: He is light essentially, and in fact He is perfect, unmixed light."[8]

3. *God is love.* The statement that God is love (1 John 4:8, 16) is clearly a qualitative one (see p. 42), and an examination of the context will show that it is also a strongly social one.[9] It represents the purest of social concerns, since there is no suggestion here or elsewhere that the acts resulting from His love are prompted by any love outside Himself. God's love, in this aspect, is radically different from the believer's love, which is entirely motivated and made possible by God's love (1 John 4:19). Nonetheless, God's love does provide a pattern for the believer's love (1 John 3:16; 4:11). Furthermore, God's love is no impersonal abstraction. Since God (who is love) indwells us (John 14:23), "we know and have believed *the love that God has in us.*[10] God is love; and he who abides in love abides in God and God abides in him" (1 John 4:16, author's translation).

We may conclude, then, that the character of God is the basis from which the Johannine teaching on the Christian life arises.

B. Jesus Christ.

1. *He is our high priest.* As presented by John, the truth that Jesus Christ is our high priest (1 John 2:1; John 17:1-26) relates primarily to Christ's work as intercessor and advocate. It is related to believers

[8]B. F. Westcott, *The Epistles of St. John: The Greek Text with Notes and Essays,* p. 16.

[9]Theologians generally define love as that in God which moves Him to self-communication.

[10]Most translations completely miss the significance of ἐν ἡμῖν, rendering the phrase as "for us," "to us," etc.

rather than to the world (John 17:9; 1 John 2:1-2) and includes not only the apostles but all believers of this age (John 17:20).

First, this ministry involves our relation to sin and the evil one. The term *παράκλητος* (advocate) refers to a friend in court, and, in a more formal sense, it refers to the attorney for the defense (counselor, in the legal sense).[11] This ministry relates to the Christian's occasional fall into sin.[12] The advocate is said to be *πρὸς τὸν πατέρα* (with the Father). He has been summoned to our aid and represents us "not simply in His Presence, but turned toward Him, addressing Him with continual pleadings."[13] In John 17:25, God is addressed by Jesus Christ as the "righteous Father," and thus the appropriateness that this advocate is "Jesus Christ the righteous" is seen. This designation points to Him as being the God-man, alive now in glory despite His having died. "Righteous" is a fact predicated of Him; that is, He is actively righteous and has no wish to abrogate the Law of God. Rather, He acts in accordance with it. This provides us with assurance that His ministry as advocate is efficacious.

If the above-described ministry of Christ relates to the presence of sin in the believer's life, His work as intercessor has to do with its prevention. In John 17:15 (cf. 1 John 5:18-19), the Lord prays regarding the believer's safety *in the world.* Τοῦ *πονηροῦ* (the evil one) is to be understood as a masculine form in light of 1 John 5:18 (*ὁ πονηρός*) and thus refers to the devil. The idea of being kept from evil is still valid, however, at least insofar as the evil is caused by the evil one. This promise of protection is spelled out in more detail in 1 John 5:18. The verse is probably best understood by seeing *ὁ γεννηθείς* (He who was born) as a reference to Jesus Christ and by reading *τηρεῖ αὐτόν* (keeps him) rather than *τηρεῖ ἑαυτόν* (keeps himself). The promise is stated both affirmatively ("He who was born of God keeps him") and negatively ("the evil one does not touch him"). "Touch" is a translation of

[11]In contrast, see the description of Satan, the prosecuting attorney, as "the accuser" (*ὁ κατήγωρ*: *κατά* + *ἀγορεύω*, from *ἀγορά* [to speak against in public, to accuse] in Revelation 12:10.

[12]Note the aorist *ἁμάρτῃ* (sin) in 1 John 2:1 in contrast to the present tenses in 1 John 3:6-9. This contrast will be more fully dealt with on pp. 131-32.

[13]Westcott, p. 43.

ἅπτεται, which means "lay hold of," "grasp"; and the implication is "to touch with the intention of harming."[14] Thus, by a comparison of these passages it seems quite apparent that the Savior's intercessory work provides for our safekeeping from sin and the evil one. Whether or not the Christian appropriates this provision and the implications thereof is an entirely different question and will be dealt with in the section on the hamartiology of the Christian life (see p. 131).

The Lord's high-priestly ministry also involves request for the Father's care (John 17:11). It seeks for realization of Christ's joy to the full (John 17:13) and for *our* sanctification in the truth, which is the Word of God (John 17:17-18). This is especially significant in light of the fact that He sends us into the world, which hates us (see v. 14). Finally, His high-priestly work relates to our glorification (John 17:24).

2. *He is our example.* John points out in John 13:1-17 and 1 John 2:6 that Jesus is our example. The one who says he abides (ὁ λέγων . . . μένειν) in Christ has a moral obligation (ὀφείλει [ought]) to conduct his life in a manner similar to His. In the final analysis, the only way to walk as He did is to search the Scriptures, especially the gospels, and act accordingly.

In this connection, one particular incident stands out in John's writing because it is particularly emphasized by the Lord. He, too, uses ὀφείλω (John 13:14)[15] and refers to what He had just done in washing the disciples' feet as a ὑπόδειγμα (example).[16] But just exactly what

[14]A. T. Robertson, *Word Pictures in the New Testament,* 6:244-45. See W. F. Arndt and F. W. Gingrich, *A Greek-English Lexicon of the New Testament and Other Early Christian Literature,* p. 102.

[15]It may very well be that John is picking up on the "oughtness" of humble service in 1 John 2:6. Undoubtedly, one of the painful lessons that John learned in the upper room that night, together with the other disciples, was that of selfless, humble service —something they all had missed until Jesus began to wash their feet. John's use of a series of present tenses as well as the great detail given in vv. 4-6 shows how vividly this incident was impressed upon his consciousness. See Luke 22:24-27 for a description of the disciples' attitude as our Lord began to wash their feet.

[16]The word may mean "pattern," "model," "example," or "copy." It is from δείκνυμι (I show) and ὑπό (under). A near synonym is τύπος, from τύπτω (to form by a blow). If a distinction between τύπος and ὑπόδειγμα may be made, perhaps it is on the basis of etymology. Τύπος gives emphasis to the idea of a pattern to follow, while ὑπόδειγμα may refer to an *animated* example.

was Jesus exemplifying? Was it the attitude of servanthood? Or was it the physical act of foot washing? Or was it both?

Some would say that Jesus was here instituting another ordinance, foot washing, which is to take its place with water baptism and the Lord's Supper. It would appear, however, that Jesus was referring to the assumption of the attitude of a servant rather than to the institution of an outward form. There are at least four things from the text itself that point in this direction. (1) Jesus' statement in verse 7, "What I do you do not realize now" (see also vv. 6, 8, 9), would seem strange and meaningless if Jesus had been referring to a mere formality, because the disciples were very much acquainted with the common practice of foot washing. (2) The fact that in verse 15 He used the word ὑπόδειγμα (an example) rather than something like παραγγελία (order, as in Acts 5:28), ἐπιταγή (command, as in 2 Cor. 8:8), παράδοσις (tradition, as in 1 Cor. 11:2), or some other word signifying a command seems to militate against the ritual concept, too. (3) The complementary teaching of John 13:10 is clearly not any more than illustrative of spiritual truth. If foot washing here is to be taken literally, then the bath must be, also. (4) Finally, in verse 15, where the actual exhortation is found, there is a simile set forth rather than a one-for-one correspondence. The use of the adverb of manner καθῶς rather than the relative pronoun ὅ is to be noted. Jesus said to do *as* He did, not *what* He did.

The Master always set a pattern of service for His servants. But His act of foot washing also illustrated a deeper theological truth. Just as one who has walked through the hot, dirty, unpaved streets of an Oriental city could not enjoy his meal until the dirt was washed from his feet and their feverishness was assuaged by the application of cold water, so one who would fellowship with Christ and His people must be prepared in mind and heart. It is a healthy thing for the church when one member assumes a place of humility in order to perform a ministry of cleansing. Since no believer has any personal power to cleanse spiritually, the most obvious way to exercise this ministry is by the application of the Scriptures to a fellow believer's life (cf. John 15:3; 17:17; see Gal. 6:1-3).

Moreover, the significance of this seemingly incidental event must not be minimized. John thought it so important that he included it in a record (20 of 155 verses in the upper room discourse) that is ostensibly intended to chronicle Jesus' preparation of His disciples for His impending death. It most certainly must, in his mind, have related in some way to the Lord's passion and our perception thereof. But even more remarkable is the fact that Jesus Christ would give attention to such an object lesson and its attendant instruction on the eve of His death for the sins of mankind. Any event or statement related to the death of a notable person is marked with special importance, but in the case of Jesus the importance is magnified to the degree of infinity. His death, and all that surrounded it, was planned in infinite detail in the counsels of eternity (see, e.g., John 12:27-36 together with 13:3). If one allows for the fact that the supper was an integral part of the experience, Jesus used all five senses as teaching tools on this occasion: taste and smell —the meal (v. 2); touch—the application of water and the wiping of the feet (v. 5); sight—Peter's intent observation of Jesus' activity until He came to him (vv. 6-9); and hearing—the accompanying instruction (vv. 7-10, 12-20). By drawing such graphic attention to the truth that He was thus illustrating, Jesus marked the experience indelibly on the minds of those present. It is quite obvious that from our Lord's standpoint no extremity, even death, should preclude the exercise of loving service to a brother.

Another indication of the purposiveness of this incident is noted by Morris. He observes "that it takes place during the meal (v. 2), not on arrival when the feet would normally be washed. This shows that it was an action undertaken deliberately, and not simply the usual act of courtesy."[17]

We certainly must not miss the fact that Jesus uses the foot washing as an occasion to give instruction about the cleansing power of His upcoming death (John 13:10). As Morris says,

> Many take the story as no more than a lesson in humility, quite overlooking the fact that, in that case, Jesus' dialogue with Peter completely obscures its significance! But those words, spoken in the shadow of the cross, have to do with cleansing, that cleansing without which no man

[17]Leon Morris, *The Gospel According to John: The English Text with Introduction, Exposition, and Notes,* p. 612.

> belongs to Christ, that cleansing which is given by the cross alone. As Hunter says, "The deeper meaning then is that there is no place in his fellowship for those who have not been cleansed by his atoning death. The episode dramatically symbolizes the truth enunciated in 1 John 1:7, 'We are being cleansed from every sin by the blood of Jesus.' "[18]

Morris continues his quotation from Hunter in a footnote as follows:

> "Many people today would like to be Christians but see no need of the cross. They are ready to admire Jesus' life and to praise the sublimity of his moral teaching, but they cannot bring themselves to believe that Christ died for their sins, and that without that death they would be lost in sin. This, as Brunner has said, is one of the prime 'scandals' of Christianity for modern man—and the very heart of the apostolic Gospel."[19]

Nonetheless, while acknowledging this emphasis, as His dialogue with Peter also shows, we also hold that this is not the end of the truth Christ was setting forth. It is true that one does not enter fellowship with Christ without cleansing. But it is also true that he cannot continue to enjoy fellowship with Christ without the ongoing cleansing that comes through the ministry of the application of the written Word of God by the believing community to one another. The interplay of λούω (bathe) and *νίπτω* (wash) in verse 10 demands that we see two types of cleansing, for λούω is properly used of the bathing of the entire body, while *νίπτω* refers to the washing of a part (in this case, a part of an already bathed body). Morris is most certainly wrong to see "you have no part with Me" (v. 8) as an indication that foot washing symbolizes the cleansing of sin at the cross.[20] Taken by itself the clause may be construed in that sense, but in light of verses 9-10 it can only be understood as a reference to fellowship—not relationship.

Further support that the foot washing incident was intended to be exemplary rather than ritualistic is seen in the overall tenor of John's gospel. Nowhere in his gospel does John dwell upon the rite of baptism,

[18]Ibid., p. 613. Morris is quoting from A. M. Hunter, *The Gospel According to John.*
[19]Morris, p. 613 footnote.
[20]Ibid., p. 617.

and even here in the upper room discourse, during which the Lord's Supper was instituted, according to the synoptics, he does not allude to the ceremony.

3. *He is our sustenance.* Three interpretations of John 6:47-58 are commonly accepted. (1) One interpretation sees the passage as a reference to the Lord's Supper. This interpretation has grammatical, theological, and historical difficulties of great proportions.[21] (2) Another interpretation sees the passage as a reference to the death of Christ for sin. This is the most common view among Protestant expositors and is based upon the future tense of δώσω (give) in verse 51 together with references to blood throughout the passage.[22] The use of "give" in this context, however, does not seem to refer so much to sacrifice as it does to the supply of spiritual nourishment (see, e.g., vv. 31-34). The tense may well refer to a future act, even the cross, or it may refer to a future continuous giving of Himself.[23] The references to the drinking of the

[21]The force of the present tense of τρώγω (eat) in vv. 54 and 56 militates against this view. The tense would call for a continuous eating of Christ's flesh (if taken in the literal sense called for by Roman Catholic theology), which would in turn call for its continuous availability. The theological problems are of equal difficulty, since nowhere in John's writings, our Lord's teaching, or the entire New Testament is the receipt of eternal life conditioned on partaking of the Lord's Supper or any other ritual. The historical problem, of course, relates to the fact that Jesus' flesh and blood are not available for ingestion, and to make them so one must resort to the excesses of Roman Catholic theology as set forth in the doctrine of transubstantiation. See Morris (pp. 373-81) for extensive refutation of the view that interprets John 6:47-58 as a reference to the Lord's Supper.

[22]Morris has shown conclusively that "blood" refers to violent death rather than to the mere release of life. See his *Apostolic Preaching of the Cross,* chap. 3, and his *Gospel According to John,* p. 378, footnote 125. That "blood" refers to violent death does not establish, however, that this discourse is referring primarily to Jesus' death as a sacrifice for sin. His death is also the basis for Christian living, as John indicates in 1 John, especially in 1:7.

[23]The future tense is sometimes aoristic in its *aktionsart,* as is seen by the sigma in its endings. There are exceptions to this, however, as the grammars will testify. Turner states that in the indicative "this is the one tense which does not express the *aktionsart,* but simply states the time of the action relative to the speaker. However, it is usually punctiliar, the periphrastic future being used when it is required to indicate linear action (Moulton Proleg. 149 f.), but the question is really a matter of opinion (Moule, p. 10)" (J. H. Moulton, *A Grammar of New Testament Greek,* 3:86). In fact, there is an example of a linear future in this very verse (John 6:51), for ζήσει (shall live) with εἰς τὸν αἰῶνα (forever) could hardly be punctiliar. The important thing

blood may be understood as being parallel to those about eating His flesh, which are much more expressive of appropriation of Christ for nourishment than of an appropriation of His death.[24] (3) The third interpretation of this difficult passage sees it as depicting spiritual appropriation and assimilation of Christ, all that He is and has done, for the sustenance of the Christian life. This views the eating and drinking in an ethical or mystical sense, and while the benefits of His death are not excluded, the primary teaching of the passage is not the atonement.[25] When John 6:48, which refers to the "bread of life," and 6:51, which refers to the "living bread," are compared, the truth of the passage is illuminated. The first phrase refers to that which the bread does; that is, it supplies life to the eater. The second phrase gives an active quality of the bread itself: it is self-perpetuating. Thus, the whole picture is of a source of life that is never used up. Verse 53 presents the picture of making Christ a part of oneself and thus having life in oneself.[26] This is the converse of faith. "Faith throws the believer upon and into its object; this spiritual eating and drinking brings the object of faith into the believer."[27] In light of this assimilation and interchange of commitment, we gain some insight into what is involved in the mutual abiding referred to here and developed later in John 15 (John 6:56). The doctrine of abiding is thus related to the believer's life in

---

to notice, however, is that *time,* not *aktionsart,* is prominent in the Greek future tense.

[24]Morris contends for the idea that the "flesh" does refer to Jesus' death and quotes C. H. Dodd *(The Interpretation of the Fourth Gospel)* to the same effect (Morris, *The Gospel According to John,* pp. 373-79). The argument is based on the use of ὑπέρ (for) in v. 51 and Barrett's conclusion that John's usage of the preposition shows "conclusively that a reference to the death of Jesus is intended—he will give his flesh in death—and suggest[s] a sacrificial meaning" (C. K. Barrett, *The Gospel According to St. John,* p. 246). Again it should be noted that even granting this valid point, one may still argue that the primary thrust of the passage may not be the initial act of justification; instead, the thrust of the passage may be the Christian life as based on Jesus' death.

[25]G. B. Stevens, *The Johannine Theology: A Study of the Doctrinal Contents of the Gospel and Epistles of the Apostle John,* pp. 159-64.

[26]The entire expression points to the ingestion of food for the *sustaining* of life. He uses the present tense of the verb ἔχω (to have) to point to the continuation of life and the phrase ἐν ἑαυτοῖς (in yourselves) to emphasize the internal nature of this truth.

[27]B. F. Westcott, *The Gospel According to St. John: The Authorized Version with Introduction and Notes,* p. 107.

Christ rather than to his coming to life; it therefore provides another support for this third interpretation of John 6:47-58.

4. *He is our victor.*

a. Jesus, the Son of God, is described as an overcomer in several places. For example, in John 16:33 He is seen as victor over the world and thus the guarantor of peace even in the midst of trouble in the world. In Revelation 3:21 and 5:5-14 He is described as victor in light of His finished work at the cross, and thus He is able to assure the believer of a place with Him in His future rule and to assume the role of sovereign ruler and judge in the future outworking of history.

b. Through faith in *the* overcomer, Christians become overcomers as well (1 John 5:4-5; cf. Rev. 2:7, 11, 17, 26; 3:5, 12, 21; 21:7; 1 John 2:13-14). It should be carefully noted that the promise has no contingency attached to it other than faith in Jesus as the Son of God. These Christian overcomers are not some select group of spiritual elite but a group that includes the humblest believer.[28] Even the humblest believer is heir to all the blessings of the New Jerusalem and has been given one of the most tender and beautiful promises ever made to man. "I will be *God* to him and he himself will be *son* to me" (author's translation [Rev. 21:7; cf. 2 Sam. 7:14]). That Yahweh should deign in a personal way to be God to us is transcending grace at its most sublime, but that He should allow us to supply the filial duties and privileges of sons to Him defies expression. It is best left in the simplicity of God's statement as recorded by John.[29]

[28]John's terminology guards against several errors. The initial clause in 1 John 5:4 shows that this overcoming is not something that is subsequent to salvation, for it is "every one who is begotten [γεγεννημένον, a perfect form indicating an existing condition based upon a completed act] of God" who "is overcoming [νικᾷ, a present form referring to an ongoing pattern of life] the world" (author's translation). The second clause, by the use of the aorist form νικήσασα (has overcome), shows that today's victory is based on yesterday's; that is, our victory is based on His. Finally, John counters the error that abstract faith (i.e., faith without the appropriate object) is efficacious by qualifying ἡ πίστις ἡμῶν (our faith [v. 4]) with ὁ πιστεύων ὅτι 'Ιησοῦς ἐστιν ὁ υἱὸς τοῦ θεοῦ (he who believes that Jesus is the Son of God [v. 5]). Faith that overcomes involves trust in Jesus (the man), who is God's Son.

[29]The passages in the seven letters to the churches of Asia Minor that present the believer as overcomer are dealt with extensively in chapter 12.

In 1 John 2:12-14 John seems to categorize his addressees as either children, fathers, or younger men in the faith.[30] One of the characteristics of vigorous young men, in addition to strength and the vital presence of the Word of God within, is that they have overcome (νενικήκατε, perfect active indicative) the evil one. Thus, not only does faith in Jesus Christ provide victory over the world; it also provides victory over the prince of the world.

But not only has the believer overcome Satan. He also is victor over Satan's servants (1 John 4:1-4). This victory is ours, John explains, because He who is in us (*the* victor) is greater than he who is in the world (the false prophet).

c. The world (κόσμος) is dealt with extensively by John. "Altogether it occurs 185 times [in the New Testament], of which 78 occurrences are in John, 24 in the Johannine Epistles, and 3 in Revelation."[31] Morris explains its root idea as follows:

> Basically the word denotes an ornament, a use which we may still see in 1 Pet. 3:3 (and which has given us our word "cosmetic"). The universe with all its harmonious relationships is the outstanding ornament, and thus the term came to be used of the universe at large.[32]

From this, the concept of a systematized and ordered whole developed; and in light of its distinctive New Testament usage this world-system is seen as basically functioning apart from and contrary to God.[33] Various definitions have been offered for this term as used in the

[30]That these are not familial distinctions is suggested from the fact that no reference is made to women (unless one is willing to suggest that John's comments in this epistle are for men and children only).

[31]Morris, *The Gospel According to John,* p. 126.

[32]Ibid.

[33]Morris writes, "It is this use of 'the world' as hostile to Christ and all that He stands for which is the significantly new use the term acquires in the New Testament. It does not appear to have such a meaning in Greek writings at large. There it is rather something attractive, the order and the beauty of the universe" (Ibid., p. 127). After a very helpful note on "the world," Westcott sums up as follows: "From this analysis of St. John's usage of the term it will be seen how naturally the original conception of an order apart from God passes into that of an order opposed to God: how a system which is limited and transitory becomes hostile to the divine: how the 'world' as the whole scene of human activity is lost in humanity: how humanity ceases to be 'of the world' by its union with God in Christ" (*The Gospel According to St. John,* p. 32).

New Testament,[34] but perhaps the following will serve our purposes here: It is a way of life ordered apart from and contrary to God, ruled by Satan, and encompassing all mankind who are not in the family of God through faith in Jesus Christ.[35]

Since the term "world" is such a complex one, it is difficult to categorize its various uses by John. In many cases there is clearly more than one shade of meaning. In general, however, the word does seem to fall into certain groupings according to usage. First, there is a somewhat general use that seems to have little moral implication. It is used in John 12:19 to describe the general mass of mankind. In several places it refers to one's coming into, going out of, or presence in this world (John 6:14; 9:5; 10:36; 13:1; 16:21, 28; 17:11; 18:37).

The majority of the Johannine references give us insight into the character and future of the world. It is the abode and domain of Satan (John 12:31; 16:11; 14:30; 1 John 5:19) and his minions, who champion its cause (1 John 4:1-5). It is, therefore, a place of moral darkness (John 1:9; 3:19; 11:9), sin (John 1:29; 1 John 2:15-16), and death (John 6:33, 51). This sin evidences itself in the form of hatred (John 7:7; 15:18-19; 17:14; 1 John 3:13), disappointment (John 14:17), and tribulation (John 16:33). As a sphere that is alien to God and His ways (John 8:23; 12:25; 13:1; 18:36) it knows neither God (John 1:10; 17:25; 1 John 2:16) nor His children (1 John 3:1). It is actively anti-Christ (John 15:18; 16:20; 1 John 4:3) and cannot receive the Holy Spirit (John 14:17). Jesus made

[34]Westcott, for example, says, "The fundamental idea of κόσμος in St. John is that of the sum of created being which belongs to the sphere of human life as an ordered whole, considered apart from God" (*The Gospel According to St. John,* p. 31). Sasse calls it "the sum of the divine creation which has been shattered by the fall, which stands under the judgment of God, and in which Jesus Christ appears as the Redeemer" (H. Sasse, "κόσμος," in *Theological Dictionary of the New Testament,* ed. G. Kittel and G. Friedrich, 3:893).

[35]Morris writes, "for John . . . the shattering thing was that the men who inhabit this beautiful and ordered universe acted in an ugly and unreasonable way when they came face to face with Christ" (*The Gospel According to John,* p. 127). Bultmann's assessment is that "the delusion that arises from the will to exist of and by oneself *perverts truth into a lie, perverts the creation into the 'world.'* For in their delusion men do not let their quest for life become a question about themselves so as to become aware of their creaturehood, but instead they give themselves the answer so as to have a security of their own. They take the temporary for the ultimate, the spurious for the genuine, death for life" (R. Bultmann, *Theology of the New Testament,* 2:27).

a particular point of noting that it is *not* the object of His prayer (John 17:9),[36] although He did come to save it (John 12:47). Since it is transient (1 John 2:17) and under judgment (John 9:39), especially in the person of its ruler (John 12:31; 16:11),[37] it is hardly the place where one should desire to remain. Thus Christ could say that for the believer it has been and now is conquered by Himself (John 16:33). And, the day is coming when its kingdom will be finally and eternally overcome by our Lord and His anointed, Christ (Rev. 11:15).

Despite the fact that the world is as described above, John teaches that it is related positively to God in several ways. Before looking at those ways, however, one must get clearly in mind the fact that the *fallen* world is the product of satanic and human doing. The world is not today as it was originally intended to be.[38]

Originally the world was created by God (John 1:10; 17:5, 24; Rev. 13:8; 17:8). Despite the fact that it fell into sin, He loves the people enmeshed in its wicked ways (John 3:16-17; 14:31; 17:23) and sent His Son to die for its sin (John 1:29; 1 John 2:2) and thus become its Savior (John 4:42; 12:47; 1 John 4:14). During Jesus' earthly ministry He spoke openly to the world (John 8:26; 18:20), making it clear that He was the light of the world (John 1:9; 8:12; 9:5; 12:46) and the life of the world (John 6:33, 51; 1 John 4:9). Upon His departure He sent the Holy Spirit to the people of the world to convict them of their sin (John 16:8) through the witness of believers (John 16:7). He prayed for the believers' witness to the end that it might be a demonstration of Godheadlike unity (John 17:21) and divine love (John 17:23) that would draw the world to faith in Him.

The world is the temporary abode of the Christian, but despite its

[36]This, together with the remainder of Jesus' high-priestly prayer in John 17, should give the Christian certain significant clues regarding his own prayer life. One of the major burdens of the believer's prayer life should be fellow believers, rather than the unbelieving per se, to the end that the fellow believers may effectively reach out to the world.

[37]John 12:47 is not a contradiction of John 9:39; 12:31; and 16:11, but simply a note that the primary emphasis of Jesus' coming was salvatory rather than judgmental.

[38]"There is only one thing certain about *the kosmos, the world*—the *kosmos* is not what it was meant to be. Something has gone wrong. What is that something? It is sin" (W. Barclay, *The Gospel of John,* 2:21-22).

animosity (John 15:19), it is a place of safety (John 17:15) due to Christ's irreproachable character (1 John 4:17; cf. John 14:30) and perfect love (John 13:1).[39] In fact, the believer is sent to the world in like manner as the Father sent the Son (John 17:18): to bear witness thereto (John 17:20). As he goes to the world, the Christian is not "of the world" (ἐκ τοῦ κόσμου) and, in fact, has been chosen[40] "out of the world" (ἐκ τοῦ κόσμου) (John 15:19; cf. 17:6, 14, 16).[41] This elective act of God leads to the new birth, after which the begotten of God continually overcomes (νικᾷ, present tense) the world (1 John 5:4) on the basis of trust in Jesus as God's Son, who has already overcome (νικήσασα, aorist participle) the world (1 John 5:4-5). If the believer keeps this in mind he will be strengthened to avoid the forbidden love[42] of the world and its "things"[43] (1 John 2:15). Anyone (τις) who exercises this kind of love for the world demonstrates the absence of the Father's love within. The reasons for this unusually strong statement are that (1) *all* that is in the world is not of the Father, but of the world, and (2) the world and its lust are in the process of passing away[44]

[39]Regarding εἰς τέλος (to the end) in John 13:1, Westcott writes, "There appears to be no authority for taking it here in the sense of *to the end of His earthly presence* (yet see Matt. x. 22, xxiv. 13 f.), and such a translation does not suit the connexion with *before the feast.* If, however, we take the words as expressing *loved them with a perfect love,* then the thought comes out clearly, 'As Christ loved His disciples, and had before shewed His love, so now at this crisis, before the day of His Passion, He carried His love to the highest point. He loved them to the uttermost' " (*The Gospel According to St. John,* p. 190).

[40]The verb ἐξελεξάμην, aorist middle indicative, points to a selective act of personal interest by God.

[41]Εκ τοῦ κόσμου (of the world; out of the world), an ablative of source in its first two occurrences in John 15:19 and in 17:6, 14, and 16 and an ablative of separation in its third occurrence in 15:19, strengthens the already intensive verb ἐκλέγω (I choose).

[42]Note that the prohibition is against *purposed* love (ἀγαπᾶτε).

[43]The phrase τὰ ἐν τῷ κόσμῳ (the things in the world) must be understood as referring to worldly ideological and philosophical things rather than to such things as the arts and sciences per se. It is the things ἐν (locative of sphere) τῷ κόσμῳ, that is, the things in the sphere of influence of the world, rather than the things τοῦ κόσμου, the things of the world themselves, that are not to be loved.

[44]The verb παράγεται (is passing away) ([1 John 2:17; cf. v. 8]) is most descriptive. It is in the present tense and the middle voice, and thus suggests that even as John was writing the world was disintegrating from within. The middle voice almost suggests a self-destructiveness. At the very least, it describes a transiency that is totally out of

(1 John 2:16-17). Then, lest anyone be left wondering what is included in "all," John gives a series of three epexegetical statements explaining it in full. In essence he says that worldliness may involve carnality ("the lust of the flesh"), that is, the inordinate desire[45] that arises from the flesh; avarice ("the lust of the eyes"), that is, the inordinate desire for gain; or pride ("the boastful pride of life"), that is, the self-sufficient attitude of boastfulness arising from one's means of living.[46] In contrast to the one who loves the fleeting world, "he who practices [ποιῶν, present participle, expressing a pattern of life] the will of God abides forever" (1 John 2:17, author's translation). He who immerses his life in God's will has found the fabled fountain of youth.

C. The Holy Spirit.

1. *He is teacher (illuminator and guide).* Both John 14:26 and 16:13 indicate that the Holy Spirit will "teach . . . all things" and "guide . . . into all the truth."[47] The context in both cases and the use of the

---

keeping with and unbecoming to one who is possessor of life that is eternal. Note the obvious contrast with the last clause of v. 17, especially μένει εἰς τὸν αἰῶνα (abides forever).

[45]'Επιθυμία may refer to any legitimate appetite, such as the desire for food, drink, or sex. In this case, however, the desire is "in the world" and "of the flesh" and therefore tends to be excessive (e.g., gluttony, drunkenness, fornication) (cf. John 8:44).

[46]The word is βίος, referring to "the means by which [life] is sustained" (G. Abbott-Smith, *A Manual Greek Lexicon of the New Testament,* p. 81). Cf. James 4:13-16.

[47]In John 16:13 the Paraclete is called "the Spirit of truth," a fitting title for one who has as one of His primary tasks the teaching of the truth. On the strength of the use of this title (Spirit of truth) in the Dead Sea Scrolls, some scholars have suggested that the Paraclete of John's writings is not the Holy Spirit at all but, as in the scrolls, an angelic being. Even a cursory examination of the pertinent passages (*Manual of Discipline* 3:18-26; *Order of Warfare* 13:9-12; 17:6-8; see the translation of A. Dupont-Sommer in *The Essene Writings from Qumran,* pp. 78-79, 189, 194) will show so many major differences as to destroy all credibility in such a hypothesis. In refutation of the idea that the New Testament Paraclete is merely an extension of the Qumran concept, R. E. Brown writes: "In our judgment, it is because the Paraclete is very carefully patterned on Jesus that the figure of the Qumrân Spirit of Truth and/or the angelic Prince of Lights has also become part of the Johannine picture of the Paraclete. If John calls the Paraclete the Spirit of Truth, we suspect that the primary factor that made this title seem fitting was that in Johannine thought the Paraclete is the Spirit of Jesus and Jesus is the truth" ("The Paraclete in the Fourth Gospel," p. 126). In a footnote

definite article in 16:13 indicate that the Holy Spirit's teaching relates specifically to truth about Jesus Christ (John 16:14). For the modern believer, this means the truth as found in the Bible, for God is no longer giving new revelations about Christ, and the Bible is the only source of truth that we know to be completely and verbally inspired by God. While John 14:26 may seem to be limited to those who heard the Lord during His earthly ministry, no such limitation is required in John 16:12-15[48] or in 1 John 2:20, 27. Verse 27 should not be interpreted as precluding the necessity of human teachers;[49] rather, it emphasizes that even when human leadership is unreliable (as in this context regarding antichrists) there is an inner witness of the Holy Spirit, and the Holy Spirit's witness is the ultimate witness.

2. *He is counselor (strengthener and advocate).* The word παρά-κλητος,[50] translated "Comforter" in the King James Version of John's gospel, has probably been mistranslated.[51] *Comforter* is from the Latin word meaning "one who strengthens," while παράκλητος means "one called to the side of another—with a view to providing help." In 1 John 2:1 the word clearly means "advocate," or "counselor" (lawyer, attorney), in the legal sense; and John 14:16 refers to the Holy Spirit as

---

he adds, "There are no citations or near-citations of Qumrân works in John" (p. 126 footnote 1).

[48]See pp. 35-36 for a fuller treatment of this passage.

[49]That John had no such idea in mind is seen from 1 John 4:1-2, which refers to spirits (true prophets) who rightly confess Jesus Christ. Also, the implication of 2 John 10 is that while false teachers are not to be received into one's home, teachers of the truth are to be welcomed. Note the following passage from the *Didache;* it closely parallels the references in John: "Whosoever then comes and teaches you all these things aforesaid, receive him. But if the teacher himself be perverted and teach another doctrine to destroy these things, do not listen to him, but if his teaching be for the increase of righteousness and knowledge of the Lord, receive him as the Lord" (11.1-2). Since this document is probably to be dated around A.D. 100 and is therefore nearly contemporary with John's writings, it reflects the prevalent views of at least a segment of the early church.

Furthermore, why should the gift of teaching (Rom. 12:7; Eph. 4:11), given to the church by the same Holy Spirit, be necessary if human teachers are prohibited?

[50]The word is peculiarly Johannine in the New Testament. It is used once of Christ (1 John 2:1) and four times of the Holy Spirit (John 14:16, 26; 15:26; 16:7).

[51]The term "Comforter" seems to have got into the English translations through Wycliffe's version. There it meant "strengthener" rather than "consoler."

"another" παράκλητον. This argues strongly for uniformity of translation. Furthermore, the Greek word is a passive form.[52] Thus, the active concept of "one who strengthens," "helper" (e.g., John 14:16) is an outgrowth or secondary meaning.[53] For these reasons the term "counselor" is used here, though in light of the multifaceted sense of the word (due as much to its usage as to its etymology) it must be admitted that no one translation does justice to its rich meaning.[54] In light of this, perhaps a simple transliteration, *Paraclete,* is safer.[55]

The purpose of the Holy Spirit's being given in this capacity is set forth in John 14:16. It is to assure us of an *ever present* counselor, in contrast to Jesus Christ, who was to return to the Father. The Holy Spirit's function as counselor is at least fourfold. (1) He represents Christ to the believer, and (2) He bears witness to Christ rather than to Himself (John 14:26; 15:26). Also, (3) as counselor He functions as

[52]Westcott, *The Gospel According to St. John,* pp. 211-12.

[53]In contrast, William Hendriksen (*New Testament Commentary: Exposition of the Gospel According to John,* 2:276) argues convincingly for "helper." See also Arndt and Gingrich (p. 102). The NEB offers "advocate" as a translation in both the gospel and the epistle. Morris objects to the NEB translation on the basis of the fact that an advocate instructs the court rather than his client. Since Morris feels that we are the clients, he rules out this translation (*The Gospel According to John,* p. 665). He has missed the picture, however, for just as Christ is our advocate before the Father, so the Holy Spirit is our advocate before Christ.

[54]Raymond Brown notes that "the Paraclete is a *witness* in defence of Jesus and a *spokesman* for him in the context of the trial of Jesus by his enemies; the Paraclete is a *consoler* of the disciples; more important, he is their teacher and guide and thus, in an extended sense their *helper.* No one translation captures the complexity of these functions. . . . In rendering this word into Latin for the Vulgate, Jerome had a choice among such Old Latin renderings as *advocatus* and *consolator* and the custom of transliterating the term simply as *paracletus.* In the Gospel he took the latter expedient (*advocatus* appears in 1 John), a course also followed in the Syriac and Coptic traditions. We would probably be wise to do the same in modern times and settle for 'Paraclete,' a near-transliteration that at least preserves the uniqueness of the title and does not emphasize one of the aspects of the concept to the detriment of others" (pp. 118-19).

[55]Westcott gives several examples of rabbinic uses of the Hebrew term פרקליט—a transliteration of the Greek word παράκλητος—in which uses פרקליט seems to mean "advocate" (*The Gospel According to St. John,* p. 212). The interesting thing to note, however, is that, as has just been noted, the Hebrew word is simply a transliteration of the Greek. Apparently, just as there is no exact English equivalent for παράκλητος, so there was no Semitic equivalent either.

instructor (John 14:26) and convictor (John 16:7 ff.). (If He is given to us as counselor and He convicts the world as counselor, then it follows that this ministry must be through us.) Finally, (4) the Holy Spirit indwells the Christian (John 14:16-17; cf. 1 John 2:27). This is another ministry assigned to the counselor that is elsewhere said to be true of Jesus Christ (see John 14:20; 15:4-5).[56] While it is treated rather fully by Paul (e.g., 1 Cor. 6:19-20; Rom. 8:1-12), this doctrine is given a relatively insignificant place in John's writings. His primary contribution to the doctrine (as he records Jesus' words) is that this relationship apparently is to be distinguished from the Spirit's previous relationship with men. In fact, this change in relationship is the key to the believer's *knowing* the Spirit (John 14:17). The reason given (ὅτι [because]) as to why Christians may know Him in this indwelling is that "He abides with you, and will be in you" (παρ' ὑμῖν μένει καὶ ἐν ὑμῖν ἔσται). The change in prepositions marks a change from nearness to inner presence,[57] and the change in tense from present (μένει [abides]) to future (ἔσται [will be])[58] indicates that with the coming of the

[56]Jesus Christ likewise teaches (John 7:14; 13:13), bears witness (John 8:14), and convicts of sin (Rev. 3:19; cf. John 3:20). As Morris notes, "There is point in Jesus referring to *'another'* Paraclete (14:16)" (*The Gospel According to John,* p. 663). The pregnant meaning of ἄλλος (another) as used of the Paraclete is highlighted by Brown in his listing of twenty-five parallels between the Holy Spirit and Jesus Christ (pp. 126-27).

[57]"The presence of the Paraclete differs from the presence of Jesus during the ministry in an essential feature: The Paraclete is invisible to the world because the Paraclete is within the disciple (xiv. 17). The only way that the Paraclete can exercise his ministry is through Christians and their way of life and the way they bear witness. The only way the world can know that Jesus' death was not the end is that the Spirit which animated Jesus is still alive in his followers. This is how the Paraclete proves the world wrong and shows that Jesus is triumphant with the Father while the Prince of this world has been condemned, namely, that two thousand years after Jesus' death, his presence is still made visible in his disciples; through Christians the Paraclete is still glorifying Jesus" (Brown, p. 132).

[58]There is a textual question about whether we should here read ἔσται, which has very strong manuscript evidence (p66, p75, ℵ , A), or ἐστιν (is [**B, D, W**]). The first edition of the Bible Societies text (K. Aland et al., eds., *The Greek New Testament*) prefers the latter but only gives it a [D] rating; that is, there exists a "very high degree of doubt" whether ἐστιν is in fact the better reading. Interestingly, the third edition has exchanged readings and gives preference to ἔσται, also with a [D] rating. Two considerations seem to favor the future tense: (1) The present tense seems more like a scribal correction to harmonize with the other present tenses in the verse (but see

counselor something that had not hitherto been true was to commence. It is questionable whether the elaborate theology that has sometimes been built on this fact is entirely legitimate.[59] If the above-suggested textual reading is indeed the proper one, some distinction between the pre-Pentecostal and the post-Pentecostal relationship between the believer and the Spirit must be maintained, but it would appear rather speculative to press it too far.[60] Certainly there does seem to be a greater intimacy of relationship suggested between the believer and the Holy Spirit today, which intimacy provides for the development of Christlike

Westcott [*The Gospel According to St. John,* p. 206], who contends that "the present tense appears to be less like a correction." (2) The movement of thought in the passage almost requires some change.

[59]L. S. Chafer, for example, writes that "the age now past is marked off by the letter of the law, in which age no provision for enablement was ever made. The present age is distinguished as a period of the indwelling Spirit, whose presence provides every resource for the realization of a God-honoring daily life" (*Systematic Theology,* 6:123). He goes on to base many other conclusions on this view. It seems as if John 14:17 teaches just the opposite, for the clear statement is that the Holy Spirit "abides with you." Two other key passages in Chafer's argument are 1 Samuel 16:14 and Psalm 51:11. First Samuel 16:14 certainly does not *necessarily* teach that God had permanently forsaken Saul or that he was left entirely to his own resources. It does, however, point to one of the distinctions that marks pre- from post-Pentecostal pneumatology. It cannot rightly be said of a believer today that "the Spirit of the LORD departed from" him. Psalm 51:11 will not bear the weight of theology that has often been placed upon it either. In the first place, there is nothing that suggests that this is a reference to the Holy Spirit's indwelling of David, and, even if that is what David had in mind, we have no indication that his concern about being forsaken by the Spirit of God is a valid one. In all likelihood, the concern expressed in this psalm relates to what we would call in the New Testament terms the filling (controlling) of the Holy Spirit rather than His indwelling. This is more in keeping with the context, in which David is confessing his sin and seeking for a renewed evidence of the Spirit's power in his life. Rather than an implicit teaching that the indwelling Spirit comes and goes from men *at will* in the Old Testament, David's cry is the cry of a genuinely contrite heart who senses that his sin is worthy of bringing separation from God's presence and separation of the Spirit from himself. Nonetheless, and no doubt absent from David's mind in the midst of his contrition, it is no more possible for God's child to be separated from Him in the Old Testament than it is in the New; it is no more possible for the Old Testament believer to lose the Holy Spirit than it is for the New Testament believer. The redemptive work of God in every dispensation is based on His changeless character and is ministered by the changeless Spirit.

[60]The pre- and post-Pentecostal distinction is especially tenuous if the correct word in John 14:17 is ἐστιν rather than ἔσται.

character; but to assign Old Testament saints to a status as less than first-rate citizens of God's Kingdom on this basis is not warranted. God works with different groups of saints in different ways in the different dispensations, but each has adequate provision by Him for the kind of life that He requires.

IX

The Hamartiology of the Christian Life

A. Introduction.

Unlike the gospel of John, which was written for the express purpose of making believers out of its readers (John 20:30-31), 1 John was written to those already believing. This epistle presumes the life appropriated by faith in the Savior set forth in the gospel. John's concern now is that the believer become a *fellowshipper* (1 John 1:3-4, 6-7) and then a convinced believer (1 John 5:13).[1]

Since it is addressed to believers, we would expect 1 John to contain positive instructions regarding such family responsibilities as fellowship with the Father and love for the brethren. Likewise, we would also expect a treatment of certain family problems of a more negative nature. And, in fact, in the course of writing 1 John, the apostle makes three affirmations of significance for a member of God's family, each of which in turn raises a serious problem. These three problem areas are readily identifiable through use of an analysis of the frequency of occurrence of the primary terms for sin in the epistle. By "primary terms" we have in mind basic theological terms of a general nature, such as "sin" (ἁμαρτία, ἁμαρτάνω), "lawlessness" (ἀνομία), and

[1]Note the ἵνα (that, *or* in order that) clauses in 1 John 1:3 and 5:13. Further evidence that 1 John is intended to be a "family letter" is seen in the over sixty occurrences of such terms as *father, children, brother, beloved,* and *fellowship*—which terms here indicate spiritual relationships—in the 105 verses of 1 John.

"unrighteousness" (ἀδικία), rather than descriptive terms such as "darkness" or specific sins such as "lie" or "hate." Note the following distribution of these primary terms:

1:5—2:6	sin (n. and v.)	8 times
	unrighteousness	1 time
2:12	sin (n.)	1 time
3:1-12	sin (n. and v.)	10 times
	lawlessness	2 times
4:10	sin (n.)	1 time
5:13-20	sin (n. and v.)	6 times
	righteousness	1 time

Of the thirty occurrences of these terms, only two are found outside of three major passages.

One other introductory observation must be made before we can proceed to suggested solutions to the three hamartiological problems mentioned above. The biblical doctrine of sin is a complex one and is not wholly expounded by any one writer of Scripture. John's contribution in his first epistle is fourfold.

First, he deals with the sin principle, or sin as a *fact.* The nearest he comes to a consideration of sin as an abstraction or principle seems to be in his use of the term "darkness" (approximately five times in the gospel and seven times in 1 John). He uses the term in a number of ways rather than uniformly, the only uniformity being the fact that it is inevitably opposed to light, love, and life. Also, it is inevitably aligned with that which is evil. First John 1 makes it quite clear that sin, here called "darkness," is in essence the opposite and absence of light. Because God is light, sin is thus the opposite and absence of God. If the statement "God is light" refers to God's holiness (see pp. 40-42, 107) "darkness" must at the least be a reference to unholiness. (See John 1:5; 3:19; 8:12; 12:35, 46; 1 John 1:5-6; 2:8, 9, 11.)

Second, in 1 John 3:4 and 5:17 John gives us some insight into the *character* of sin. The statement "sin is lawlessness" is the more important of the two, because it views sin from the divine standpoint and because it is a comprehensive statement.[2] Lawlessness must be understood as contrariness to law rather than merely as the breaking of *a* law.[3] Law, in the most absolute sense, represents God's character, and lawlessness represents the antithesis of God's character. Sin (ἁμαρτία) is a missing of the mark, which mark, as Paul points out in Romans 3:23, is ultimately the glory of God. Thus sin is that which falls short of the standard of God's character. In effect, then, John has said that that which falls short of the standard of God's own character is contrary to God's character. Thus the damning character of sin is brought into bold relief.

The other statement John makes about the character of sin is that "all unrighteousness is sin." This statement views sin more from the human standpoint. "The essence of righteousness lies in the recognition and fulfillment of what is due from one to another." Thus, "failure to fulfill our duty one to another" is unrighteousness.[4]

The third item John contributes to the doctrine of sin has to do with its *root:* the sin nature. Two of the three references to the sin nature relate to the believer, while the third has to do with Christ (1 John 3:5*b*) and states that there is no sin resident in Him.

First John 1:7 is a conditional statement containing a protasis—"if we walk in the light as He Himself is in the light"—and a double apodosis—"we have fellowship . . . and the blood . . . cleanses us from all sin."[5] Thus the last clause does not describe the ground of fellowship (although it is inextricably bound up with our enjoyment of fellowship) but a coordinate result of walking in the light. When the last clause of verse 7 is contrasted with verse 9, the significance of the statement becomes more apparent. Notice the following analysis:

[2]The statement "sin is lawlessness" is a convertible one because of the use of the definite article with both substantives (cf. H. E. Dana and Julius R. Mantey, *A Manual Grammar of the Greek New Testament,* p. 149). Thus it is probably the most definitive biblical statement regarding sin.

[3]Charles C. Ryrie, *Biblical Theology of the New Testament,* pp. 333-34.

[4]B. F. Westcott, *The Epistles of St. John: The Greek Text with Notes and Essays,* pp. 24, 192.

[5]The καί (and) is best understood as being coordinate (Ibid., p. 21; cf. Henry Alford, *The Greek Testament,* 4:427-28).

The Condition	The Agent or Agency	The Act	Those Dealt With	That Which Is Dealt With
if we walk in the light	the blood of Jesus	cleanses	us	from all sin
if we confess our sins	He	forgives	us	our sins
(if we confess our sins)	He	cleanses	us	from all unrighteousness

The statement of verse 7 is to be distinguished from those of verse 9, which have carried the argument a step further. Verse 7 speaks of the blood (a reference to the death of Jesus Christ at the cross) cleansing from all sin (ἁμαρτίας [sin], anarthrous, singular) as a result of our walking in the light. On the other hand, verse 9 speaks of God forgiving specific acts of sin (τὰς ἁμαρτίας [our sins], articular, plural) and cleansing from all unrighteousness as a result of confession. This is not to imply that the forgiveness and cleansing of verse 9 are possible apart from the cross (see 1 John 2:2); rather, the two verses are describing two entirely different things. Observe that the sin of verse 7 is not forgiven—it is cleansed; whereas the sins of verse 9 are forgiven and the resultant unrighteousness is cleansed. Forgiveness, in verse 9, deals with the defilement caused by sinful acts, whereas cleansing, in verse 7, deals with defilement caused by the sin nature. Verse 7 is setting forth a promise of cleansing and thus of control of the sin nature in order that it may not assert itself in sinful acts. On the other hand, that there is no suggestion of an absolute or final negation of the sin nature is seen in the present tense of the verb, which is both a promise of continual cleansing and a reminder of a continual need.

The other verse in which the sin nature is dealt with is 1 John 1:8. Contrary to Lenski's suggestion,[6] there is a very significant difference between verse 8 and verse 10. To claim to have no sin—that is, to deny

[6]R. C. H. Lenski, *The Interpretations of I and II Epistles of Peter, the Three Epistles of John, and the Epistle of Jude,* p. 391.

the presence of the sin principle in one's nature—and to claim to "have not sinned" (ἡμαρτήκαμεν, perfect tense)—that is, to deny the past performance of sinful acts—are two different things. Some scholars say that the error John is dealing with in this verse is the denial of guilt rather than the denial of sin as an inherent principle.[7] If the error is the denial of guilt, the verse is an answer to those who deny responsibility for sin. If, however, the error is the denial of sin as an inherent principle, the verse is an answer to those who believe in sinless perfection. Perhaps the key to the whole matter is found in Westcott's statement: " 'To have sin' includes the idea of personal guilt: it describes a state both as a consequence and as a cause."[8]

And, fourth, in addition to his insights into the fact, character, and root of sin, John has a good deal to say about the *fault* of sin: an uncontrolled sin nature, which produces personal acts of sin. This is the primary burden of 1 John and brings us to the three problems previously alluded to. Two important truths must be held in balance in a consideration of these problems. In light of 1 John 1:10, the presence of personal sin in the Christian life is undeniable. If we do not continually walk in the light, and our sin nature is thus not continually controlled, its activity will bear fruit in sins. If instead of confessing these sins we deny that we have committed them, we likewise deny God's witness to the contrary and betray the absence of His Word in our lives. Likewise, in light of 1 John 2:1, the presence of personal sin is undesirable. Here John declares that the purpose (ἵνα) for his having written the preceding truths (1 John 1:6-10) is that the believer may not commit a single act of sin (ἁμάρτητε, aorist tense).[9] This is not a declaration that believers *will* live sinless lives; it is a reminder that provision has been made so that we do not *have* to sin (1 John 1:7). The next clause

[7]John R. W. Stott, *The Epistles of John: An Introduction and Commentary,* p. 77, footnote; cf. Moffatt's translation of 1 John 1:8.

[8]Westcott, p. 22.

[9]What sins were these things written to keep them from? 1. Claiming fellowship with God while walking in darkness (1 John 1:6). 2. Failing to walk in the light with God and thus not realizing continual cleansing from sin (1:7). 3. Claiming the absence of a sin nature (or guilt) (1:8). 4. Failing to confess sin when it has been committed (1:9). 5. Claiming not to commit acts of sin (1:10). While we probably should not limit the sins referred to in 1 John 2:1 to these five, they surely would be prominent in any list.

makes it clear that when an occasional act (ἐάν τις ἁμάρτῃ [if anyone sins], another aorist) of sin is committed, God has also made provision for our resultant need.

B. How Can a Sinner Enjoy Fellowship with a Holy God?

The apostle declares that we may have fellowship with God (1 John 1:3), that God is absolutely holy (1:5), that sin destroys fellowship with God (1:6), that everyone sins (1:10), and that sin deceives the sinner (1:8) and dulls his discerning abilities (2:9, 11). How, then, can a sinner enjoy fellowship with a holy God?

The provision is twofold, consisting of a primary and secondary answer. The primary provision, found in 1:7, is that the sin nature from which personal sins arise may be controlled by walking in the light (see above). When the first provision is not utilized and as a result we commit personal sins, there is yet another provision (1:9—2:2). It has both a human and a divine aspect to it. Our responsibility is to confess our sins. That is, we are to take the same attitude and action toward our sins that God takes by acknowledging them to be what He says they are. This brings forgiveness of the guilt and cleansing of the defilement by the faithful and righteous God. The foundation upon which confession may be made by man and acted upon by God is stated in 2:1-2. Divine provision is based upon Christ's present work as advocate, upon His past work of propitiation, and upon His unchanging person. This One is faithful, and so we continually have (ἔχομεν, present tense) an advocate with the Father. Because He is righteous, the just nature of His work is guaranteed and God's just and holy demands are met and fully satisfied.

C. How Can a Sinner Be Conformed to the Image of Christ?

In 1 John 3:2 it is stated that when Christ is manifested, we shall be like Him.[10] Yet we are also told in 1 John 3:6*b* that everyone who is

[10]Likeness to Christ is not to be construed in terms of essential deity; rather, it is to be understood in terms of a pure, sinless, righteous character like His (1 John 3:3, 5, 7) and in terms of a glorified body like His (Phil. 3:20-21). Cf. Rom. 8:29; Eph. 5:27.

sinning (ἁμαρτάνων, present participle) as a pattern, or bent, of life has not ever seen Him and does not now see Him, and has not ever known Him and does not now know Him (both ἑώρακεν [has seen] and ἔγνωκεν [knows] are perfects). This does not mean simply that he who sins does not *now* abide in Him. It means, rather, that he who sins never has abode in Him, since he has never known Him. How, then, can a sinner be conformed to the image of Christ?

As incredible as it may be, John gives us two reasons why it is possible to be conformed to the image of Christ. The first makes the second possible, and the second must follow the first.

1. *By a divinely given relationship in the family.* The first provision for such a conformation is a divinely given relationship in the family (1 John 3:1-2). John speaks of our present place in the family. That the issue is birthright, or relationship, rather than legal standing, or sonship, is evident from the repetition of τέκνα θεοῦ (children of God), which is emphatic both times. Despite the utter wonder of it all, this is a present reality.[11] He then points out our place in the family in the future. Present relationship is the assurance of future likeness.[12] We do not await a day when we shall become His children. We await a day when, as children, we shall give perfect evidence of His likeness.[13]

2. *By a divinely given responsibility in the family.* The second provision for this conformation is a divinely given responsibility in the family. In light of our family privileges there are family duties. One of them is the maintenance of an active hope (1 John 3:3). Hope that is focused on Christ will lead to present self-purification.[14] But responsible

[11]Note the use of νῦν (now) in 1 John 3:2, the perfect form of δέδωκεν (has bestowed) in v. 1, and the repetition of ἐσμέν (we are) in vv. 1-2.

[12]Note the change of tense to ἐσόμεθα (we shall be) and the contrast between νῦν and οὔπω (not . . . as yet).

[13]John uses the neuter interrogative pronoun, τί (what), rather than the masculine form, τίς (who).

The last ὅτι clause of v. 2 (because we shall see Him just as He is) introduces an interesting question. Does it refer to the necessary condition for the divine vision or does it refer to the actual consequence of the divine vision? See Westcott, pp. 99-100, for discussion.

[14]The prepositional phrase translated "in him" in the KJV is ἐπ' αὐτοῦ. While ἐπί with the locative case is locational in force, it answers the question Where? rather than Wherein?, as ἐν might do. Thus ἐπ' αὐτοῦ means "set upon Him" ("fixed on

Christian living is not merely an expression of occasional purification. It is the maintenance of a life of purity.[15] This ongoing experience may be realized by fulfilling at least two obligations.

The first obligation is that we must abide in the Sinless One (1 John 3:6). *Abiding* in Christ is to be distinguished from *being* in Christ, although ideally there should be no practical difference between the two. We may observe the distinction by noting John 15:1-11, where the "in Me" branch of verse 2 is seen to be different from the "abide in Me" branch of verse 4. To *be* in Christ is to be born again, to be regenerated, to have had forgiveness of sins through Christ. Thus the disciples are in Christ (v. 2) because they have been cleansed of their sins (v. 3). To *abide* in Christ, however, is to be an obedient follower in fellowship with Christ the Savior and Lord (vv. 4-5, 9-11).[16] An examination of

---

Him," NASB) and is a reference to Christ rather than to the believer. This is in accord with the general New Testament teaching on hope, which is presented as an objective certainty related to the promise of God and the person of Christ rather than as a subjective feeling residing in the believer (cf. Col. 1:27; 1 Tim. 1:1). The words "this hope fixed on Him" refer back to φανερωθῇ (He appears) in v. 2, which should be understood (as the NASB rightly does) as having a masculine subject ("He").

[15]One might ask whether hope itself purifies one or whether hope leads one to the purification of self. Vv. 4-9 seem to suggest the latter alternative.

[16]Arminian theology, which for the most part rejects the doctrine of the perseverance of the saints, would typically interpret the "abiding" passages as relating to salvation rather than to fellowship. Because one may not necessarily always abide in Christ, advocates of this theological position see such passages as teaching the possibility that a believer can lose his salvation. The Arminian writer Robert Shank, in his discussion of 1 John 3:6 and 9, says: "What John attributes in verse 6 to 'abiding in him' he attributes in verse 9 to being 'born of God.' John thus implies that 'abiding in Him' and being 'born of God' are equivalent" (*Life in the Son: A Study in the Doctrine of Perseverance,* pp. 94-99). Although this is a frequently held position, it is unwarranted for several reasons. In the first place, Shank's statement that one of the major theses of 1 John is "the Apostle's insistence that there are specific conditions under which the new birth *can* exist, and other specific conditions under which it *cannot* exist" is not demonstrable, as will be shown in the discussion of v.9 on pp. 135-36. Second, his discussion of the word μένω (to abide) fails to consider John's other usage of that word. Third, he overlooks the fact that the argument of v.6 has to do with the believer's relationship to the sinless Savior (3:5), while the argument of v.9 is based on the presence of the divine seed in the believer. What John is saying is that the reason the begotten of God does not sin is that he has become a partaker of the divine nature. The person who lives a life characterized by sin is not one who is out of fellowship or one who has lost his salvation, but one who was never born again in the first place (3:6*b*).

1 John 3:24 will reveal that obedience is the condition for abiding. Moreover, in John 15:10 our obeying Christ and thus abiding in Him is compared to the Son's obeying the Father and thus abiding in Him; the Son was already *in* the Father by virtue of His sonship, but the Son *abided* in the Father by obeying Him. We see, then, that just as Christ's abiding in the Father was the maintenance of personal fellowship with the Father, so our abiding in Christ is the maintenance of personal fellowship with Christ. Just as Christ's abiding in the Father was the continuous enjoyment of the position that was His, so our abiding in Christ is the continuous enjoyment of the position that is ours. Paul writes of this same truth when he points out the need for the control of the Holy Spirit in the Christian's life (Gal. 5:16; Eph. 5:18). Furthermore, a study of John 15:4-11 will show that abiding is the condition for fruitbearing (vv. 4-5), that abiding brings the confidence of answered prayer (v.7), and that abiding is commanded of Christians (v.9).

Three things must be grasped if this obligation to abide in Christ is to be fulfilled. First, the nature of sin must be understood. Sin is lawlessness. The one who practices sin practices lawlessness. The person whose life is characterized by lawlessness has never seen or known the Savior (vv. 4, 6*b*). Second, the relation of the person and work of Christ to sin must be understood (v. 5). He was manifested to take away sin and thus to take away lawlessness. In light of the context, this must be understood as a reference to sanctification rather than to justification. Also, there is no sin and thus no lawlessness in Him. Third, the need for abiding in Christ must be understood. The continually abiding saint does not continually sin. Sin is not a prevailing habit for him, because as he abides in Christ he abides in the one in whom there is no lawlessness. As Ryrie puts it:

> The person who is abiding in Christ is not able to sin habitually. Sin may enter his experience, but it is the exception and not the rule. If sin is the ruling principle of a life, that person is not redeemed (Rom 6); thus a saved person cannot sin as a habit of life. When a Christian

---

The one who fails to abide is in line for discipline, not damnation (see the discussion of 1 John 5:16-17 on pp. 136-40); the one who is begotten of God cannot undo his birth, for he had nothing to do with it in the first place (John 1:12-13; cf. Eph. 2:8-9).

> does sin, he confesses it (I Jn 1:9) and perseveres in his purification (3:3).[17]

The second obligation that must be fulfilled is the maintenance of a true doctrine of sin (1 John 3:7-9). We as believers are not to read this passage and then be led astray by the false doctrine that the presence of sins in our lives disproves salvation. That this false doctrine is not being set forth in this passage is seen by a comparison with 2:1 and by noting that:

> the phrase ποιεῖν τὴν ἁμαρτίαν regularly means, to lead an habitually sinful life. It is important to bear this in mind for the right understanding of the statement that the Christian 'does not' and 'cannot sin' (I. iii. 6, 9). The meaning is that the Christian life and sin are, in principle, contrary to each other, and that the true disciple of Christ cannot, in the nature of the case, lead a life characteristically sinful, although he still commits acts of sin (I. i. 9,10).[18]

A true doctrine of sin recognizes that paternity is proven by practice (3:7-8). A life of righteousness is proof of a righteous heart. "The 'doing righteousness' reveals the character and does not create it."[19] Likewise, a life of sin is a guarantee of a sinful heart. In addition, a true doctrine of sin recognizes that practice is made possible by paternity (v. 9). Legitimate spiritual birth precludes the practice of sin because of the presence of God's seed (i.e., His nature; see 1 Pet. 1:23, which shows that the divine life is planted through the agency of the Word; cf. 2 Pet. 1:4). Not only is the Christian one who does not continually sin, but he cannot continually sin, because "of God he has been begotten" (cf. Rom. 6:1-2).[20] The point is that divine sonship and sin are mutually

[17]Charles C. Ryrie, "The First Epistle of John," in *The Wycliffe Bible Commentary,* ed. C. F. Pfeiffer and E. F. Harrison, p. 1473.

[18]G. B. Stevens, *The Theology of the New Testament,* p. 586. Cf. Stott: "In this whole section John is arguing rather the incongruity than the impossibility of sin in the Christian" (pp. 126-27).

[19]Westcott, p. 105. In v. 7, John does not intend to say, with the phrase ὁ ποιῶν τὴν δικαιοσύνην [the one who practices righteousness], that by doing good a man becomes a righteous man any more than he intends to say that by doing sin a man becomes a sinful man. (In addition, v. 7 is further proof that John is discussing habitual rather than occasional sin.)

[20]"It is not satisfactory to say that it is only the divine seed, the new nature or new

exclusive. When the relationship with God is genuine, sinful acts can be committed, but not as a basic way of life. This is not to excuse them, but merely to account for them.[21]

D. How Can a Sinner Know He Has Eternal Life?

The believer can know that he has eternal life (1 John 5:13). The apostle later asserts just as definitely that there is sin leading to "death" (v. 16). Is this to be construed as evidence that the believer not only cannot be sure of eternal life but that he may even lose it? Emphatically, no! As will be explained later, the "death" referred to here is not physical death. God has made provision that enables the sinner to know that he has eternal life.

1. *The persuasion of prayer.* First, the believer can know that he has eternal life because of the evidence of two types of prayer (1 John 5:14-17).

a. In verses 14-15 the apostle speaks of *petitionary* prayer and indicates that confidence in God's answering prayer is evidence of our possession of life. Only the fearful, the uncertain, the unassured are not confident in their praying. The one who knows his birthright is bold. This kind of prayer has a condition, "if we ask . . . according to His will,"[22] and when the condition is met we have the confidence that "we have the requests which we have asked from Him." A prayer heard is a prayer answered. In light of the juxtaposition of the statement of verse

---

life within the soul, which is unable to sin, while the flesh continues to be sinful (3:9). Grammar obliges us to assign as subject of the words, 'And he cannot sin, because he is born of God,' the individual who is in view in the opening words of the verse—'Whosoever is born of God.' The whole person is in view throughout" (E. F. Harrison, "A Key to the Understanding of First John," p. 43).

[21]See William Barclay, *The Letters of John and Jude,* pp. 96-97. In contrast, Shank characteristically finds conditions in 3:9 where there are none. He is forced to that inaccurate exegesis because of his belief that one must perform certain gook works to remain saved. Actually, the statement of verse 9, as that of verse 6, is a declaration rather than a condition.

[22]Praying according to God's will involves delighting oneself in Him (Psalm 37:4), asking in Jesus' name (John 14:13-14; 15:16), abiding in Christ (John 15:7), and obeying God's Word (1 John 3:22-23). More particularly, this context would teach that praying according to God's will is asking for those things that accord with His will.

13 with the teaching of verses 14-15, the strong implication is that answered prayer is an assurance of the possession of eternal life.

b. Similarly, in verses 16-17 John mentions *intercessory* prayer for a sinning brother as an evidence of our possessing eternal life.

There is, initially, an invitation to prayer addressed to the brother who observes the sin. It is to be noted that this invitation is based upon what is seen, not what is suspected (cf. Gal. 6:1). The present participle ἁμαρτάνοντα is probably temporal and may be translated "while he is sinning," or "as he is sinning." Two things are stated regarding the observer: "he shall ask" and "he shall give" (KJV).[23] These verbs set forth affirmations, not commands. That is, the spiritually sensitive person will *spontaneously* respond this way when he becomes aware of such a need. The continuance of life for the sinning brother is conditioned upon the intercession of the observing brother. The point is that God, in answering prayer, will stop the sinning brother short of that which may become "sin leading to death." In light of the above, verse 16*a* could be paraphrased: "If a person sees his brother committing a sin not leading to death, he (the person) shall ask God and he (the person) will 'give' life to the sinning brother."

But what is "sin leading to death"? Both the King James Version and the New American Standard Bible, by placing the article "a" before "sin," suggest that it is some identifiable sin. This is grammatically misleading. The Revised Standard Version, with the translation "a mortal sin," and the New English Bible, with "a deadly sin," are theologically misleading.[24] The absence of the definite article before the word "sin" emphasizes the character of the sin rather than identity, specificity, or degree of sin. The fact that the sin is seen and recognized as sin does not mean that it may be identified as one "leading to death." Most commentators, although acknowledging the difficulty if not the

[23]While both the NASB and the RSV make "God" the subject of δώσει (will . . . give), the proximity of αἰτήσει (he shall ask) makes this a rather forced exegesis. It is better to understand the subject of the second verb to be the same as that of the first—namely, the observing brother. James 5:15 and 20 are similar examples of a brother's "giving life" to another brother. See Stott, pp. 186-87.

[24]The distinction between venial sins and mortal sins, the latter so-called because they supposedly are deadly, killing the soul and subjecting it to eternal punishment, is a Roman Catholic doctrine that has no basis in the Scriptures.

impossibility of identifying the particular sin in view here, understand John's words to be a reference either to apostasy (which they define as the denial of Christ by a believer, which denial leads to the loss of eternal life)[25] or to the unpardonable sin (which Scripture tells us is the blasphemy against the Holy Spirit [Matt. 12:31-32]).[26] However, John's words cannot refer to apostasy in the sense described above, since a true believer cannot persist in sin (1 John 3:9); and they cannot refer to the blasphemy against the Holy Spirit, since that sin was related to our Lord's earthly ministry and since the circumstances that made it possible are not reproducible today.[27]

Because Scripture does not plainly tell us what sin leading to death is, any definition of sin leading to death is a matter of conjecture. Barclay's explanation probably comes as near to the truth of the passage as it is possible to come. "The sin unto death is the state of the man who has listened to sin so often, and refused to listen to God so often, that he has come to a state when he loves his sin, and when he regards sin as the most profitable thing in the world."[28]

This leads to a second question. What kind of life and death is involved? The answer comes in two ways. Scripture teaches that one

[25]Cf. G. B. Stevens, *The Johannine Theology: A Study of the Doctrinal Contents of the Gospel and Epistles of the Apostle John,* pp. 153-55; H. Willmering, "The Epistles of St. John," in *A Catholic Commentary on Holy Scripture,* pp. 1188-89.

Other commentators, recognizing that in a more biblical sense apostasy is a falling away from a superficial profession that was never a genuine salvation experience, would relate sin leading to death to Gnostic false teachers, whom John is refuting (see 1 John 2:19). Thus these commentators would view sin leading to death as the continuing practice of sin, hatred, and adamant rejection of the incarnate Christ. While this is an attractive possibility, it does not seem to suit the context, for the sin in view is one committed by a true believer.

[26]Cf. Stott, pp. 188-90; Alexander Ross, *The Epistles of James and John,* p. 221.

[27]Charles C. Ryrie, *The Holy Spirit,* pp. 53-54; A. C. Gaebelein, *The Gospel of Matthew,* 1:251.

If the blasphemy against the Holy Spirit is the rejection of every overture of the Spirit and thus the removal of oneself from the only power that can lead to forgiveness, as is suggested by Homer Kent, Jr. ("The Gospel According to Matthew," in *The Wycliffe Bible Commentary,* ed. C.F. Pfeiffer and E.F. Harrison, p. 950), then it may throw some light on 1 John 5:16-17. The problem with Kent's interpretation is that it largely ignores the historical context of the Matthew passage. The Lord is not present in the earth today; so the sin described in Matthew cannot be committed.

[28]Barclay, p. 143.

who is a brother—that is, a born-again believer in Christ—can only die physically (John 10:27-29; Rom. 8:38-39). Also, in the other passages that deal with sin leading to death (Acts 5:1-11; 1 Cor. 5:1-5; 11:29-30; James 5:19-20), the death in view is always physical.[29]

Following the invitation to intercessory prayer, there is a limitation given. We are not to seek from God an answer as to whether or not a given sin may be sin leading to death. Intercession, not evaluation, is our responsibility. There are two different words for *ask* in this passage. In 1 John 5:14-16*a* John several times uses the verb ἀιτέω, which means "ask for," or "seek for," something as you would in prayer, while in verse 16*b* he uses ἐρωτάω, which in some passages means "inquire of," "question," "interrogate," or "make request of," as one seeking information.[30] The limitation, then, is not in praying for someone who unknown to us may have committed sin leading to death, but in seeking such information from God. The first clause of verse 16 must be understood in light of this last clause. If this is true, it would seem that it is not some particular sin, from a list of possibilities, that is a sin leading to death, but that any sin may become such. We are to pray for anyone whom we know to be sinning, whether or not we think the sin is "leading to death," because sin "leading to death" is πρὸς θάνατον,

[29]Stott (p. 187) dismisses the possibility of this being physical death without offering any support for his statement that "the life with which it is contrasted is clearly spiritual or eternal life." Building on this assumption, he presents the view that sin leading to death is the blasphemy against the Holy Spirit. Since he does not believe that a true believer can apostasize, he suggests that both the one who commits sin not leading to death and the one who commits sin leading to death are unbelievers. He does this by giving the term "brother" the sense of "neighbor" or "professing brother." Sin leading to death is not, however, to be identified with the unpardonable sin (blasphemy against the Holy Spirit), which was a sin related only to the Lord's earthly ministry. For an extended discussion, see W. R. Cook, *Systematic Theology in Outline Form,* 2: 78-80.

[30]See the NASB translation of this passage and of John 16:26, where the two words are contrasted with one another. Also, note the helpful comments on the latter passage by R. C. Trench (*Synonyms of the New Testament,* pp. 140-41). John 16:17-26 in the Greek demonstrates that the distinction between ἀιτέω and ἐρωτάω is a legitimate Johannine usage (note especially vv. 18-19). In fact, it seems that John 16:17-26 makes better sense when the distinction between the two words is maintained throughout. While the sharp distinction is not always maintained in passages in which no contrast of ideas for *ask* is required (e.g., John 14:16), when distinction is called for it seems that one term is played against the other.

that is, *tending* to death, not guaranteeing it. "Death is, so to speak, its natural consequence, if it continue, and not its inevitable issue as a matter of fact."[31] The implication is, then, that "sin leading to death" will sometimes lead to untimely physical death despite the prayers of other Christians, because God knows that severe chastisement, not forgiveness in this life, is the best answer.

2. *The persuasion of absolute perseverance.* In addition to the assurance that comes to the believer as a result of prayer, there is the persuasion of absolute perseverance (1 John 5:18-20). In these verses, John makes three confident statements, each of which is introduced by the verb οἴδαμεν (we know). First, the redeemed sinner is confident of eternal life on the basis of divine birth. In light of 3:9, we are reminded that everyone who is begotten of God lives a life that excludes the practice of sin as a way of life. However, instead of bringing forward the same reasons as given before, John gives further explanation to account for this fact. "He who was born of God keeps him." Ὁ γεννηθεὶς ἐκ τοῦ θεοῦ (He who was born of God [1 John 5:18]) probably refers to the Savior, especially in light of the fact that the most likely reading two words later in the Greek text is αὐτόν (him) rather than ἑαυτόν (himself).[32] The secret of perseverance is that He keeps us. The verb "keeps" may refer to either the first or last clause of verse 18, or to both. He keeps us from a life-pattern of sin and from the evil one.

Second, confidence is based upon divinely imparted character (5:19). We are of God, in contrast to the whole world, which lies (helpless) in the evil one. In the first half of the verse, there is no expressed subject in substantival form, while in the last half there is. This serves to throw the emphasis in the first half upon ἐκ τοῦ θεοῦ (of God), which underscores the divine source of our life. In the last part of the verse, the emphasis is upon ὁ κόσμος ὅλος (the whole world), indicating that all unbelievers are in a vastly different relationship. The change of

[31]Westcott, p. 210.

[32]Westcott, p. 194; A. Plummer, *The Epistles of John,* pp. 169-70. This interpretation is not without its difficulties, as are pointed out by Alford, pp. 512-13, and Stevens, *The Johannine Theology,* pp. 245-48, but it has fewer problems than the other interpretations.

preposition from ἐκ to ἐν (in) also changes the focus from source of life to sphere of life, or position, in the evil one.

Finally, confidence is based upon divinely given understanding (5:20). We have been given the ability to follow facts to their right conclusions. This understanding relates to our experiential knowledge of and our position in Him who is true. The use of the perfect tense in the verbs translated "has come" and "has given" indicates that the basis of our assurance at this point is not merely historical fact but the continuing effect of that fact.[33] Personal appropriation of the abiding fact of the incarnation carries with it an understanding involving knowledge of Him who is true. Furthermore, we not only know this true God and His Son: we are also *in* this true God and His Son.

[33]Westcott, p. 195.

X

The Ecclesiology of the Christian Life

First, it must be noted that John does not present a formal ecclesiology. There is no didactic portion of John's writings treating the subject of the church. It is for this reason that the following treatment is dealt with under the section on the Christian life rather than in a separate section of its own. John's only references to the local assembly by use of the term ἐκκλησία (church) are in 3 John and Revelation 2-3. There are also a few other passages in which the body of believers is alluded to, as will be seen below.

A. Jesus Christ's Appraisal of the Churches.

1. *The Lord of the churches* (Rev. 1:10-18; 2:1, 8, 12, 18; 3:1, 7, 14). In Revelation 1, John gives an extensive description of Jesus Christ as the Lord of the churches. In Revelation 2-3, that description is drawn upon and expanded in the introductions to the seven letters. When all the descriptive data are collated, they seem to fall into three categories: His clothing, which seems to highlight the role of judge-king He plays throughout the book (Rev. 1:13; cf. 19:13, 16); His personal features and characteristics, which are related to the various churches and their particular needs (1:14-16; 5:6; cf. 19:12, 15); and His solemn declaration, which contains words of encouragement to John and the churches (1:17-18; cf. 1:5; 19:11).[1]

[1]Commentaries should be consulted for exposition of the various symbolisms used and for discussion of certain literary features that distinguish the description of Revelation 1 from the parts of the description repeated in Revelation 2-3. In Revelation 1:13,

It is quite apparent that the particular description of the Lord given in the introduction to each letter is suited to that church's peculiar need. To the *apathetic* Ephesian church He is presented as one whose concern is maintained despite the church's cooled love for Him. He continues to hold each church's messenger[2] in His authoritative and protective right hand (cf. John 10:28), and He continues to walk among the churches, thus showing His ongoing interest. To the *suffering* Smyrnian church He is presented as the one who both predates and postdates all suffering and as the one who has conquered the greatest trial of all: death. To the church in Pergamum, *partially compromised by failure to remain separate from the unbelieving,*[3] He is presented as the one whose word judges error. To the Thyatiran church, *compromised by immorality and cultic practices,*[4] He is presented as the discerning judge, God's true Son, as over against the false gods of lust and demonic tyranny. To the *complacent* Sardian church, which was satisfied with the spiritual status quo, He is presented as the one with plenary power and knowledge,[5] the one who is sovereign in the life of the pastor of the church, at least. He who has full knowledge of the

---

John states that the One he saw was "son-of-man-like" (ὅμοιον υἱον ἀνθρώπου—note the anarthrous construction), suggesting that He was both Messianic (cf. Dan. 7:13-14) and juridical (cf. John 5:22, 27; Acts 17:31).

[2]The term ἄγγελος at the beginning of each letter probably refers in each case to the pastor or chief elder of that church. He was the divinely designated point of contact between the church and the apostle, who had been appointed by God to deliver His messages to the seven churches (Rev. 1:1-2, 10-11).

[3]One of the chief characteristics of Balaam's error seems to have been the intermingling of God's people with the heathen, and the result was idolatry (Num. 25:1-2; 31:16).

[4]In light of the fact that the Old Testament associates Jezebel with witchcraft (2 Kings 9:22) as well as with immorality and idolatry, it may be that there are intimations here of this church's dabbling in the occult.

[5]The significance of the "seven Spirits of God" (Rev. 3:1) is difficult to determine. In Revelation 1:4 "seven Spirits" may be a reference to the Holy Spirit, in light of the fact that "seven Spirits" is mentioned between a statement concerning the Father (Rev. 1:4) and a statement concerning Jesus Christ (Rev. 1:5). Revelation 4:5, however, seems to be more like a description of some quality or qualities of God than a reference to a member of the Godhead, and Revelation 3:1 and 5:6 seem to indicate that the seven spirits are something that belong to the Lord of the churches, the Lamb. In an attempt to interpret the symbolism, the "seven" has been taken as a reference to completeness or fullness, the "horns" (Rev. 5:6) to power, and the "eyes" (Rev. 5:6) to knowledge.

status quo and full power to change it will surely not be satisfied to leave things incomplete. To the *steadfast* Philadelphian church He is presented as the morally pure and essentially genuine one who has regal authority (stemming from His lineage from David)[6] to permit or deny as He will without fear of reversal. Because of the Philadelphian church's steadfastness, He will open for it opportunities of service that others do not enjoy. Finally, to the *blasé* Laodicean church, which not only is smugly satisfied with its condition but also has desperate needs of which it is unaware, He is presented as the one with God's affirmative approval, the one who will accurately testify to things as they are, and the one who is the source of every need the church experiences. Since His credentials come from God and since His witness regarding the condition of the Laodicean church is true, the believers there will do well to heed His message. Furthermore, since He is the origin of God's creation, the gold, clothing, and eyesalve the church needs are all His to supply.

This composite picture John gives of Christ as He walks among the churches shows His relation to local assemblies no matter where they are or what their circumstances.[7] The church that ignores the instruction contained in these letters does so at peril of the removal of its lampstand (2:5), that is, at peril of losing its raison d'être and thus at peril of its own demise.

2. *The message to the churches.* Many things about the Lord's messages to the churches are worthy of consideration, but only a few of particular theological note will be mentioned. Each of the seven churches of Asia Minor (and each of today's churches) is taken note of by the Lord[8] and addressed with an exhortation and an evaluation or promise that is commendatory, condemnatory, or both.

a. In these seven letters are mentioned twenty-five things that the Lord of the churches knows.[9] While inward qualities (four are named) and outward circumstances (four are noted) are not overlooked in

[6]In light of the clear allusion to Isaiah 22:22, it seems that Revelation 3:7 has Messianic overtones (cf. Luke 1:31-33; 2:4-5, 11).

[7]See page 158 and footnote 1, page 158, for a statement regarding the addressees of the seven letters.

[8]Notice the repetition of οἶδα (I know) in Revelation 2:2, 9, 13, 19; 3:1, 8, and 15.

[9]This figure is based on construing ὅτι in Revelation 3:1, 8, and 15 as declarative rather than causal.

the listing of things of which He takes note, the predominant emphasis is upon the deeds (ἔργα [deeds], six times; κόπον [toil], once; διακονίαν [service], once) and actions (note the verbs describing actions He knows, twelve in all) of the churches. Of all the items listed, only four involve derogation of the churches, and they are all in the area of deeds and actions. Christ is pleased with a working church when those works are undertaken properly (as will be demonstrated below).

b. The exhortations (2:5, 10, 16, 25; 3:2-3, 11, 18-19) range from the very simple ("repent"), in the case of Pergamum, to the very elaborate, in the cases of Sardis and Laodicea. In two cases, Smyrna and Philadelphia, there is no call to repentance, since the Lord is apparently satisfied with the status of both churches; in the other five situations repentance is called for since some change is in order. Four of the five calls to repentance are addressed to faithful remnants within the local assembly, with Ephesus apparently being the only wayward church in which the entire group may be restored. In regard to the five churches in which repentance is urged, it is clear that both the need and the possibility for repentance exist. This is seen from the fact that in every case the threatened judgment is conditional. In the two letters in which there is neither an urge to repent nor a reprimand of any other sort, the spiritual milieu in each church seems to be one of great extremity. In the one church, persecution will reach diabolical proportions and may lead to physical death (2:10). In the other, the danger of submitting to the rigors of witness is so great that there is the possibility of loss of reward (3:11).

c. As the Lord turns from exhortation to the message proper, He has open words of commendation for only three churches (Ephesus, Sardis, and Philadelphia), while there is tacit commendation for all in the "I know" sections or in the promises given each.[10] There are condemnations for all but Smyrna and Philadelphia, the two churches that are thoroughgoing in their faithfulness.[11]

An analysis of the things commended or condemned will reveal that

[10]Even the most thoroughly negative of all the letters, those to Pergamum and Laodicea, have in them a small positive note. The possibility of repentance is held before each of them.

[11]Each exhortation likewise contains explicit or implicit commendation or condemnation following the pattern outlined above.

in the message proper of each letter there is a complete reversal from the type of items emphasized in its "I know" section. Whereas in the opening sections of the letters the activities of the churches were most conspicuous, here in the evaluative portions condition, attitude, and doctrine are emphasized.[12] While Christ is desirous of a serving church, service must arise out of a proper spiritual condition, a God-honoring attitude, and correct doctrine.

While many aspects of the promises made to the churches are distinctively eschatological and are therefore dealt with in chapter 12 ("The Future of the Church"), others must be considered here to the extent that they reflect the Lord's evaluation of each situation. These promises fall into two categories: (1) warnings and (2) assurances of blessing.

Five of the churches (Smyrna and Philadelphia are excluded) are given warnings of imminent judgment if there is a failure to repent. These judgments vary in form and essence, but in general they range from selective punishments of the unfaithful ones in the given assembly (2:16, 22-23; 3:3) to the actual elimination of the local church at Ephesus (2:5) and at Laodicea (3:16).[13] In all, to the five churches there

[12]Of the twenty-six instances of commendation or condemnation, only six refer to deeds, which are commended twice (Rev. 2:5, 19) and condemned four times (2:5, 20; 3:2, 18). Condition is commended four times (2:25; 3:2, 4, 11) and condemned four times (2:5, 20; 3:2, 17); attitude is commended once (2:6) and condemned four times (2:4, 20; 3:16, 17); and doctrine is commended four times (2:13, twice; 3:3, twice) and condemned three times (2:14, 15, 20).

[13]Because the threatened action in these two cases is so severe, the occasion for each warning should be noted. In the case of Ephesus, the threat came because the church had forsaken its first love. While πρῶτος frequently means first in order of time, on occasion it means first in order of importance (see Luke 15:22; 1 Cor. 15:3; Eph. 6:2). This seems to be the sense here. Christ is not simply rebuking the Ephesians for leaving the first in a series of loves; He is rebuking them for leaving the most important love of all. The exhortation of Revelation 2:5 for the Ephesians to recall the level at which they had operated supports this interpretation. The call to "do the deeds you did at first" is a call to reinstitute former works that are more important in a scale of values than the works the Ephesians are now doing.

This forsaking may take two possible forms. It may involve the cooling of one's fervor for Christ (e.g., the apostle Peter [John 21:15-17]) or a decline in love for a brother in Christ (cf. 1 John 3:17-18). In the final analysis, however, defection in one area inevitably affects the other (1 John 4:20-21).

Laodicea's errors lay in two areas. First, the church is said to be lukewarm. It

are ten warnings, all of which relate potentially to the immediate future rather than to the eschatological future. The aim of the warnings is immediate rather than eventual repentance.

There are many more assurances of blessing than there are warnings. When the promises to the overcomers are included, all seven churches are assured of some blessing, either in the near or eschatological future. In contrast to the warnings, in which the emphasis is upon more immediate action, the promises of blessing have the end times as their primary focus.[14] Sin in the life of the church needs prompt attention. The development of the kind of service and character deserving of blessing requires time.

B. The Doctrine of Fellowship.

It seems quite apparent that John's doctrine of fellowship is conceived of by the apostle as relating to the Christian life, and within this larger category it most nearly fits within the believer's life in the church. The conclusive support for placing this doctrine within the section on the Christian life is the fact that John's treatment of the subject is almost totally limited to the epistles. That it should be viewed as an aspect of ecclesiology is seen from the fact that fellowship is set forth as something that takes place among a believer, His God, and other

---

cannot be distinguished as being either cold or hot. Just as tepid water has no distinctiveness of its own, having assumed the temperature of its environment, so this church has no distinction from the world in which it lives, having assumed its temperament. The exhortation "be zealous" (Rev. 3:19) answers to this condemnation. The second indictment against the Laodiceans is that they have a sense of absolute self-sufficiency because of their accumulated wealth, while they are unaware of their desperate misery, poverty, blindness, and nakedness. This second indictment is answered by the exhortation of Revelation 3:18. Graciously, the Lord offers the opportunity for repentance (Rev. 3:19) and the provisions to rectify the Laodiceans' wretched condition (Rev. 3:18), but, from a human standpoint at least, the Laodiceans are so insensitive to their condition that there seems to be scant hope of correction. The grace of God is further highlighted in v. 20, where the invitation to repentance is elaborated upon by way of an invitation to renewed fellowship, a feature unique to this letter.

[14]The seven churches are given a total of nineteen eschatological promises, and three of the churches are given a total of six near-future blessings.

believers. That is, it is a community experience rather than a private one (see 1 John 1:3-4, 7).[15]

In light of John's usage of the term, its broader New Testament usage,[16] and its etymology,[17] the following working definition of *biblical fellowship* is offered: it is active intercourse between God and His child and among His children, whereby interests and possessions[18] are shared on a continuing basis in light of common life and life-style.

1. *The participants in fellowship.* John names the participants in fellowship in 1 John 1:3. Believers ("we") fellowship both with other believers ("you," plural) and with the Father and the Son.[19] In this verse the apostle makes it quite clear that proper fellowship with other believers also involves fellowship with the Father and Son. This is reiterated in verse 4 in different words: "and these things we write, so that our joy may be made complete." In other words, the circle of fellowship will be completed when believers-Godhead-believers are involved. The statement in verse 7 that "we have fellowship with one another" is sufficiently ambiguous, probably by design, to allow "one another" to

[15]I cannot agree with Ryrie's reasons for treating the subject of fellowship under the topic of soteriology. He claims to "follow John's own emphasis," for "salvation is the cause of which [fellowship], according to Johannine theology, is the effect" (*Biblical Theology of the New Testament,* pp. 340-41). It certainly is true that the Christian life is the effect of salvation, but if one were to follow Ryrie's logic, one would have to subsume *all* John's theology, including eschatology, under soteriology.

[16]The term κοινωνία is used once by Luke, fourteen times by Paul, once by the author of Hebrews, and four times by John. Of its twenty occurrences, one is in reference to the Lord's Supper (1 Cor. 10:16), four refer to the sharing of one's material possessions (Rom. 15:26; 2 Cor. 8:4; 9:13; Heb. 13:16), and the other fifteen, with one exception, relate to some facet of Christian fellowship such as that of believer with believer or that of believer with a member of the Godhead. The exception, 2 Corinthians 6:14, forbids believers to fellowship with unbelievers.

[17]Κοινωνία is from κοινωνός, an adjective used only substantivally in the New Testament and meaning either "partner" or "partaker." Κοινωνός in turn, is from κοινός, which may mean "common" in the sense of "generally shared" (as in the Latin *communis*) or "common" in the sense of "profane" (as in the Latin *vulgaris*). Coming as it does from κοινός through κοινωνός, κοινωνία follows the sense of "generally shared."

[18]Ryrie (p. 123) offers helpful distinctions between fellowship and Communism. Biblical sharing was, among other things, voluntary, and the right of private ownership was never revoked.

[19]It seems that 1 John 2:27 suggests that the Holy Spirit (alluded to in the term "the anointing") is also involved in this fellowship. Paul explicitly speaks of the fellowship of the Holy Spirit in 2 Corinthians 13:13 and Philippians 2:1.

refer both to the other parties implied by the "we" and to God Himself.

2. *The recipients of fellowship.* Fellowship is not one-directional (man to God) but two-directional (man to God and man to man). As the word κοινωνία itself suggests, sharing is at the heart of fellowship. This is evidenced in two ways.

a. One example of fellowship in the form of sharing is the exercise of love toward brothers in Christ, especially those in need (1 John 3:14-18). This is a testimony to ourselves of the validity of our salvation (3:14) and to others of the reality of our love (3:17). Genuine love is not evidenced by mere statement (λόγῳ [word]) or oral expression (γλώσσῃ [tongue]) but rather "in deed and truth," that is, in action that conforms to and reflects reality (v. 18).[20] Although not limited thereto, such love is tangibly reflected when one has some of "the world's goods" (v. 17) and shares them with one in need.

b. A second evidence of fellowship in the form of sharing is the exercise of a very particular kind of love in the form of hospitality, especially for itinerant preacher-teachers (3 John 5-8). When one thus provides for the needs of such, he in turn shares in their ministry.[21]

It may be wondered at that no Godward matter is listed here under this heading. We must remember, however, that it is *evidence* of which we are speaking, and according to John this must take concrete, tangible form (1 John 4:20).[22]

[20]The phrase ἐν ἔργῳ καὶ ἀληθείᾳ (in deed and truth), being governed by just one preposition, shows a close intertwining of "deed" and "truth."

[21]The *Didache,* in addition to referring to this practice (11.1-2), also urges hospitality to Christian travelers in general. "Let everyone who 'comes in the Name of the Lord' be received; but when you have tested him you shall know him, for you shall have understanding of true or false. [This clause literally reads "for you shall have right or left understanding." Lake's translation is interpretive and may very well have obscured the point. The test mentioned is with a view to approval (δοκιμάσαντες), so it may well be that "right and left" refer to *complete* understanding as a basis for knowing him.] If he who comes is a traveler, help him as much as you can. . . . And if he wishes to settle among you and has a craft, let him work for his bread. But if he has no craft provide for him according to your understanding [this word, both here and in the preceding verse, almost has the sense of discernment], so that no man shall live among you in idleness because he is a Christian. But if he will not do so, he is making traffic of Christ; beware of such" (*Didache* 12.1-5).

[22]The "love of God" of 1 John 3:17 is in all likelihood a reference to the believer's love for God (τοῦ θεοῦ is probably an objective genitive), as is seen when this verse is compared with 1 John 4:20.

3. *The basis of fellowship.* John proclaimed the gospel in order that believers may have fellowship with other believers (1 John 1:3). His statement in verse 3 indicates both a major aim of the preaching of the gospel and the basis of fellowship. The proclamation of the gospel is designed to lead to fellowship based on the incarnate Word and eternal life through Him (1 John 1:1-3).

4. *The condition of fellowship.* While there are two conditional statements in 1 John 1:6-7, they both relate to the same thing. *The* condition of fellowship is right association with God, who is light. To claim to have fellowship with God while going on walking in darkness is a lie, because God is light and there is no darkness in Him. On the other hand, if we do indeed go on walking in the light (the sphere of holiness)[23] as He is in the light, fellowship with God and fellow believers will automatically follow (ἔχομεν [we have] is present active indicative, signifying the apodosis, or conclusion, that may be expected if the condition of walking in the light is met). This metaphorical use of περιπατῶμεν (we walk) in the present tense pictures an ongoing pattern of life, and since the figure is of a "walk" it relates to progress.

5. *The preservation of fellowship.* By its very nature—in that it depends upon a minimum of two parties, one of whom is human—fellowship is a fragile thing. The fact that fellowship usually involves not one but two human beings even intensifies its fragility. Its preservation may be accomplished by both negative and positive means.

a. From a negative standpoint, corporate fellowship is preserved by maintaining a believing group in the local assembly. A believing group is one that affirms rather than denies the incarnate Christ (1 John 2:18-26).[24] Corporate fellowship is also maintained by the discipline of erring members of the assembly (3 John 9-10; cf. Rev. 3:19). In 3 John 9-10, John points out for all to read that Diotrephes had rejected both him and his previous message to the assembly because of his sense of self-importance. In addition, John says that when he visits the church

[23]See the discussions of the phrase "God is light" (pp. 40-42) and of 1 John 1:7 (pp. 128-29).

[24]There are two signs of an "antichrist" attitude or person: 1. Refusal to confess the historical reality of the union of absolute deity and genuine humanity that formed the God-man, Jesus Christ (1 John 4:2-3). 2. Failure to obey the apostolic word (1 John 4:6). See Ryrie, p. 343.

he plans to make a public issue of this matter.[25] The specific sins for which Diotrephes will be censured are slander, inhospitality, and autocracy.[26] John thus sets a pattern for the church to follow in maintaining its own discipline after he passes off the scene.[27]

The preservation of personal fellowship is also treated by John as he deals with the confession of personal sin (1 John 1:9). It is the believer's responsibility, when he sins by stepping out of the light, where God is (i.e., out of the sphere of holiness, where fellowship is experienced; see 1 John 1:7), to confess his sin and thereby experience forgiveness of that sin and cleansing from all (other) unrighteousness.[28] This concept has created a difficulty in the minds of some persons because it seems to suggest a kind of "yo-yo Christianity" whereby the believer bounces in and out of fellowship on the basis of every sin committed and its subsequent confession. It is also claimed that the ongoing necessity to confess sins demeans the grace and love of God by ignoring that the Christian was given full pardon of sins when he was saved.

Peter Gillquist is perhaps the most popular advocate of the view that the grace and love of God are demeaned by continual confession of sins. Gillquist (in *Love Is Now*) and other writers who hold this view would say that because all of the believer's sin is already forgiven in Christ, when he sins he need merely recognize that the sin already *has been forgiven* in Christ. Gillquist further tries to demonstrate that 1 John 1:9

[25]Both the NASB, with the translation "call attention to" and the RSV, with "bring up," interpret ὑπομνήσω as referring to a public action.

[26]"Evidence for the existence in Asia, in fact, if not also in name, of a bishop with monarchical powers is found in III John. The exact position held by the writer of the letter, who calls himself 'The Elder,' is obscure; but it is clear that the Diotrephes mentioned is not merely one who 'loveth to have the pre-eminence' in the church to which the letter is addressed; he is a person who has actually secured it. He has the power to decline to receive in the church brethren recommended by outsiders like the writer of the letter, and also to 'cast out of the church' members who differ from him; that is, he has the right of excommunication" (B. H. Streeter, "The Rise of Christianity," in *The Cambridge Ancient History,* ed. S. A. Cook, F. E. Adcock, and M. P. Charlesworth, 11:290).

[27]It may be wondered why John did not urge the church to discipline Diotrephes as Paul urged the Christians in Corinth to discipline the immoral man among them (1 Cor. 5:1-13). John may be silent on the matter because Diotrephes was the pastor and had taken to himself authority that was not his and was using it to intimidate the members, who therefore may have found it hard to assert their authority.

[28]See pp. 128-36 for an extended discussion of this subject.

is not addressed to believers. His argument will not stand the scrutiny of the context, which clearly presupposes believers, because the discussion concerns fellowship. Furthermore, 1 John 2:1 is addressed to "my little children" and refers back to "these things" that John has just written. Gillquist's contention (p. 64) that "confess" means agreeing with God regarding forgiveness is pure eisegesis. The text of Scripture says "if we confess our sins", not "if we confess our forgiveness." The desire to exalt the grace of God in Christ is noble and worthy, but when it is done at the expense of biblical doctrine the price paid is too high. Denial of the believer's need to confess his sins does not honor the grace of God because it fails to distinguish between forensic and family forgiveness. The legal claims of sin on the believer were dealt with once and for all at the cross (through *justification*), but the moral and ethical debilitation of sin must be dealt with on a continuing basis (through *sanctification*).[29]

Certainly it must be admitted that if fellowship is a continual on-again-off-again experience something is amiss. The question is, is it the doctrine, the believer's conception of the doctrine, or the believer himself wherein lies the problem? Unless one is willing to rewrite the biblical teaching on fellowship and the confession of sin, it cannot be that the problem lies with the doctrine. John clearly teaches that a Christian may or may not enjoy fellowship (1 John 1:6-7),[30] and it is equally clear that one's being or not being in fellowship is not to be equated with the possession or loss of eternal life.[31] The idea that the

[29]For a helpful study of this subject, see Zane C. Hodges, "Fellowship and Confession in 1 John 1:5-10," pp. 56-59.

[30]The phrases "in fellowship" and "out of fellowship" are not found in John's writings, but they certainly are accurate expressions of the concept taught in 1 John 1:6-7. The actual picture given is of one who is in or out of the light, and being in or out of the light is tantamount to being in or out of fellowship with God.

Although at first glance the teaching of 1 John 2:9 may seem to run counter to the teaching of 1 John 1:6-7, there is no contradiction when 1 John 2:9 is properly understood. You cannot hate a "brother" unless he is indeed of the same family. The one who hates his brother is in the family of God but not in fellowship in the family. To "still" (RSV, NIV) be in darkness means only that he is there at this time, not that he has always been there.

[31]The truth of this statement is seen in John 10:27-29 (see pp. 96-97, 131-36) and from acknowledgment of the intended audience of 1 John (see p. 126 and footnote 1, p. 126).

believer's being in and out of fellowship at various times is unacceptable betrays a presumption on the grace of God rather than an honoring of it. No one but an indulgent father ignores continual infractions of family standards and leaves them unpunished. On the other hand, only a tyrannical and insecure father would punish such infractions with harshness or even disinheritance. God is neither indulgent nor tyrannical, and therefore His grace is to be honored by the confession of family sin and enjoyed as He in response provides forgiveness and cleansing. It is not that God is reluctant to forgive or that the death of Christ did not deal with all sins. Rather, the nature of God *and* the nature of man require that experiential sin must be dealt with at an experiential level if the Christian life is to be enjoyed. Moral transformation, within the grace of God, comes through obedience to the divine commands (cf. John 14:21). The initial perception of the heavenly vision comes through faith in Jesus Christ and is demonstrated by a turning to righteousness from sin (John 3:3; 1 John 3:6-7; 3 John 11), but its continual enjoyment is contingent upon ongoing cleansing and confession (1 John 1:7, 9).

The believer who has a frustrated sense of continually being in and out of fellowship has probably never come to grips with the truth of 1 John 1:7[32] or has failed to understand the intent of 1 John 1:9. God's intent is that we remain in the light with Him and thus enjoy ongoing fellowship and cleansing. When we step into the darkness, that is, when we sin, there is immediate remedy at hand to deal with both the human (1 John 1:9) and divine (1 John 2:1-2) complications. Confession is necessary for the Christian, not to avoid disinheritance, for that is dealt with by our advocate, but it is necessary to appropriate His family forgiveness and cleansing, which bring us back into the light of His holiness and thus back into fellowship.

The supposed problem of "yo-yo Christianity," then, lies either in ignorance of, misunderstanding of, or failure to appropriate the biblical teaching. More careful attention to Scripture rather than indulgence of our personal grievances will lead much more rapidly to God's norm: an abundant life.

b. When looked at from a positive standpoint, fellowship is pre-

[32]See pages 128-29.

served by the continuous control of the sin nature, which control comes from walking in the light (1 John 1:7),[33] and by the practice of righteousness (1 John 2:29; 3:7). The practice of righteousness is equated by John with the exercise of love for our brothers in Christ (1 John 3:11-14), which love, as was demonstrated above, will evidence itself in acts of material sharing (1 John 3:17). "All unrighteousness is sin" (1 John 5:17) since it is, among other things, a failure to love. This gives another insight into why confession of sin is so important for the Christian. Personal sin is basically a failure to share, in love, with God or a brother, and therefore it is unrighteousness. In addition to forgiveness, we receive cleansing "from all unrighteousness" when we confess our sins. Thus, by means of this cleansing of the stain left by our unloving failure to share, the barriers to fellowship that are within us are removed. Channels of communication between Father and child and between brother and brother are reopened and allow for the flourishing of life and fellowship in the family of God.[34]

[33]Ibid.

[34]J. Grant Howard, Jr., notes that "Psalms 51 and 32 support the concept of confession with Psalm 32 detailing the experience of the man struggling with unconfessed sin. The longer he hid it, the more miserable he became. When we are listening carefully to God, we will examine our lives and deal with those things that are wrong. To deal with them adequately we must openly and honestly confess them to Him. He forgives.

"Usually sin involves others. We have sinned against them. They have sinned against us. How do we communicate with each other about sin? The same way we communicate with God—openly and honestly. We are to confess to one another (James 5:16). We are to forgive one another (Ephesians 4:32). If we have been communicating with God, we have been experiencing His forgiveness and thus we can more adequately forgive others. If we have been communicating with God, we have been confessing our sin, and thus we can more easily confess to others.

"The person who is not openly and honestly talking to God about his sin will tend not to share openly and honestly with others about his sin. As a result he won't identify as easily with people, nor will they relate to him as readily. The Word says that temptation is common to all men (1 Corinthians 10:13). If we, by our silence or our superficiality, give the impression that we don't really have weaknesses, problems, and temptations then we don't communicate on their wave length, because they have them. But if I am talking with God openly and honestly, then I have been sharing everything with Him, including my sin. This prepares me to communicate relationally and helpfully with others" (J. Grant Howard, Jr., "Interpersonal Communication: Biblical Insights on the Problem and the Solution," p. 253).

Part Four:
Eschatology

XI

Introduction to John's Eschatology

While all of the New Testament writers give us some insights into the future, John is without question *the* seer of the New Testament. He alone gave an entire book to what to him, at least, was the prophetic future. This is most fitting for at least two reasons: (1) he was by nature suited to apocalyptic vision, and (2) he was selected by the Holy Spirit to be the writer of the climactic revelation of the New Testament in all areas of theology. (Perhaps, indeed very possibly, in the providence of God he was selected for this writing because of his nature.)

A. Its Distinctive—Christocentricity.

The one distinctive mark of John's treatment of the future is that it is in every way associated with the second person of the Godhead, Jesus Christ (Rev. 1:1). Thus the theology of the Apocalypse is a theology of the future as it relates to Jesus Christ. While different entities or groupings may be identified in their future relationships to Christ (e.g., individuals, the church, Israel, the nations, etc.), the emphasis is not upon the church as a group, Israel as a group, and so forth, but upon Christ as the sovereign of the future. John deals with several doctrinal themes of an eschatological nature, such as death, resurrection, Christ's return, and the rule of God in the affairs of men, but again the unifying principle is the predominance of Christ in each area.

B. Its Frame of Reference.

1. *The churches.* Our Lord had in mind a twofold frame of reference when He set forth this "Revelation of Jesus Christ" (Rev. 1:1) through John. First, the information contained in this apocalypse was intended to instruct the seven churches of Asia Minor (Rev. 1:11; 22:16); and, second, it was intended as instruction for the church throughout the church age, as well.[1] That is not to say that all the information contained in the book of Revelation is *about* the church in the church age. Rather, it is all *for* her learning.

2. *The chronology.* The second aspect of the broad frame of reference in which this eschatological truth is placed is chronological. (Note well that the chronology is incidental to the theology that is being developed by John, but it is necessary as a framework for the unfolding of the future and its significance.) This frame of reference is very general and purposefully vague, as are most allusions to time, whether indicating movement or setting forth increments, throughout the book (see, e.g., Rev. 1:3; 3:10; 4:1; 6:9-11; 8:1; 9:15; 10:6; 14:13; 15:5; 17:10, 12, 17; 18:1, 8, 10, 17, 19; 19:1; 20:3, last clause; 22:12, 20). It is set forth in Revelation 1:19 and divides John's vision into three nonspecific parts. Only from the contextual development of the message of the book can

[1]That the information contained in Revelation is also for the instruction of the church throughout the church age may be arrived at by following two separate lines of thought. First, just as the other books of Scripture, although addressed to specific peoples, churches, and individuals, are intended to have as their wider audience the church throughout the church age, so the letters to the seven churches of Asia Minor are intended for the entire church throughout the church age. Second, the seven churches represent seven conditions that prevailed in the church of the first century, and those seven conditions also prevail and have prevailed in the church throughout the church age; therefore, all believers ought to heed each message as well as the larger message of the whole book. (It is quite apparent that the seven letters were written to historical churches of the first century [Rev. 1:4, 11]. That the seven churches are intended to be representative of the entire church of their time is suggested by the fact that only seven out of a larger available number were selected. [Note, e.g., that no church from eastern Asia Minor was selected and that such a prominent church as the one at Colossae, in western Asia Minor, was excluded.] Also, in every case [Rev. 2:7, 11, 17, 29; 3:6, 13, 22] the reader is called to heed "what the Spirit says to the churches," not what the Spirit says to one specific church.)

The often suggested "foreview of church history" interpretation of Revelation 2-3 is too contrived for acceptance. The facts of history simply do not support it.

any particularity be given to the elapsed time in each of the three segments. Thus it is from the logical rather than the chronological notes given by John that the time frame is to be ascertained.

a. The first element, designated as "the things which you have seen" (1:19), can only refer to the vision recorded in 1:12-16, since at this juncture that was the only vision John had had. Likewise, this initial vision is the necessary introduction to all the other visions since it identifies and describes the one who is the dominant figure throughout the remainder of the letters and visions (Rev. 2:1, 8, 12, 18; 3:1, 7, 14; 5:5-6; 6:1, 3, 5, 7, 9, 12, 16-17; 7:10, 14, 17; 8:1; 11:15; 12:10-11; 13:8; 14:1, 4, 10; 15:3-4; 16:1; 17:14; 19:7, 9, 11-16; 20:4, 6; 21:9, 22, 23, 27; 22:1, 3, 16). As far as historically elapsed time is concerned, it would be minimal, that is, merely long enough for the vision itself to be given.

b. The second part of this time frame, "the things which are" (Rev. 1:19), must follow the first and exist in John's day. The letters recorded in chapters 2-3 clearly form a self-contained unity, or entity, that was revealed after the vision of Revelation 1. Revelation 1:4, as well as the address in each letter (Rev. 2:1, 8, 12, 18; 3:1, 7, 14), shows that these are churches then in existence. Since they are representative as well as historical churches, we may logically assume that the elapsed time intended in these letters will extend from the beginning of the church on the day of Pentecost (not dealt with at all in Johannine literature) to the rapture of the church at an undisclosed time in the future (to which event John makes oblique reference in John 14:2-3; 1 John 3:2-3; Rev. 3:10-11).

c. Finally, the third part of the broad chronology of the book embraces "the things which shall take place after these things" (Rev. 1:19). As far as the book itself is concerned, this includes the material from Revelation 4 through the end of the last vision (Rev. 22:7). This is obviously the major part of the book and constitutes the primary focus of the Apocalypse. It is here that the sovereign and exalted Christ is most graphically seen to exercise His role as judge and ruler of the universe.

In this portion of the book there are two levels of activity—earthly (e.g., Rev. 6:8-9; 13:16-18; 20:1-10) and heavenly (e.g., Rev. 4-5; 15;

19:1-10)—with a gradual movement toward the climax when the two are interrelated, that is, when they are seen to have regular and ongoing association as the usual rather than the unusual (e.g., Rev. 19:11-16; 21:1—22:5). Likewise, there are four distinguishable periods, or, it is better to say, movements of thought and action, all of which in actuality form but four parts of one great whole. These four movements are (1) divine judgment on the nations of earth (cf. Rev. 5 with Rev. 6; 8-9; 16-18) and divinely permitted judgment upon Israel (Rev. 12), (2) the return of the Judge-King to the earth following the judgment (Rev. 19:11-16), (3) the reign of the Judge-King in the earth for one thousand years (Rev. 20:1-6) and His final triumph over Satan and his followers after the thousand-year reign (Rev. 20:7-15), and (4) the grand finale, the climax and consummation of history, when time and eternity coalesce, with evil having been finally and decisively judged and righteousness being manifestly in control of the universe. This is designated as a new heaven and a new earth, wherein is a New Jerusalem, where God Himself will dwell among men (Rev. 21:1—22:5).

It is most interesting to note that it is only in this last major segment of the Apocalypse that John gives any specific references to time. These references are to duration rather than to sequence and point in time, so we are still left to the logical development of the material for the determination of these items. (Other parts of Scripture, such as Dan. 9:24-27, the Olivet discourse, 1 Thess. 4:13—5:11, 2 Thess. 2:1-12, give much data with which to ascertain chronological sequence, which data are not to be ignored, but our burden in this study is Johannine.)

Before a possible time frame for this third major segment of the Apocalypse is suggested, the overriding theme of this material should be noted. It was suggested above that the four discernible movements of this third major segment of the book were in reality but four parts of a whole. This grand theme is set forth in the two introductory chapters (Rev. 4-5), which are the key to all that follows. In these chapters we look upon a scene in the divine throne room of the universe. God is enthroned and attended by various beings who ceaselessly extol Him and who engage in a dialogue relating to the final subjugation of all things to their rightful sovereign. In the midst of this sublime setting the spotlight is shifted to the crucified and glorified Christ. He steps forth as the one with authority, by virtue of His being the crucified and glorified Messiah-King of the Jews and Savior of the world, to initiate and consummate the subjugation of the universe.

The theme, then, is the establishing in a *manifest* way (not in a purely spiritual or inward way, as during this age) of the reign of God among all moral beings, both human and angelic. The four movements of thought and action are thus seen to be four steps in the final establishment of this Kingdom of God.

The first of these four movements is one of judgment, and while it is primarily punitive, it will include both punishment and reward. This is to prepare the earth for the advent of the Judge-King in person and will include the decimation of the satanic substitutes: first, in the form of secular religion (a religio-economic cartel that will fill the vacuum left when the church is raptured [Rev. 17-18]), and, later, in the form of a monstrous demonic attempt to counterfeit the Godhead (Satan [the dragon], anti-Christ [the beast], and the false prophet [Rev. 16:13]) and require universal worship of this satanic trinity through economic sanction (Rev. 13:15-17). This is the day of God's wrath (see Rev. 6:16-17), sometimes referred to as the Tribulation.

In light of the promise given to believers in Revelation 3:10-11, this time of God's wrath will not begin until the church has been raptured. How soon after the rapture the judgments will begin is not disclosed, but it will be after the heavenly scene of Revelation 4-5 transpires.[2] Since this is heavenly rather than earthly and since time is not a part of the eternal dimension, the events of Revelation 6 and following may well begin hard upon the removal of the church. This period will last for approximately eighty-four months (seven years), in light of time

[2]Revelation 4:1 ("I will show you what must take place after these things") may be the introduction to the exposition of the future things John was commanded in Revelation 1:19 to record ("Write . . . the things which shall take place after these things"). It is important, however, to distinguish between the μετὰ ταῦτα (after these things) of Revelation 4:1 and the μετὰ ταῦτα of Revelation 7:9; 15:5; 18:1; and 19:1. In all likelihood the μετὰ ταῦτα of the four verses last noted is merely a literary device used to continue the narrative. On the other hand, the ἃ μέλλει γενέσθαι (the things which shall take place after these things) of Revelation 1:19 and the ἃ δεῖ γενέσθαι μετὰ ταῦτα (what must take place after these things) of Revelation 4:1 refer to the *entire sequence* of future events set forth in the Apocalypse.

data given in Revelation 11:2-3 (relating to the first part of the Tribulation) and in Revelation 13:5 (relating to the last part). (Cf. the order of things as they unfold in Rev. 17, which shows that the beast will not come into prominence until about the middle of the Tribulation period, since the great harlot will be prominent during the first half.)

The second movement likewise involves judgment, but it primarily reveals the Judge-King returning to assume His rightful reign in the earth (Rev. 19:11—20:3). After the general population of the ungodly (those "who dwell on the earth" [Rev. 11:10; 13:8; 17:2, 8]) has been largely destroyed and Israel has been prepared for the advent of her Messiah by the outpouring of God's wrath, the Judge-King will come in person to "tread . . . the wine press of the fierce wrath of God, the Almighty" (Rev. 19:15). At this point, as the time of wrath is consummated and the time of the King's reign is begun, the diabolically inspired human leadership will be summarily dealt with (Rev. 19:17-21) and Satan himself will be bound for a thousand years (Rev. 20:1-3). It is at this point that the prophetic statement of Revelation 11:15 will be realized as the King of kings begins this first phase of His eternal reign (Rev. 11:17).

With the advent of the Judge-King the third movement is introduced. This is the millennial (Rev. 20:4), or Messianic (Rev. 11:15), aspect of the Kingdom of God, which, although it will last only a specified period of time (Rev. 20:4) and will relate to this-worldly, time-space history, is merely the prelude to the second and final phase of the Kingdom of God among men (cf. Rev. 20:4 with 22:5). The Kingdom, in this phase, will be composed of the King (Rev. 11:15; 19:15-16; 20:4, 6); His royal priests, that is, glorified saints from Pentecost through the Tribulation (Rev. 5:10; 20:4, 6); willing subjects from the nation Israel (Rev. 11:15; cf. 1:7) and, by implication, from the nations of earth (see, e.g., the reference to the camp of the saints in Rev. 20:9); and a group of rebels who will rally to Satan upon his release from prison at the end of the thousand-year period (Rev. 20:7-8).

At the close of this thousand-year period, six incidents transpire that form a transition from the Messianic to the eternal aspects of the Kingdom. Satan is released from the abyss (Rev. 20:7); he rallies a large group of unbelievers from among the nations of earth for one final act of defiance against God (Rev. 20:8-9); this last group of God-rejectors in the history of earth is destroyed by a heavenly judgment (Rev. 20:9); Satan is finally sent to eternal punishment (Rev. 20:10); the ungodly dead of the ages are sent to the same eternal punishment (Rev. 20: 11-15); and the present heaven and earth are supplanted by a new heaven and earth (cf. Rev. 20:11 and 21:1).

At this juncture the fourth and final movement of this eschatological drama is set forth. With all ungodly elements dealt with (Rev. 21:8, 27), the Kingdom of righteousness will assert itself in its final and eternal form (Rev. 21:2—22:5). While there will be a pristine universe in which this final scene is unfolded (Rev. 21:1), the one thing that dominates this final vision is the New Jerusalem (see, e.g., Rev. 21:24-27). This is the designation for the eternal residence of all glorified saints (cf. Rev. 21:3 and 13:6) and accomplishes the joining of the new heaven (Rev. 21:3, 22; 22:3) and the new earth (Rev. 21:24).

In light of this development of the third (future) segment of the Apocalypse, the following outline of events is offered for consideration:[3]

I. The shape of the future determined (Rev. 4-5)
 A. The heavenly throne room of the universe (4)
 B. The Judge-King (Messiah-Savior) of the future identified (5)

II. The earth prepared for the advent of the Judge-King; the period of the wrath of God and of the Lamb (6-18)
 A. The first forty-two months[4]
  1. The securing of a witness
   a. Sealing of 144,000 Israelites (7:1-8; cf. 14:1-5)
   b. Ministry of the two witnesses (11:3-6)
  2. The rise of godless authority
   a. The religio-economic cartel designated as Babylon, the great harlot, is dominant (17:1-7, 15, 18)
   b. The ten-kingdom confederacy, led by the beast, will begin to emerge (17:8-13)

[3]This outline includes only events covered in Johannine theology. A number of prophetic events mentioned only in other parts of Scripture are not included.

[4]The following items should be viewed as taking place simultaneously rather than successively.

3. The outpouring of divine judgment; the six seal judgments (6:1-17)

B. The middle of the Tribulation

1. Satan is cast out of heaven into earth (12:7-12)

2. The beast overthrows the great harlot and asserts himself as supreme ruler in the earth (17:16-17; 12:1-2)

3. The two witnesses are slain, raised from death, and taken to heaven (11:7-13)

C. The last forty-two months

1. The consolidation of satanic authority in the earth

a. The beast's kingdom established

(1) Beast- and Satan-worship set up (13:3-15)

(2) Economic control of earth set up (13:16-18)

b. The religio-economic dominion of Babylon destroyed (18:1-24)

c. Persecution of Israel on an unprecedented scale (12:13-17)

2. Divine judgment intensified

a. The trumpet judgments (8-9)

b. The bowl judgments (15:1, 5-8; 16:1-21)

3. Plans are laid for what becomes the Battle of Armageddon (16:13-14, 16; 17:14; 19:19)

III. The advent of the Judge-King (19:7—20:3)

A. Heavenly preparation for His coming; the marriage of the Lamb will precede His return, although the exact time is not specified (19:7-9)

B. The denouement (19:11-16)

C. Events surrounding His arrival

1. Destruction of the armies of earth (19:15; cf. 14:17-20; 19:17-18, 21)

2. Final judgment of the beast and false prophet (19:19)

3. Imprisonment of Satan (20:1-3)

IV. The millennial reign of the Judge-King (20:4—21:1)

A. The administration of the Millennium

1. The King (11:15; 19:15-16; 20:4, 6)

2. His royal priests (5:10; 20:4, 6)

B. Transition from millennial to eternal Kingdom
1. Release of Satan (20:7)
2. The last great battle (20:8-9*a*)
3. The final judgment of the nations (20:9*b*)
4. Final judgment of Satan (20:10)
5. Great White Throne Judgment (20:11-15)
6. A new heaven and earth supplant the present order (21:1; cf. 21:11)

V. The eternal Kingdom of God (21:2—22:5)
A. Its exclusions
1. The ungodly (14:9-10; 20:14-15; 21:8, 27; 22:15)
2. The beast and false prophet (19:20)
3. Satan (21:10)

B. Its inclusions
1. The Godhead (21:3-7)
a. God the Father (21:22; 22:1, 3, 5)
b. The Lamb (21:22; 22:1, 3)
c. The Spirit (22:17)

2. Glorified saints; this group seems to include all believers of all times up to the return of Christ, all of whom will inhabit the New Jerusalem (21:2-3; cf. 13:6; 21:7, 9)

3. The nations and kings of the earth; possibly nonglorified saints who inhabit the new earth (21:24-27)

Finally, by way of recapitulation, let it be noted that as the following material is considered, three things must ever be kept in mind: the key person of the future is Jesus Christ (Rev. 1:1-7), the key theme of the future is the manifest Kingdom of God (Rev. 11:15), and the Johannine key to understanding the future is truth set forth in Revelation 4-5. In these chapters, where the divine throne room of the universe is depicted with the holy, omnipotent, eternal Lord of the creation in absolute control, the decisions are made and actions taken that both initiate the coming of and determine the shape of the prophetic future.

XII

The Future of the Church

Immediately upon embarking on such a line of consideration as the future of the church, certain decisions have to be made that are at best problematical and that will in no wise please all who consider them. One of these decisions relates to the categorization of material under this heading. It is the conviction of the writer that unless John designates a given experience or characteristic of the future as relating to a specific entity (church, Israel, nations) or certain spirit being (Satan, demon, angel), it should be related to individual persons, regardless of their implied ecclesiastical, religious, or national association. This accounts for the limited material given under this heading, since the only place John specifically relates the church as church to the future is in Revelation 2-3.

As pointed out in footnote 1, chapter 11 (p. 158), the seven letters of Revelation 2-3 must be viewed as relating concurrently to seven churches of John's day and to seven conditions in which the church will always find herself throughout the age. As a consequence, the interpretation and application of all this material must be related to the church in general, too. Thus all material that relates to the prophetic future (in contrast to the prophetic past [relating to fulfilled prophecy] and the prophetic present [relating to prophecy now being fulfilled]) should be viewed as (1) a special promise to that particular church in John's day and (2) a general promise to the church at large. To put it another way, when the seven letters are viewed as a unit rather than as separate entities they give a composite picture of the church and Christ's promises thereto.

One final introductory note is in order regarding John's use of the term "the bride, the wife of the Lamb" (21:9; cf. 19:7). Contrary to traditional dispensational interpretation, the text does not seem to support the contention that this term applies to the church exclusively. It is only by implication that church saints are seen to be included in the term, although as will be seen below there is little question about this implication.

A comparison of 21:9 with 21:10 will show that the bride of verse 9 is identified by John with "the holy city, Jerusalem, coming down out of heaven from God" of verse 10.[1] Revelation 21:2-3 show that "the holy city, new Jerusalem," is a metaphor used by John to describe "the tabernacle of God" come to be among men, that is, His people. The people so described, who will enjoy the blessings of residence in this city (see 21:4-6), are said to be those who overcome (21:7). John gives us a twofold description of the overcomer: he believes that Jesus is the Son of God (1 John 5:4-5), and he is one of the brethren who are victorious in resisting Satan because of the blood of the Lamb and because of the word of their testimony, who did not love their lives to death (Rev. 12:10-11). In light of the context and the last clause of Revelation 12:11, the second description of an overcomer quite clearly relates to martyred Tribulation saints, while the first description shows that church saints are also overcomers. There is one final qualification, however, that must be noted. The tabernacle of God, which is the New Jerusalem, is said to be "those who dwell in heaven" (Rev. 13:6).

Thus, we may conclude that the bride, the Lamb's wife, is composed of glorified saints of the church and Tribulation periods, at least, and probably from all previous ages as well (see pp. 232-33 for further discussion). This conclusion is verified by the context of 19:5-8, which describes the Lamb's wife in a heavenly scene. Also, the reference to the nations and kings of the earth in 21:24-27 shows that other believers (nonglorified) will enter the city from the outside (the new earth).

In light of these observations, it seems highly tenuous to maintain that the church has a future that is wholly distinct from other glorified

[1] While Revelation 21:2 simply says that the New Jerusalem is bridelike, Revelation 21:9-10 actually calls her the bride.

saints. That she may be continued as a distinct group of believers as a part of a larger whole seems entirely reasonable, but to separate her from the bliss enjoyed by other saints seems to be biblically unwarranted.

A. The Church and the Return of Christ (Rev. 3:10-11).

It is generally acknowledged by all premillennialists that Revelation 3:10-11 refers to two events: (1) the return of Christ for the church and (2) the Tribulation. Among premillennialists it is disputed as to whether this passage teaches that Christ's coming for the church will be before or after the Tribulation.

The text of verse 10 naturally divides itself into two parts both grammatically and logically. The first part, which deals with the reason for the promise to the church, is introduced by the conjunction ὅτι (because). The second part, introduced by κἀγώ (I also: καί [also] + ἐγω [I]), sets forth the promise in five parts. By the repetition of the same main verb in both clauses, by the use of κἀγώ, and by the use of the subject of the first clause as the object in the second, the close relationship of thought of the two clauses is established. The glorified Christ says to the church, "Because you have been obedient to the word which assures you of my steadfast endurance on your behalf, I will, in turn, demonstrate that steadfastness to you by keeping you from the hour of testing."

Note carefully that this is nothing more or less than an ethical commitment of one party to another. At this juncture, at least, it is not a matter of God's playing favorites with one group of saints as over against another. God gave His people a pledge of His steadfast endurance regarding their safety and security.[2] They, in turn, have responded

[2]See John 10:27-30. Note the interesting use of ἁρπάζειν ἐκ (to snatch out of) twice in this passage (vv. 28 and 29). Ἁρπάζειν ἐκ clearly means "to remove from." In vv. 28 and 29 ἁρπάζειν ἐκ is negated: a person cannot snatch a believer from God's hand. Also see John 17:9-26, where Christ's prayer for the believers is that they be kept safe in the world so that various experiences and truths listed in vv. 9-26 may be realized. Our Lord's purpose for us is most clearly stated in v. 15, where the contrast between αἱρεῖν ἐκ (to take out) and τηρεῖν ἐκ (to keep from) is drawn. Christ's intention is to leave believers in the world while preserving them from the evil one. John appeals

to His pledge by keeping, or being obedient to, His Word. Thus the period of testing for church saints is fulfilled (Rom. 5:1-5; James 1:2-4, 12; 1 Pet. 1:3-9; 4:12-13) and the hour of testing for the world is about to come. If the truth of this first clause is recognized, then any apparent "respect of persons" whereby church saints are spared the Tribulation period and other saints suffer death for the faith is shown to be nonexistent. It is simply a matter of the fulfillment of God's purposes in different ways for different periods of history.

The second clause of verse 10 sets forth the promise itself. Christ first indicates the action to be taken and the historical period when it will take place. "I also will keep you from the hour of testing." As has been pointed out by others, the words "keep from" (τηρήσω ἐκ) may be construed as "preserve in the midst of" (see John 17:15) or as "keep out of."[3] If "preserve in the midst of" prevails, a posttribulational rapture of the church is taught here; but if "keep out of" is established, a pretribulational rapture is set forth. Because the only other Johannine use of τηρεῖν ἐκ (John 17:15) is properly translated by "preserve in the midst of," some scholars adduce it as proof that Revelation 3:10 should be given the same meaning.[4]

---

to this same truth with somewhat different terminology in 1 John 5:18. "He who was born of God [Jesus Christ] keeps him [the believer] and the evil one does not touch him."

[3]Certainly no one is denying Gundry's contention that in many cases ἐκ should be given a sense of motion. All we are calling for is recognition that it does not always have that sense. An examination of listings in lexicons like J. H. Thayer's *Greek-English Lexicon of the New Testament* or W. F. Arndt and F. W. Gingrich's *Greek-English Lexicon of the New Testament and Other Early Christian Literature* will show that there are more than just a few examples of ἐκ with other senses. While they do not necessarily promote the viewpoint set forth in this discussion, both Henry Alford (*The Greek Testament,* 4:585) and James Moffatt ("The Revelation of St. John the Divine," p. 368) recognize that the meaning of ἐκ in Revelation 3:10 is not a foregone conclusion. In addition see Alva J. McClain, *The Greatness of the Kingdom,* pp. 464-65; J. Dwight Pentecost, *Things to Come,* pp. 216-17; and Henry Clarence Thiessen, *Introductory Lectures in Systematic Theology,* pp. 478-79.

[4]See Robert H. Gundry's *The Church and the Tribulation,* pp. 54-61. He notes that the parallels between John 17:15 and Revelation 3:10 are "very impressive" (p. 58), making it very probable that Revelation 3:10 and John 17:15 are of similar usage and meaning. Gundry recognizes the importance of Revelation 3:10, because he spends seven pages on it. He then comes to the conclusion that the hour of testing refers to the end of the Tribulation. However, it is questionable whether his study is accurate.

There are two reasons, however, why this need not, and in this case does not, hold true. First, in John 17:15 a contrast is set up by the use of ἀλλά (but) and the use of ἄρῃς ἐκ (take out of) as over against τηρήσῃς ἐκ (keep from). This is not the case in Revelation 3:10, where a contrast is not even suggested. Second, by the interjection of τῆς ὥρας (the hour) the focus of the "keeping from" is greatly narrowed and defined. If the statement were simply τηρήσω ἐκ followed immediately by τοῦ πειρασμοῦ (testing), it most certainly

---

First, he concludes that the primary idea conveyed by ἐκ is that of "emergence"; hence, he makes ἐκ to mean "coming out through" and τηρέω to mean "protect" or "guard" (p. 59). The conclusion he reaches concerning these two terms is based on their independent usage rather than on their joint usage, except for his discussion of John 17:15. While it is acknowledged that this combination of terms has this sense in John 17:15, the broader context of the Apocalypse must be considered before one assigns that sense in Revelation 3:10. As McClain notes, "The notion that those who become believers on earth during the period of pre-Kingdom judgments will be divinely guarded *from* the afflictions entailed, in alleged fulfilment of the promise in Rev. 3:10, is simply false to the record. In that hour the physical judgments will generally fall upon the saved and unsaved alike. But, excepting the 144,000 sealed Israelites, in the supreme 'trial' those who choose Christ will be killed, while those who reject Him will live! Even the two great prophets of the hour, having borne their faithful witness for 1260 days, will at last suffer martyrdom and the diabolical indignities which attend it (11:7-10)" (McClain, p. 465).

If, as Gundry claims, ἐκ does mean "emergence" here, he is implying that the church will actually be *in* the hour of testing. Yet, later in the same chapter of his book (pp. 62-63) he presents the concept of a prewrath rapture that will take place near the end of the seven-year period. He does this by stating that "no saint can suffer divine wrath" and "divine wrath . . . concentrates at the close." Further, with respect to his use of John 17:15, the differences surely outweigh the similarities. In addition to the differences noted in the text above, John 17:15 tells about a person, whereas Revelation 3:10 tells of a time.

Second, Gundry takes τῆς ὥρας τοῦ πειρασμοῦ (the hour of testing) and concludes that a mere presence on earth will not necessarily bring one into testing. "The hour of testing" may refer to the last crisis. It appears, however, that he has essentially redefined the Tribulation. In ὥρας (hour) there is a temporal factor, and this would emphasize complete exemption from being anywhere around during the time. "Hour" refers to a time period, whether long or short.

Finally, the objects of the hour of testing are "those who dwell upon the earth." These words refer to people of a godless society who have surrendered themselves to the worship of Antichrist (cf. 6:10; 8:13; 11:10; 13:8; 17:8). Judgment is therefore reserved for the earth-dwellers; God's people are distinguished because they have been raptured and are no longer of the earth. On the basis of these facts, it would seem reasonable to conclude that Revelation 3:10 is *clear* support for a pre-Tribulation rapture.

could mean that Christ was promising preservation in the midst of a given situation or period of time. But since the promise is "I also will keep you from the *hour* of testing" (italics added), the sense of "preservation in the midst of" is not suitable. The only way one may be preserved from a time of testing is by being kept out of it. In John 17:15 the Lord prays for the believer to be preserved from the evil one while he (the believer) is yet in the world. But in Revelation 3:10 the promise is that Christ will keep the church from the *time* of testing, and since matters of time and space cannot be separated in this world, the "keeping" in this passage requires a removal from the dimension of time and space to that of eternity.

The next aspect of the promise relates to the calendar and is very general (τῆς μελλούσης ἔρχεσθαι [which is about to come]). The auxiliary verb μέλλω points to something in the indefinite future from the vantage point of the speaker. Thus the exact time of this hour of testing, the Tribulation, is clearly future but not specified.

The extent or magnitude of this πειρασμός is suggested by the words "upon the whole [inhabited] world" (Rev. 3:10; cf. 12:9, where τὴν οἰκουμένην ὅλην [the whole world] also occurs; see also 16:14). This is no ordinary or localized period of testing. Whereas other testings may relate to the church and may bring tribulation for a relatively short time (2:10) or may be the general experience of various individuals here and there (cf. James 1:12-15), this testing relates to the whole earth and to unbelievers specifically (see discussion below on τοὺς κατοικοῦντας ἐπὶ τῆς γῆς).

The aim of this "hour of testing" is set forth in πειράσαι (to test), which is an infinitive of purpose. As earth's population, particularly those persons who are of this world, is put to this one final test of supreme magnitude, it will be shown to be deserving of eternal judgment. The consistent response of the earth-dwellers to God's judgment upon sin is graphic proof of their inherent perversity.[5]

[5]See Revelation 6:15-17; 9:20-21; 11:9-10, 18; 16:10-11, 21. Time after time as judgment comes from God upon sin, the men of earth refuse to repent. In fact, they go to great lengths, even to the point of seeking death, to avoid His presence. They keep this attitude even with full knowledge that the incidents are from God and are not merely natural catastrophes. The unrepentant response continues despite the fact that one-

Finally, the objects of the testing are described as "those who dwell upon the earth" (τοὺς κατοικοῦντας ἐπὶ τῆς γῆς). This phrase is used eight other times in the Apocalypse (8:13; 11:10, twice; 13:8, 14, twice; 17:2, 8; and possibly 13:12), and in every case it refers to the unbelieving. (A fuller study of this phrase is given on p. 215.) Two of these passages are of particular significance at this point. Revelation 13:8 indicates that these earth-dwellers worship the beast (and thus the dragon [v. 4]), while 14:9-11 makes it clear that *only* unbelievers will do this. Verse 12 shows that believers cannot do it. A comparison of 13:8 with 17:8 shows that John wanted especially to stress one thing about the earth-dwellers: their names have not been written in the book of life *from the foundation of the world.*

There are a variety of ways used in the Apocalypse to describe the unbelieving residents of earth during the Tribulation. Each underscores some aspect of their character. This description focuses on their abode and the place of their primary attachment: earth rather than heaven. It is interesting to note that the focus of the various judgments throughout the book is the earth (ἡ γῆ; note, e.g., 6:4, 8; 8:7; 9:1, 3; 11:9, 12; 14:15, 16, 18, 19; 16:1) and the kings of the earth (6:15; 17:2, 18; 18:3, 9; 19:19). The significance of this fact is highlighted all the more by two notes given in conjunction with the consummation of all things in the eternal Kingdom of God. In Revelation 21:1 special notice is given of the supplanting of the present earth with a new (καινή, i.e., qualitatively new, fresh, unworn) earth. Also, in 21:24 the "kings of the earth" are referred to again, but because of the pejorative sense already attached to the phrase earlier in the book, John adds a note in verses 25-27 that explains that these kings are different from the others in that their names are written in the Lamb's book of life (as indicated by the fact that they will be allowed to enter the city).

---

fourth of the world's population is killed (Rev. 6:8) and later another one-third (Rev. 9:18), leaving only one-half of the original number. A crescendo of this diabolical insanity is reached when the men of earth display a sadistic sense of joy over the slaying of the two prophetic witnesses. There seems to be a momentary softening in 11:13 due to the terror struck in the hearts of the men of earth by the great earthquake in Jerusalem, but that apparent softening is soon supplanted by wrath when they hear of the coming of Christ's Kingdom.

B. The Church and Her Reward.

1. *The time of reward.* Revelation 11:18 suggests that rewards will be given in conjunction with the establishment of the millennial Kingdom. An examination of each of the rewards listed for the seven churches in Revelation 2-3 (see below) will show that most of them are associated in some way with either the Millennium or the New Jerusalem.[6]

2. *The nature of the rewards.* An initial comment regarding the phrase "he who overcomes," which occurs at the end of each of the seven letters and introduces the reward section, is in order. A comparison of these passages with 1 John 5:4-5, Revelation 12:11, and Revelation 21:7 will reveal three significant facts. First, "overcoming" basically relates to faith in Jesus as the Son of God, which results in being born of God (1 John 5:4-5; cf. Rev. 12:11*a*). Thus, every church saint is an overcomer in standing even if not in practice. Second, Tribulation saints will be considered as overcomers in their struggle with Satan on the basis of the finished work of Christ and their own testimony regarding this truth. In many cases (excluding those sealed especially by God [Rev. 7:3; 8:4; 14:1]) their testimony will lead to martyrdom (12:11). Third, both church and Tribulation saints will inherit the blessing of the New Jerusalem (21:7). (See also p. 115.)

a. *The church at Ephesus* (2:7). The reward granted to the church at Ephesus is the privilege of eating of the tree of life. The only other references to this tree are Genesis 2:9, 16; 3:22-24; and Revelation 22:2 and 22:14, and in none of them are we specifically told of its significance. It is in the Paradise of God, which is a reference to the New Jerusalem (Rev. 22:2). The tree originally appeared in the Garden of Eden (Gen. 2:9), and prior to the Fall was accessible to Adam and Eve for sustenance (Gen. 2:16). Following the Fall, God expelled man from the garden and from access to the tree lest he eat of it and live forever in his fallen condition, knowing good and evil (Gen. 3:22-24). In the New Jerusalem, the tree of life will be in the center of the city (on the main street; cf. Rev. 21:21 and 22:2), it will bear fruit monthly (perpetu-

[6]In some cases the statements are so enigmatic that it is difficult to suggest with any degree of certainty the significance of the reward.

ally?), and its leaves will provide healing (medical service) for the nations of the new earth (Rev. 22:2; cf. 21:24, 26). Perhaps this is the way the physical life of the nonglorified saints who inhabit the new earth will be maintained. Privilege of access to the tree is limited to those who have washed their robes in the blood of the Lamb (Rev. 22:14; cf. 7:14).

In light of the above, it would seem that the tree is a real entity that in some way has medical powers to maintain longevity; and it would seem that this real tree symbolizes the eternal life and its sustenance, which reside in God alone.

b. *The church at Smyrna* (2:11). The church at Smyrna is promised that the overcomers will not be hurt by the second death. The only other references to this phenomenon are Revelation 20:6, 14; and 21:8. From these passages we learn that those over whom the second death has no power will take part in the first resurrection, will be priests of God and Christ in some special way in the future, and will reign with Christ during the Millennium (20:6). Revelation 20:14 discloses that the second death refers to the lake of fire, the place of eternal torment for unbelieving men and spirits (19:20; 20:10, 15). The fact that this is not the destiny of believers is reiterated in Revelation 21:7-8, where the contrast between inhabitants of the New Jerusalem and those of the lake of fire is sharply drawn.

c. *The church at Pergamum* (2:17). The overcomers at Pergamum will be rewarded with hidden manna and with a new name on a white stone, which name will be known by none but the recipient.

There are no references to hidden manna in the Apocalypse, so we must go elsewhere for an insight. The significant passages are Exodus 16:8; Psalm 78:24-25; John 6:31-35, 48-51; and Hebrews 9:4, with the references in John being the most important. It is emphasized over and over in these passages that the manna was a miraculous, heavenly provision for the physical sustenance of the Israelites while they were traveling in the wilderness (Ex. 16:4; Psalm 78:24; John 6:31) and that there was all the manna they needed to be satisfied (Ex. 16:18; Psalm 78:25) on a given day or for a given period (forty years). Nonetheless, the people still died (John 6:49). As a memorial of God's provision for Israel in the wilderness, Aaron was directed to place a jar of manna alongside the Tables of the Covenant in the Ark of the Covenant (Ex. 16:33-34; Heb. 9:4). Thus it was *hidden* beneath the Mercy Seat.

In His bread of life discourse, the Lord used the manna as an illustration, both by comparison and contrast, of Himself as God's ultimate provision for the sustenance of His people (see John 6:31-51). Like manna, He may be viewed as bread, and He originated in heaven from God (John 6:32-35). Unlike manna, He gives life to the world rather than to Israel only (John 6:33); He will finally, rather than momentarily, satisfy hunger (John 6:35); He delivers from death as well as hunger (John 6:50); and He provides eternal rather than merely physical life (John 6:51).

From this information it would appear that "hidden manna" is a token, or memorial, for the believer alone (it is hidden from the eyes of others) of the spiritual life and sustenance he has in Christ.

The second aspect of the reward for the overcomers in the church at Pergamum is a new name written on a white stone. The significance of the white stone is nowhere explained, although a possible clue is found in Acts 26:10. In that passage the ψῆφος (stone) is used to describe the casting of a vote. It is known that in ancient times a black stone signified a vote of disapproval and a white stone a vote of approval. The meaning of the new name on the stone is also problematical, although there are some clues to follow. If the white stone is a symbol of Christ's approval, then the name written thereon personalizes the approval. In Revelation 3:12; 14:1; and 22:4 reference is made to Christ's (the Lamb's) new name written on the foreheads of the members of various groups of saints. This must be another name than that of 2:17, since it is a different name—Christ's rather than the believer's—and since it is written in a different place—on the believer rather than on a white stone. Apparently the believer will have two names in that day.

One other passage gives some light on the matter. In Isaiah 62:2 we find that Israel in the future will receive a new name (cf. Rev. 22:4). The context shows that it is a special name of endearment, such as a bridegroom may use of his bride.

When all this information is collated, the following tentative conclusions may be reached. Since this new name is known only by the giver and the receiver, it is obviously a very intimate one. Since it is associated with the white stone, it must be a name of approval, or, perhaps better, endearment. Since it differs from the new name of Christ that all believers will receive, it must be distinctively individual. It could be, then, that our being called by His name will identify us with Him (much as a bride assumes the new name of her husband), while this private name will show us His special, individual love (much as a husband and father may have special terms of endearment for each member of his family).

d. *The church at Thyatira* (2:26-28). There are two promises to the overcomers in Thyatira, and the first has a corollary. Because of other helpful passages and because of the straightforward nature of this first reward, it is one of the easier ones to understand. The concept of ruling the nations with a rod of iron is set forth in three other passages, all of which relate to Christ the Shepherd-King. Psalm 2:8-9 is the initial setting forth of the truth that in eternity past the Father gave authority to the Son to rule the nations with a rod of iron (cf. Rev. 2:27*c*). As the Son received authority from the Father, so He extends that authority to the saints (Rev. 2:26-27*b*). The Son's exercise of this authority was contingent upon His first (Micah 5:2, 4; cf. Matt. 2:6) and second (Rev. 19:15) advents, that is, upon His incarnation and glorious return to reign. On the other hand, the believers' exercise of this authority is contingent upon their participation in the first resurrection (Rev. 20:6), that is, upon their glorification as church or Tribulation saints.

Some further instruction regarding this iron-rod rule is found in the term used to set it forth. There is no question that the rule will be with absolute and righteous standards, since it will be with an *iron* rod that will shatter the vessels of disobedience. "Rod" (ῥάβδος) is variously used in the New Testament to refer to a staff such as one would use on a journey (e.g., Matt. 10:10), a ruler's sceptre (e.g., Heb. 1:8; Rev. 19:15-16), and an instrument of chastisement (1 Cor. 4:21; cf. 2 Cor. 11:25). The last two senses are combined in this passage. On the other hand, the verb translated "rule" (ποιμαίνω) gives another dimension to this picture. The word literally means "function as a shepherd," or "tend a flock." This ruler will be firm but have a shepherd's heart. And, just as a pastor today serves as an undershepherd in relation to Christ, the good chief Shepherd (see 1 Peter 5:1-4; John 10:14-16), so in that future day believers will serve as shepherd-princes under the Shepherd-King (since the word for "rule" in Rev. 2:27 is the same term used of Christ in Rev. 19:15). This aspect of the believer's future apparently relates both to the Millennium and to the eternal Kingdom of God (Rev. 20:4, 6; 22:5). While we are given little detail as to the specifics of this role, certain terms are suggestive. As coregents (Rev. 20:4, 6; 22:5) we shall have administrative responsibilities of both a judicial and a pastoral nature (Rev. 2:27). As priests (Rev. 5:10; 20:6) we shall have certain worship responsibilities.

The second reward to the church is "the morning star." Revelation 22:16 is the only other reference to this in the New Testament, and from it we discover that Jesus is the morning star. In light of the fact that the morning star is the harbinger of dawn, and thus of a new day with its new hopes and opportunities, there may be the suggestion here of a new order of things to be ushered in by the triumphantly returning Jesus.[7]

e. *The church at Sardis* (3:5). As with the church at Thyatira, so there are two promises to the group of overcomers at Sardis, with the second having two parts: a negative and a positive. The first reward is that the overcomers will be clothed in white garments. The first, and clearest, insight into the significance of this act is found in Revelation 3:4, where it is stated that being clothed in white garments is a mark of honor. It signifies worthiness because of some position or act of distinction. In this case the honor is given in light of holy living in this life.[8]

Revelation 19:14 (cf. 19:8) seems to identify this reward with association with the returning, conquering Christ as He comes to establish His

[7]Note should be taken here of 2 Peter 1:19, where reference is also made to the morning star but by use of different terminology (φωσφόρος rather than ὁ ἀστὴρ ὁ πρωϊνός). In 2 Peter 1:19 we discover that with the rising of the morning star (Christ), presumably when He comes again, the prophetic Word will yield to the living Word.

[8]Of the twenty-five occurrences of the word "white" in the New Testament, all but one signify distinction or prestige; all but three relate in some way to heaven; all but six relate to clothing as a sign of distinction or honor; and seventeen are Johannine, with fifteen being found in the Apocalypse.

millennial Kingdom. If, as seems likely, this army of 19:14 is to be identified with the bride of 19:7-8, then the reward of being clothed in white garments relates not only to the millennial but also to the eternal Kingdom of God, since the bride so clothed is the New Jerusalem (21:2, 9-11; cf. 22:14).

The second reward is that Christ "will not erase his name from the book of life" and that He will "confess his name before [His] Father, and before His angels." This is one promise stated in two ways for emphasis. The second statement, in addition, serves to heighten the significance of the first.

The term translated "erase" (ἐξαλείφω) is used two other times in the Apocalypse (7:17; 21:4), and both times it refers to the wiping away of tears by God. It is also used in Acts 3:19 of the wiping away of sin. Thus, while it is clearly figurative, it is to be taken in a straightforward sense as signifying an actual removal. Since it is negated here, it becomes an assurance that the overcomer's (believer's) name will emphatically not (οὐ μὴ) be removed from the book of life.

A number of significant references in both the Old Testament and the New Testament to the "book of life" (or "My book," "the book") give light on this promise. The term is first used in Exodus 32:32-33 in regard to Israel's forsaking Yahweh to worship the golden calf. This breach of the second commandment was clearly a repudiation of the true God. Moses' selfless plea that God blot out his name in exchange for Israel's forgiveness was rejected. He was told instead that those who sinned would be blotted out. In Psalm 69:28, a psalm of imprecation, David calls upon God to blot his enemies' names out of the book of life. This is explained in the second line of the parallelism as "may they not be recorded with the righteous." Perhaps this helps explain the Exodus 32:33 passage as meaning that God would not record the names of those idolators with the righteous. Daniel is told (Dan. 12:1) that in the Tribulation Jews whose names are in the book will be rescued (cf. Rev. 12), and Paul shows from Philippians 4:3 that the names of Christians in general are recorded in the book.

In the Apocalypse there are five other uses of the term. Revelation 13:8 and 17:8 show that the ungodly citizens of the Tribulation (earth-dwellers) have had no place in this record from the foundation of the world (i.e., in the eternal counsels of God). While the ungodly will be judged finally "according to their deeds," the basis of their eternal punishment will be that their names were not written in the book of life (Rev. 20:12, 15). From a record-keeping standpoint, the purpose of the book seems to be that it is the basis for right-of-entrance to the New Jerusalem.

Further understanding of the meaning of not having one's name erased from the book is given in the last clause of Revelation 3:5. Instead of having his name erased from his visa to the New Jerusalem, the believer will be confessed in the courts of heaven as being worthy of admittance.

Three passages of significance in the New Testament allude to the confessing (from ὁμολογέω [I am acknowledging with approval]) of the name. (A number of passages refer to confessing Christ; seven are in Johannine writings.) In Matthew 10:32 it is stated that the one who confesses Christ before men will be confessed by Christ before God. Luke 12:8 states the same thing, while substituting "the angels of God" for "God." This confessing is explained by the following verse in each case as being the opposite of denying Christ. Hebrews 13:15 helps explain the meaning of "confessing His name," which will in turn help explain the meaning of His confessing our name. The verse literally translated reads, "through Him, then, let us offer up a sacrifice of praise continually to God, that is, fruit of lips confessing His name." That is, fruit borne through the confession of His name is viewed as a sacrifice of praise. Not the confession, but the fruit coming from the confession, is the sacrifice.

His confession of our name before the Father and His angels will likewise bear fruit in the form of a sacrifice of praise. We, the redeemed thus vouched for by the Son to the Father, will join with the hosts of heaven in extolling Him who alone is worthy (cf. Rev. 5:11-14).

In summary, then, this second promise to the overcomers in Sardis is a doubly enforced assurance of the saint's perseverance because of the Savior's faithfulness.

f. *The church at Philadelphia* (3:12). The believers in Philadelphia also received a double promise of reward. The first promise has two parts and the second three. First, Christ states, "I will make him a pillar in the temple of My God, and he will not go out from it any more." While there is no statement quite like this elsewhere in Scripture, it is clear that the figure of a pillar is intended to represent support (cf. Gal. 2:9; 1 Tim. 3:15)—support of a vital rather than decorative nature. Revelation 7:15 indicates that the temple of God here in view is a place of service and safety, while 21:22 shows that in the New Jerusalem this temple is conceived of as a person rather than a place. That is, the center of worship, service, and safety in that day will be "the Lord God, the Almighty, and the Lamb."

The second half of the statement, ἔξω οὐ μὴ ἐξέλθῃ ἔτι, is a very strong affirmation of permanence. Not only will he be a pillar in God's temple, but he will never (οὐ μή, emphatic negative) go outside (ἔξω ἐξέλθῃ—note the repetition of the preposition for emphasis) any more (ἔτι—added for reinforcement of the already emphatic statement).

The second promise has to do with the writing on the believer of a threefold name to identify him and to indicate ownership. Notice in each case that it is God's or Christ's name rather than his own that is affixed to the believer (in contrast, see the discussion of 2:17 above).

Throughout the book of Revelation repeated reference is made to various names, some of which have bearing on this passage. In 14:1 the 144,000 select Jews are said to have the name of the Lamb and His Father on their foreheads. Likewise, the inhabitants of the New Jerusalem are so marked with the Lamb's name (22:4). It is somewhat difficult to determine what the name of "the city of My God" is if it is not "new Jerusalem." Revelation 21:2-3 and 9-11 give much information about this city by use of descriptive terms and epithets such as "holy," "tabernacle of God," "bride," "costly stone," but none of these is really a name. In describing the city of Jerusalem during the Millennium, Ezekiel says that its name shall be "The LORD is there" (Ezek. 48:35).

The third name, designated by Christ as "My new name," is also problematical. In Revelation 19, three names of the returning Christ are given, but none is designated as being "new." He is called by a name "which no one knows except Himself" (v. 12), by the name "Word of God" (v. 13), and by the name "KING OF KINGS, AND LORD OF LORDS" (v. 16). The question is, to whom is the name new? If it is new to Him, we are left without a certain identification. If it is new to us, it may be considered to be something like the new name a bride receives when she takes her husband's name.

From the rest of Scripture it is clear that *the* name of God is *Yahweh* (LORD, Ex. 3:13-15) and that *the* name of the Lamb is *Jesus* (Matt. 1:21), or *Immanuel* (Matt. 1:23). Whether these names are what is alluded to here is uncertain. It is clear, however, that believers will wear a spiritual name-tag, so to speak, on which will be inscribed their immediate family name as part of the bride of Christ, their broader family name as being related to the Father in the family of God at large, and their address in the New Jerusalem. There is no question left as to whether they will belong.

g. *The church at Laodicea* (3:21). The overcomers in the Laodicean church are promised one reward: to be seated with Christ on His throne. This is likened to Christ's enthronement with the Father following His victorious conquest of the world (John 16:33) and of sin (Rev. 5:5-6; note that the Lion of v. 5 is the slain Lamb of v. 6). His victory at the cross makes possible two truths of cosmic significance. First, He has declared a *Pax Christi* (peace of Christ) for the believer of this age even though he lives in a world that is set to trouble him (John 16:33). Second, and this relates more directly to Revelation 3:21, He has thereby established His throne rights as sovereign of the universe (Rev. 5:5-14; cf. 17:14). The slain Lamb of the first advent (Rev. 5:6, 9) demonstrated His worthiness to exercise dominion as the regal Lion (Rev. 5:5) who is yet a Lamb (Rev. 5:11-14). Having overcome, He sat down with His Father, assuming the heavenly position as co-King of the universe (Rev. 3:21*b*).

This reference to the Father's throne, as with most references to a throne in Revelation, is to the throne of God in heaven. Almost without exception, when θρόνος is used in the New Testament it is used metaphorically to refer to a seat of authority or metonymically to refer to regal power and sovereignty. Since the grand theme of the Apocalypse is the ultimate manifestation of God's universal Kingdom, it is fitting that there be many references to thrones in this book. In addition to the diabolical pseudosovereignty asserted by the beast (Rev. 13:2), who will be overcome by the Lamb (Rev. 17:12-14), there are at least three aspects of genuine divine sovereignty seen in the book. First, there is the heavenly manifestation of God's Kingdom, as seen in Revelation 3:21*b*; 4:2; 5:1; and so forth. The heavenly sovereign is attended by several ministers of court who are likewise enthroned (Rev. 4:4; 11:16) yet subservient to the Lord God of all things (Rev. 4:10-11).

Second, there will be the Messianic manifestation of God's Kingdom when Christ sits on His throne, reigning in this earth over Israel and the other nations (Rev. 3:21*a*; 11:15; 19:12-16; cf. Matt. 19:28). During this time He will be attended in His royal court by several groups that will aid Him in administering His Kingdom. Revelation 20:6 and 5:10 give a general statement indicating that all who have been purchased by the blood of Christ and who experience the first resurrection (which seems to include all saints from the beginning up through the Tribulation, as well as Christ) will reign with Him. Matthew 19:28 shows that the apostles will have a responsibility especially to Israel at that time; Revelation 3:21*a* shows that church saints will be involved in some way; and Revelation 20:4 indicates that Tribulation saints are included.

Finally, the universal Kingdom of God will be manifest in the New Jerusalem, in the context of the new heaven and new earth. Here, again, is seen the shared reign of Father and Son (Rev. 11:15; 22:3). Once again the glorified saints are seen sharing in His reign (Rev. 22:5), perhaps aiding Him in the administration of the new heaven and earth (cf. 1 Cor. 6:2-3, which may, however, describe duties performed by the saints during the Millennium).

One final word of repetition is in order before this chapter is closed. While the promised rewards considered above do relate to the variously named historico-geographical churches of the first century, they also relate to any church so characterized throughout this church age. Further, the combination of all the promises provides a composite reward for every church saint. All will enjoy the blessing of life eternal that resides in God alone; all will be delivered from eternal torment; all will be provided with private nourishment for their spiritual life by Christ; all will receive an intimate name of endearment indicating His special love; all will serve as shepherd-princes under the Shepherd-King; all will share in the new order of things established by the return of Christ; all will be honored with garments of distinction; all will be kept safe and secure, which keeping will in turn be occasion for great praise; all will be a functional and permanent part of the service and worship of God; all will be identified by name with Christ, the Father, and the whole company of the redeemed in the New Jerusalem; and all will graciously be given a part in the administration of the millennial and eternal Kingdom of God, together with the Son and the Father. It is no wonder that each of the seven letters closes with the exhortation, "He who has an ear, let him hear what the Spirit says to the churches."

XIII

The Future of Israel

When the historico-grammatical system of interpretation of Scripture is applied consistently to the Old and New Testaments, especially to the Abrahamic and Davidic covenants, one is irresistibly led to the conclusion that Israel has a national future.[1] John gives a good deal of information regarding Israel's future as it relates to the period of the Tribulation on through the Messianic Kingdom.

A. Israel and Her Future Ministry.

The ministry of Israel during the time of Tribulation is set forth in two very unusual passages: Revelation 7:1-8 and 14:1-5. Whatever is being taught here is rather enigmatic, and the particular service in which these 144,000 persons engage is only to be determined by implication. As Revelation 7:4-8 shows, the group is merely representative of the nation rather than all-inclusive.[2] A specific number of persons are selected by God for a very particular task, although that task is nowhere named in explicit terms.[3]

[1]See Charles C. Ryrie's *The Basis of the Premillennial Faith* for a development of this concept.

[2]Because of the humanly insurmountable problem posed by the absence of tribal distinctions in modern Israel, there is a great temptation to explain the phrase "one hundred and forty-four thousand sealed from every tribe of the sons of Israel" (Rev. 7:4) as simply an apocalyptic way of saying that every tribe of Israel will be represented in the 144,000. The specificity of Revelation 7:5-8 and the fact that the sealing is ordered by God (Rev. 7:2-3), however, show that the 144,000 comprises literally 12,000 persons from each of the twelve tribes of Israel.

[3]They are often called the 144,000 witnesses, but μάρτυς (μάρτυρ)—the Greek word for witness—and its related words are not used in reference to this group.

Those persons selected are designated as "bond-servants of our God" (7:3). It is quite clear that the sealing relates to a special task that requires divine protection in order to be accomplished (cf. 7:3 with 9:4; see the parallels between the sealing of the 144,000 and the protection and ministry of the two witnesses in 11:3 ff.). The fact that the seal is the name of the Lamb and His Father (14:1) and the fact that the 144,000 "follow the Lamb wherever He goes" suggest that they are His special emissaries and are working under His authority.

There are four clues as to the nature of their bondservice. First, they are numbered among the redeemed (14:3-4) and join with the retinue of the heavenly King in singing the praise of the Lamb (cf. Rev. 5:9 and 14:3). Second, and as an extension of this emphasis upon redemption, they are described as "first fruits to God and to the Lamb" (14:4). The figure of "first fruits" is taken from the Old Testament (Ex. 23:16,19; 34:22,26) and carried over metaphorically into the New Testament (Rom. 16:5; 1 Cor. 16:15; James 1:18). Just as the Old Testament Feast of the First Fruits was a reminder that there was more of the same crop yet in the field to be harvested, so the New Testament figure signifies that there are yet more people to be brought into the family of God.[4] The implication in this passage is that there are yet others to be redeemed from among men during the period of great tribulation with which they may be identified. Third, it is most interesting that the statement about first fruits is immediately followed by (and associated with, by means of the connective καί) a statement regarding the 144,000's oral (ἐν τῷ στόματι [in their mouth]) integrity (οὐχ εὑρέθη ψεῦδος [no lie was found]), a quality of absolute necessity for a witness. Finally, the close association made in Revelation 7 (μετὰ ταῦτα [after these things] [v.9]) between the description of the 144,000 and the "great multitude" suggests something more than coincidence. The implication is that the presence of the latter group in heaven is in some measure accounted for by the activity of the former on earth. Here we may have the full harvest of which the 144,000 were the first fruits.

[4]Ἀπαρχή (first fruits) is also used of the relationship between Christ and the believer (1 Cor. 15:23), the Spirit and the believer (Rom. 8:23), and the believer and the resurrection (1 Cor. 15:20).

Here may well be the crop reaped by the witness of God's sealed bondservants.[5]

B. Israel and Her Future Judgment.

1. *Future persecution.* Revelation 12 describes in very abbreviated form both the history of Israel as the bearer of Messiah and the satanic persecution that arises in relation thereto. The persecution is described as an attempt to destroy the Jewish race (vv. 13, 15), which attempt is forestalled only by divine intervention (vv. 14, 16). In his frustration, the devil then turns to persecution of the Messianic Jews, described by John as those of Israel's seed "who keep the commandments of God and hold to the testimony of Jesus" (v. 17). In light of this statement there seems little question that there will be two distinct groups of Jews during this period: (1) those who have responded in faith to the redemption message of the 144,000, and (2) those who, at this point at least, have not yet received the gospel of Jesus Christ and yet are being preserved by God.[6]

2. *Future reward.* In Revelation 11:18 there is a general statement made regarding reward from God to His "bond-servants the prophets and to the saints and to those who fear [His] name." In the context, this act is associated with the time when Messiah will assume His Kingdom and the dissident factions will be judged. There is little reason to doubt that Israel will be numbered among those so rewarded.

A more tangible and specific form of reward, or perhaps providence, is described in Revelation 12:6, 14, and 16. During the time of the Tribulation when there are intense anti-Semitism and attempted genocide, God will protect and nourish the nation in the wilderness at a

[5]This multitude is described in Revelation 7:9 as comprising representatives "from every nation and all tribes and peoples and tongues"; so without question it includes Jews as well as persons from other ethnic, tribal, and linguistic groups.

[6]In all likelihood, one of the reasons for this preservation is to provide the nucleus for the population of the Messianic Kingdom, for John makes it clear that many Jews will turn in faith to Christ at the time of His second advent (Rev. 1:7; cf. Zech. 12:10—13:1). The "day" when the fountain will be opened for the cleansing of sin for David's house (Zech. 13:1) is the same "day" that the Lord's feet will "stand on the Mount of Olives" and "the LORD [our] God, will come" (Zech. 14:4-5).

location designated as "a place prepared by God" (v. 6), a place that is particularly "her place" (v. 14).[7]

C. Israel and Her Returning Messiah.

Because Israel was the national vehicle God chose to bring Messiah into the world, she has been the object of intense satanic activity throughout her history. As was noted above, the future will be no different. At the same time, since it is Satan's desire to establish his own kingdom in lieu of God's, he has inaugurated a plan that in many details counterfeits God's. One of the similarities is an antimessiah whom the true Messiah will vanquish at His return (see 2 Thess. 2:8).

1. *Antimessiah.* The initial problem to be settled before the matter of the antimessiah can be examined is the sense to be given the prefix ἀντί in the word ἀντίχριστος (antichrist). There are two basic ideas that can be conveyed by the preposition when it is not used in compound form: "instead of" and "against," and both of these meanings are reflected in compound nouns and verbs. As Ryrie points out, when ἀντί is used in compound form to indicate substitution "it does not have the sense of an unlawful substitute but of one who rightly acts in the place of another."[8] (See, for example, ἀνθύπατος [proconsul] in Acts 13:7-8, 12.) On this basis he contends that "the scriptural picture of antichrist is of one who usurps authority" and that the prefix therefore conveys the idea of opposition rather than substitution. There are, however, two problems with this conclusion. In the first place, as is seen in the text telling of Antichrist's installation to office, he is a lawful substitute, since he is given his position under Satan's auspices (see 2 Thess. 2:9). In this way, then, he is the devil's substitute for Messiah.[9] Second, the passages in John in which the term is used refer to antichrist as a

[7]No hint is given as to where this place will be, although some scholars have tried to associate it with the ancient Nabatean stronghold of Petra, in the Jordanian desert east of the Arabah.

[8]Charles C. Ryrie, *Biblical Theology of the New Testament,* p. 351.

[9]The contention that the concept of usurpation is expressed by ψευδόχριστος (false christ) somewhat misses the mark, too. While similar in meaning to ἀντί, ψεῦδος emphasizes more the *spurious* character of the pretender; ἀντί, however, when it means "instead of" emphasizes the fact that the pretender has taken *another's* place.

deceiver as well as an opposer (1 John 2:26; 2 John 7). Certainly there is no question that he opposes Christ, as will be seen below, but to shut up the force of the prefix to this alone seems unnecessary. He is a substitute who both opposes and imitates.[10]

a. The manifestations of antichrist. John uses the term *antichrist* in several different ways. There is *the* Antichrist (1 John 2:18*a*; 4:3), who epitomizes everything that is anti-Christian. John uses this term in the epistles, describing the Antichrist from the standpoint of what he does: namely, he stands against and takes the place of Christ. In the Apocalypse (11:7; 13:1 ff.) the title used—the (wild) beast—describes his character as evaluated by God. It is quite apparent from the way John makes reference to him (1 John 2:18) that the coming of this person in the future is common knowledge to John's readers. This archetypical person already had precursors in John's day (1 John 2:18—καὶ νῦν [even now]), both in multiple and individual manifestations (1 John 2:18, 22). Furthermore, there was already in the world in his time (1 John 4:3) a permeating "spirit of the antichrist" whereby the basic doctrine of the Antichrist and his many antichrists (1 John 2:22; 2 John 7) was influencing many.[11] The references to πᾶν πνεῦμα [every spirit] and τὰ πνεύματα [the spirits] in 1 John 4:1-3 seem to be references to personal beings whose message and ministry accomplish today what the Antichrist will do on a grand scale in the future. Ryrie suggests that this spirit of antichrist of which John speaks

> is evidently a superhuman spirit working through the Antichrist. [John] is suggesting that those of his own day are demonically inspired men, and the future Antichrist is likewise. In the Revelation it sometimes appears as if the Antichrist were only a man and sometimes as if he were the Devil himself. Evidently this concept of the spirit of antichrist explains that seeming contradiction (11:7; 13:8; 17:11).[12]

[10]This conclusion is corroborated by Paul when he says that the man of lawlessness (Antichrist) "opposes and exalts himself above every so-called god or object of worship, so that he takes his seat in the temple of God, displaying himself as being God" (2 Thess. 2:4).

[11]Paul describes the same phenomenon as the "mystery of lawlessness" (2 Thess. 2:7).

[12]Ryrie, *Biblical Theology of the New Testament,* p. 352.

It is the believer's responsibility to "test the spirits to see whether they are from God" (1 John 4:1)[13] so as to protect the church, to watch themselves lest they lose (ἀπολέσητε [destroy]) the work they have accomplished and not receive full reward (2 John 8); and to refuse them hospitality and even the civility of a common greeting (χαίρειν) lest the believer participate in any way[14] in their evil deeds and thus encourage such teaching (2 John 10-11).

b. The marks of antichrist. The distinguishing features of antichrist in John's day, and in the future as well,[15] are ecclesiastical and theological. The antichrists concerning whom John was warning his readers originated (ἐξ ἡμῶν ἐξῆλθαν [they went out from us]) in the local assembly (1 John 2:19) and were seeking to influence the other members to go along with them (2 John 7-11). The proof that their relationship to the churches was superficial rather than organic is seen in that they did not remain with the assembly (1 John 2:19). The other mark of antichrist is defective theology. The antichrists deny that Jesus is the Messiah, obviously claiming that Messiah is yet to come in the person of Antimessiah; they deny the Father and the Son; and they deny that Jesus was incarnate deity (1 John 2:22; 4:2-3; 2 John 7). Their doctrine is thus anti-Christ, anti-trinitarian, and anti-incarnational.

c. The ministry of Antichrist. Since the work of Antichrist is quite extensively treated by John, it will be dealt with separately in chapters 14-15. Some observations about the work of contemporary antichrists are in order at this point, however. It is, first of all, a work of deception (1 John 2:26; 2 John 7). Their aim is to lead astray by the promulgation of error. This error takes a variety of forms, including the questioning

[13]This is probably what Paul describes in 1 Corinthians 12:10 as the spiritual gift of "distinguishing of spirits."

[14]The use of κοινωνεῖ (participates) here is most instructive. Κοινωνεῖ is related to κοινωνία, and the Christian's fellowship is with the Father and His Son and with fellow believers (1 John 1:3). There is no way that his fellowship can be with those who deny the Father and Son. What does he have in common with them? John feels so strongly about the matter that he forbids believers to extend even the basic human courtesies of a pleasant greeting, food, and shelter.

[15]See pp. 200-207.

of the truth that a pattern of righteous living is an evidence of Christian life (1 John 3:7-8), the denial that Jesus Christ as the eternal Son took to Himself genuine humanity (2 John 7), and the encouraging of personal unchastity and impiety (Rev. 2:20).[16]

2. *The Messiah of God.* Rooted in the Old Testament and coming to flower in the New is the doctrine of God's anointed, the Messiah who would come to deliver and to judge. Jesus, while teaching in the synagogue in Nazareth, made it clear that He was the one of whom Isaiah wrote as being the Lord's anointed to preach the good news to the poor, release to the captives, recovering of sight to the blind, and the acceptable year of the Lord (Luke 4:16-19; cf. Isa. 61:1-2*a*). By stopping in the middle of the Isaianic prophecy (Isa. 61:1-3) and by stating that this first part of the prophecy was fulfilled in Himself (Luke 4:21), Jesus was also showing that Messiah's two tasks—deliverance and judgment—were to be fulfilled at different times.[17] It is most striking that the very next clause in Isaiah's prophecy, which Jesus did not read, is "and the day of vengeance of our God." Daniel 9:25-27 shows us that the two tasks of Messiah will be performed at two distinct advents separated by an undisclosed period of time, while the New Testament describes these two comings in great detail. His second coming is not related to Israel only,[18] but as the Old Testament prophecies show (see, e.g., Isa. 2; 61:1—63:6) and as John himself indicates (Rev. 1:7; cf. Zech. 12:10-14), it does especially involve her.

[16]By repeated use of πλανάω (deceive), John emphasizes that deception is one of the chief works of Satan, the beast, and the false prophet (Rev. 12:9; 13:14; 19:20; 20:3, 8, 10).

[17]While the Old and New Testaments teach that there will be two advents of Messiah—the first advent for deliverance, the second advent for judgment—one rabbinic teaching that is still widely held today is that there will be two messiahs: messiah ben-Joseph and messiah ben-David. Messiah ben-Joseph will precede messiah ben-David and will die in combat with the enemies of God and Israel. The one who will finally restore the people of Israel to their land and to spiritual blessings is messiah ben-David (Gerald J. Blidstein, "Messiah in Rabbinic Thought," p. 1411). An earlier two-messiah tradition saw a Davidic messiah as king and an Aaronic messiah as priest (David Flusser, "Second Temple Period," p. 1409). (See Psalms of Solomon 17:23—18:10 for a first century B.C. example of a concept of the Davidic messiah.) The hope of the coming of a personal messiah is yet alive in the hearts of some Jews today even though others have transmuted the teaching into a purely nationalistic concept.

[18]See pp. 208-9, 229-31 for discussion of other aspects of the second coming.

a. The fact of Jesus' coming again and its particular relation to Israel is set forth by John in Revelation 1:7. It will be a publicly witnessed event ("EVERY EYE WILL SEE HIM") marked by several celestial phenomena (see Matt. 24:29-30), the most frequently noted of which is His being accompanied by clouds (Rev. 1:7; cf. Dan 7:13; Matt. 24:30; Mark 13:26; Luke 21:27; 1 Thess. 4:17[19]). The most notable statement of this passage, however, is "EVEN THOSE WHO PIERCED HIM." While all will behold Him, Israel, especially, will mark His return with mourning in light of her particular involvement in His death as she finally comprehends that she instigated the crucifixion of her own Messiah.[20]

[19]While 1 Thessalonians 4:17 in all probability refers to a different aspect of His coming from that described in Revelation 1:7, both views have this one attendant circumstance in common.

[20]Zechariah 12:10, from which John is here quoting, shows that Revelation 1:7 is a reference to the "house of David and . . . the inhabitants of Jerusalem." In light of John's reference to Zechariah 12:10 in John 19:34 and 37, it is seen that even though the legal act of execution was performed by a representative of the Roman government the Jews are viewed as those who pierced Christ. Thus the historical fact is given its theological significance and the Jews are thereby seen to have a special accountability for Christ's death. It is true that the early church recognized that Herod, Pilate, and the Gentiles shared the guilt for Christ's death with the people of Israel (Acts 4:25-27; cf. Psalm 2:1-2), and the contemporary church must remember this, too. It is also true that John and Peter considered Israel as having particular responsibility for Christ's death (Acts 2:22-23; 3:12-18; 4:8-11; cf. Matt. 27:25, where the people themselves assume such responsibility). This is further supported by the exhortation given by Peter indicating a need for national repentance (Acts 3:19-26) as well as for individual repentance (Acts 4:12; cf. 2:37-39). It will not do to say that the responsibility for Christ's death relates only to the generation who lived in Jesus' day and called for His blood or to a small group of religious bigots in the Sanhedrin. Such an explanation does not account for Zechariah's prophecy (Zech. 12:10—13:9) or for John's (Rev. 1:7).

Some readers will immediately cry "anti-Semitism," but to do so is to misunderstand both the record of Scripture and the preceding remarks. What the Scriptures record and what has been here acknowledged is a matter of history. That Israel is accountable in some national sense for Christ's death is a matter of New Testament *and* Old Testament theology. Such is God's evaluation, and He is not anti-Semitic. Anti-Semitism is the mind-set and resultant action that make these facts of history and theology an occasion for discrimination and persecution. Nowhere in Scripture are Christians, or anyone else, charged with the responsibility of punishing the Jew for the death of Christ. All Christians should abhor and repudiate with shame the various notable and less notable atrocities perpetrated against the Jews throughout the history of the church. We can afford neither to be ignorant of the facts of history nor to be intimidated

The time of Messiah's return is fixed by John in relation to events that surround it.[21] It will be preceded by the overthrow of the great harlot, Babylon (Rev. 19:1-3), the outpouring of the bowl judgments (16:1-21), and the gathering of the armies of earth in a place called Armageddon (16:13-16); it will be attended by the destruction of those armies (19:17-19, 21) and the incarceration of the beast, the false prophet, and Satan (19:20; 20:1-3); and it will be followed by Messiah's millennial reign (20:4-6).

b. As He returns in regal splendor, Messiah is identified by certain designations that relate especially to the denouement. He is first called "Faithful and True" (Rev. 19:11; cf. 1:5; 3:14), reminding us that He fulfills His covenant promises, for it is as one so designated that He evaluates and punishes in righteousness (see, e.g., Gen. 12:2-3). Second, it is said that He will have a name that He alone knows (Rev. 19:12; cf. 2:17). Since this is a private name, it is useless to conjecture as to what it may be. It appears from the text to be inscribed on His many diadems,[22] which may suggest that it is in some way associated with His right to reign. The third designation given is "The Word of God" (Rev. 19:13; cf. John 1:1, 14), which unmistakably shows Him to be the incarnate Son of God. He is God's message to the world in personal form, first as Savior and then as Judge-King. Finally, on His robe, which is dipped in blood (Rev. 19:13; cf. Isa. 63:1-3), and on His thigh

---

by them. Both God's assessment of Israel's part in the crucifixion and the professing church's horribly misguided zeal to be the scourge of God are eloquent statements from which we ought to learn. The grace and love of God for Israel still stand, "for the gifts and the calling of God are irrevocable" (Rom. 11:29; see Rom. 11:25-31) and He has loved her with an everlasting love (Jer. 31:3). The most tangible evidence of this love and an example that we have too often overlooked is found in Jesus' own words from the cross: "Father forgive them; for they do not know what they are doing" (Luke 23:34).

[21]Matthew records Jesus' statement (Matt. 24:29) that the coming of the Son of Man will be "immediately after the tribulation of those days" described in Matthew 24:3-28.

[22]The Greek word for diadem used here is διάδημα, the mark of royalty, rather than στέφανος, the mark of bestowed honor. (Not all scholars grant this distinction, however. See, e.g., J. B. Mayor, *The Epistle of St. James: The Greek Text with Introductory Notes, Comments, & Further Studies in the Epistle of St. James,* on James 1:12 or G. Milligan, *St. Paul's Epistles to the Thessalonians: The Greek Text with Introduction and Notes,* on 1 Thessalonians 2:19).

is written "KING OF KINGS, AND LORD OF LORDS" (Rev. 19:16; cf. Deut. 10:17; 1 Tim. 6:15; Rev. 17:14). Here without question His right to conquer and reign is signified, for He is sovereign of all sovereigns.

c. The activity associated with Messiah's return is set forth in the same passage (Rev. 19:11-16) by means of several figures. He is seated on a white horse (19:11), in keeping with the martial setting that follows.[23] In this role as conquering warrior He will judge and wage war in righteousness (19:11; cf. Isa. 11:4), which acts will be marked by insightful omniscience ("His eyes are a flame of fire" [Rev. 19:12; cf. 1:15; 2:18]) and executed with sovereign right ("upon His head are many diadems" [Rev. 19:12], signifying fullness of royal authority). As He comes He will be accompanied by "the armies which are in heaven" (Rev. 19:14), which term, in light of verse 8, probably refers to the glorified saints who in Revelation 17:14 are identified as "the called and chosen and faithful." The sole weapon of His warfare will be a sword that proceeds from His mouth (Rev. 19:15; cf. 1:16; 2:12, 16) and is in all probability a reference to His spoken words (John 12:48; cf. Eph. 6:17),[24] with which He will smite the rebellious nations of earth (Rev. 19:21; cf. Psalm 2:9). Having thus subdued the nations, He will assume the position of Shepherd-King[25] (Rev. 2:27;[26] 12:5) and Judge-King (Isa. 63:3; Rev. 14:20; cf. Lam. 1:15; Joel 3:13).

D. Israel and Her Future Kingdom.

Actually, John gives very little information about the Messianic Kingdom from a distinctively Jewish standpoint. That it is particularly

[23]See footnote 15, p. 221.

[24]It may seem that Revelation 19:21 argues for a literal sword; but because the sword is said to come out of Christ's mouth, it is obviously a metaphor for the sentence of death He pronounces on the wicked (John 3:36; cf. John 5:24; see also Ezek. 18:4).

[25]The Greek verb translated "rule" is ποιμαίνω, which means "to tend a flock" (ποίμνη) or "to govern." It was used in post-Alexandrian times of a warrior-king who was considered an exemplary ruler. This post-Alexandrian usage is reflected in that period's "good-shepherd" figurines, whose physiognomy was patterned after Alexander —the ruler par excellence.

[26]See discussion on pp. 176-77.

Jewish is clear from the Old Testament (e.g., Isa. 2, especially vv. 1-3; Isa. 11, especially vv. 10-12) but is only implied from the Apocalypse. These implications are found in Revelation 11:15-17 in the reference to the Messiah and His Kingdom, which very strongly reflects Old Testament teaching (see Isa. 61:1-3; Dan. 9:25 for references to Messiah, and Exod. 15:18; Psalms 10:16; 22:28; Dan. 2:44; 7:13-14 for references to the future Kingdom). There is little question that these announcements signal the heavenly inauguration[27] of the Messianic Kingdom and Israel's consequent exaltation among the nations. The earthly installation of the new King is described in Revelation 19:15-16. The use of the title "KING OF KINGS" is not distinctively Jewish in light of its use in 1 Timothy 6:15 and Revelation 17:14, but it should not be overlooked that this new sovereign, who will rule over kings as well as other people of earth, is Himself a Jew and Israel's Messiah. The title "LORD OF LORDS" is more a Jewish designation in light of its usage in Deuteronomy 10:17.

The particular contribution that John makes to the doctrine of the Messianic Kingdom is in the area of chronology. The Old Testament passages referred to above relate the Messianic Kingdom to the last days and to the Day of the Lord, but nowhere in the Old Testament is it as carefully related to other eschatological events or is its duration specified. The Messianic Kingdom is preceded by a seven-year period of unprecedented tribulation in the earth, which period will be climaxed by Messiah's return (see above) and the imprisonment of Satan and his chief henchmen. It will last for a period of one thousand years (Rev. 20:4, 6) and will come to an end with the release of Satan and the final rebellion of unregenerate mankind (Rev. 20:7-9).[28]

[27]Notice the tense change from aorist (*ἐγένετο* [has become]) to future (*βασιλεύσει* [will reign]) in Revelation 11:15. The transfer of regnancy is seen as having taken place and the reign of the new monarch is about to begin.

[28]Many other promises of the Old Testament covenant to Israel will likewise be fulfilled during the last days, but John does not deal with them in his writings.

XIV

The Future of the Nations

There is a sense in which Israel is simply one among the nations of the earth, and as with each of them, so she, too, must give answer to the God of creation and to His Son, Jesus Christ. There is, also, a sense in which Israel is distinct among the nations, not only in the past but in the future as well. This uniqueness stems from the unconditional pledge of God to Abraham (Gen. 12:1-3; 15:1-21; 17:1-21) and its reiteration to David (2 Sam. 7:4-17; cf. Psalm 89:-1-37). In each case the enduring character of the covenant promises is given such great emphasis that there is no question left but that they will yet have a future fulfillment. The book of Deuteronomy is God's theological commentary through Moses upon His covenant relationship with Israel, and here again her distinction from the other nations is emphasized. He indicates that it was for no merit of her own that God chose Israel; rather, it was because of His elective love and covenant faithfulness (Deut. 7:6-11, note especially v. 8; cf. Amos 3:2[1]).

If Israel is viewed by God as being this distinct from the other nations, both in the past and the future, it stands to reason that the nations may be considered separately, as well, when the future is considered. John does just this and gives a good deal of information relating thereto.

[1]The verb translated "chosen" would literally be translated "known." It is used here in the sense of "take special note of" and suggests loving choice.

A. Future Gentile World Power.

The political ascendancy of godless Gentile world power will continue throughout the Tribulation period. It will grow from a religio-economic cartel under the aegis of Babylon the Great, which will exercise hegemony over the kings of earth, including the beast (Rev. 17:2-3, 7, 9-11, 18) and the peoples of the earth in general (17:1, 15), to a worldwide dictatorship under the beast (13:1-18).

1. *Babylon the Great.*[2] In the end times there will arise a world power that in John's thinking is best compared with ancient Babylon[3] for purposes of identification and characterization (Rev. 17-18).[4] This power is variously designated as a great harlot (Rev. 17:1, 5) and a great city[5] (16:19; 17:18; 18:21). These two descriptions mark the two major

[2]The following discussion will view the future of the nations from the standpoint of the *system* represented by the term "Babylon the Great." Chapter 15 will view the same subject from the standpoint of the *people* involved in this system.

[3]The Bible traces the Mesopotamian empire of Babylon in broad strokes back through Nimrod, Cush, Canaan, and Ham to Noah (Gen. 10:1-10). In light of the Tower of Babel incident recorded in Genesis 11:1-9, Babylon is viewed by Scripture as the epitome of human self-assertion against God (cf. Gen. 1:28 ["fill the earth"] and 9:7 ["populate the earth abundantly and multiply in it"] with 11:4 ["lest we be scattered abroad"]) and the fountainhead of all inappropriate religious practices. The tower was undoubtedly a ziggurat adjoined to a temple and thus a supremely religious edifice (see U. Cassuto, *A Commentary on the Book of Genesis,* 2:227-30). God's assessment of the abominations of Babylon is found in Isaiah 14:3-23. The seriousness of her sin is seen in the fact that He sees the king of Babylon as a figure of Satan himself (vv. 12-14) and in the severity of her punishment (v. 22).

[4]Many expositors attempt to distinguish between the Babylon of Revelation 17 and the supposedly different entity described in Revelation 18. In light of the unified nature of the various passages (Rev. 14:8; 16:17-21; 17; 18; 19:2) and the absence of any clear separation into two distinct entities in the text of Scripture, it is our conclusion that there is one Babylon with a variety of characteristics.

[5]Because of Babylon's designation as a city, and because she is said to sit on seven mountains, many people have tried to see in her a veiled reference to Rome, and more particularly to the Roman Catholic Church. However, such attempts at identification are fruitless and serve no good purpose. While it is true that Rome has been known since ancient times as a city built on seven hills, and while some people think that Peter referred to Rome as "Babylon" already in the first century (1 Pet. 5:13), it is also true that there are several other prominent cities of the world built on seven mountains, including Jerusalem. In Revelation 11:8 John described Jerusalem as "the great city" —thus using the same phrase as the one he used to describe the great power of the end times. But the one usage (Rev. 11:8) does not necessarily call for the identification of Jerusalem with the Babylon of Revelation 17-18. Other people think that Revelation

features of her rule and are so interwoven in the record as to suggest interdependence and argue strongly for one Babylon.

a. The first feature of this future Babylonian Empire is decidedly religious. As strange as it may seem, it is the designation "harlot" that most directly supports this concept. Time after time throughout the Bible the state of spiritual infidelity and impurity is described as a fornicatious relationship (see, e.g., Hosea; Matt. 12:39; Mark 8:38; James 4:4; Rev. 2:20-22), and it was a characteristic of pagan religion to associate cultic rites with immorality. John is undoubtedly describing a religious system that has prostituted its original purpose through syncretism (Rev. 17:15),[6] secularism (note the repeated references to her consorting with the political rulers of the earth [Rev. 17:2; 18:3, 9]),[7] and the systematic effort to destroy all vestiges of biblical religion left in the earth (Rev. 17:6; 18:24; cf. 18:20).[8]

17-18 refers to a rebuilt Babylon. Their conjecture is a possible one, but it is not without its problems in light of the divine curse placed on Babylon (Isa. 13:19-22). It is more likely that the term is intended to characterize an empire as much as a place (see Jer. 50-51). The best that can be said for the view that holds—on the strength of the reference to seven mountains—that "Babylon" is a reference to the Roman Catholic Church is that it shows an active imagination. This identification of the Roman Catholic Church with Babylon is usually linked with an overall interpretation of the passage that sees in it reference to Roman Catholic doctrine and practice. The conclusion that John used "Babylon" to indicate "Rome" is the product of Reformation overkill and misses the broader implications of the passage altogether.

[6]It would appear that if the harlot is acceptable to all these various groups, she must promulgate a religious system acceptable to all. It would seem, therefore, that instead of some sectarian emphasis (e.g., Roman Catholicism, Protestantism) or some sub-Christian emphasis (e.g., apostate groups within Christendom, such as various unitarian and modernistic bodies), her emphasis will be upon a religious system that will amalgamate aspects of various major world religions at the lowest common denominator. It is notable that the redeemed group described in Revelation 7:9 ff. is composed of converts from the same multitude as that from which the harlot's followers will come.

[7]This feature is motivated by predominantly economic interests, as will be seen below. Two of the world's great religions, Christianity and Judaism, are already well on their way to secularization, while the Arab countries, which are for all practical purposes 100 percent Islamic, are rapidly moving in the same direction as a result of their newfound wealth from petroleum.

[8]Brutal religious repression and persecution are not in themselves an indication of the religious feature of the harlot-system, as may be seen from the example of modern atheistic Russia and her notorious treatment of the Jews. Nonetheless, reli-

A second, and less obvious, indication of Babylon's religious activity is the statement in Revelation 18:23 that "all the nations were deceived by your sorcery." The word translated "sorcery" is φαρμακεία. It was used by Xenophon of drugs or spells, by Polybius of poisoning, and in the New Testament of witchcraft, probably with drug overtones (Gal. 5:20; Rev. 18:23). Two related words, φάρμακον and φαρμακός, are used in Revelation 9:21 to refer to drug-induced enchantments and in 21:8 and 22:15 to refer to magicians. In the Old Testament, God expressly forbade Israel to have anything to do with such practices (Deut. 18:9-13) on theological grounds (Deut. 18:14-18).[9] Throughout the history of religion, sorcery has been associated with various forms of demonism and satanism.[10] It is also proscribed in the New Testament (Gal. 5:20) as being against the Holy Spirit (Gal. 5:17 ff.) and as being a practice of those who oppose the truth, have corrupt minds, and are disapproved concerning the faith (2 Tim. 3:8; cf. Ex. 7:11-12).

The final item that relates to the religious aspect of Babylon's rule is found in the description given in Revelation 17:4. It appears at first glance simply to be a picture of regal splendor, which may very well be present, but it seems that there is more than this involved. The fact

---

gious repression and persecution do make up one facet of Babylon's religious system.

[9]One of the key distinctions between the monotheistic Jew and his pagan neighbors was that they practiced witchcraft and listened to divination, which things Israel was forbidden to do (Deut. 18:14). Isaiah, in his vision of the last days (Isa. 2:6) reprimands Israel for falling into such practices and thus abandoning her distinctiveness among the nations. Even Balaam recognized witchcraft and divination as forbidden religious practices whose eschewal by Israel was a mark of her distinction (Num. 23:23). While S. Mowinckel holds that the incantations of Babylonian liturgical poetry have become imbedded in the biblical record, especially the Psalms (*Psalmenstudien,* 1:29, 78, 157), Y. Kaufmann rejects this as "nothing more than scholarly romancing." He states that "the absence of a literature of therapeutic incantations complements the absence in Israel of a native magic. This implies that the Israelite world view was essentially non-magical" (Y. Kaufmann, *The Religion of Israel: From Its Beginnings to the Babylonian Exile,* pp. 108-10).

[10]See, for example, Peter's evaluation of Simon Magus in Acts 8:9-11, 18-23. The words of v. 20 are especially strong; translated literally, they are: "May your silver perish with you into perdition." Peter's words also reflect his revulsion at the idea that the gift of the Holy Spirit be associated with magic. See also 2 Thessalonians 2:8-10; Revelation 9:20-21; 16:13-14.

that she is pictured as holding a golden cup filled with abominations and the unclean things of her fornication (i.e., her religious practices) suggests that these garments are sacramental as well as regal. She is not only a queen; she is also a priestess.[11] The holding of the cup is probably symbolic of the cultic liturgy in which she engages.

b. The second distinctive feature of Babylon the Great is economic. The key verse here is Revelation 18:3, which indicates that the merchants of the earth have become wealthy on the basis of the financial strength of her wanton luxury. The future Babylonian rule will make its greatest worldwide impact through a vast commercial system (Rev. 18:11-16). The goods thus traded will range from precious metals and gems to rich clothing, expensive building materials, spices, scents, foodstuffs, military equipment, and, finally, human lives.[12] Those involved in this system include the merchant-financiers (18:11, 15), the ship

[11]There seems to be more than a coincidental similarity between the great harlot and Ishtar, the ancient Akkadian goddess of fertility. In the "Hymn to Ishtar" and the "Prayer of Lamentation to Ishtar" (the translation of which text follows a translator's introduction that includes the information that the text was the property of the temple of Esagila in Babylon), Ishtar is described both as a queen and as a goddess (J. B. Pritchard, ed., *Ancient Near Eastern Texts Relating to the Old Testament,* pp. 383-85). The Sumerian name for Ishtar was *Inanna,* who was one of the major deities of the Sumerian pantheon. One of the notable things about Ishtar-Inanna is the great variety of forms she took. She was goddess of the power of the storehouse, a harvest fertility cult; rain goddess, in which form she aspired to marry the god of heaven and consequently became the queen of heaven; goddess of the evening star, in which role she was protectress of harlots, who begin their work with the rising of the evening star; and the harlot, who indiscriminately consorts with any and all whom she will. In the various myths she is seen as a beautiful but wanton young girl of aristocracy, a sweetheart, a happy bride, and a sorrowing widow. Thus she filled all the roles a woman may have except those of maturity. She is never portrayed as a responsible wife or suitable mother. Her wants are always immediate, and when she receives the thing or the lover she desires she soon casts it aside. It was her characteristic to destroy those whom she "loved." See Thorkild Jacobsen, *The Treasures of Darkness: A History of Mesopotamian Religion,* pp. 135-43.)

When the picture of Ishtar-Inanna is viewed as a composite whole, it becomes apparent that John is drawing upon the ancient pagan Ishtar-Inanna cult to describe the great harlot system of the end times: she will enter into fornicatious relationships with the kings of earth and will ultimately be the occasion of their destruction.

[12]The last phrase in Revelation 18:13 is *σωμάτων καὶ ψυχὰς ἀνθρώπων* (bodies and souls of men, author's translation). There is evidence from Polybius in the second century B.C. that *σῶμα* (body) was sometimes used in the sense of "slave."

captains, the crews of the ships, and other businessmen whose enterprise is subsidiary in some way to the transport of these goods. Also, there is the related pleasure transportation industry (18:17).[13] Of lesser importance, but a part of the system described, will be the cultural community (18:22), the industrial complex (18:22 *b-c*), and the day-to-day functions of the home (18:23 *a-b*).

The climax of the description comes in Revelation 18:23*c,* where the interlocking relationship between temple and marketplace is seen. The reason the merchants of Babylon were viewed as the great men of the earth is that all the nations were deceived by their sorcery. This will be no mere state church but a true ecumenical (worldwide) religion with socio-politico-economic ramifications.

2. *The kingdom of the beast.*

a. While Gentile world power in the end times will initially find its manifestation in a form John describes as Babylon, the great harlot, its culmination will be in the beast and his kingdom. The genesis of this kingdom is more emergent than irruptive, although the transfer of power from the harlot to the beast is certainly violent (Rev. 17:16). The beast himself[14] is introduced by John as being under the control of the harlot (Rev. 17:3, 7). The harlot's authority seems to be official but not absolute, and the subkingdoms over which she exercises hegemony are pictured as being in a constant state of flux (Rev. 17:9-13). The beast, one of a line of kings, comes to the fore under the domination of Babylon and at the same time has lesser kings and their kingdoms under his dominion (cf. Rev. 13:1; 17:3, 9-10).

Protobeast is said to emerge from the sea, in contrast to deuterobeast, who comes up out of the earth (Rev. 13:1, 11). There may be intended some suggestion of association between protobeast's coming and the "many waters" upon which the harlot sits in control and which are

[13]The phrase πᾶς ὁ ἐπὶ τόπον πλέων is somewhat ambiguous. It means "everyone who sails upon the sea" (author's translation). The RSV has the translation "seafaring men," while the NASB gives "every passenger." The latter translation seems more likely since the former is comprehended in one or both of the next two categories (sailors and those who make their living by the sea).

[14]John refers to two beings called beasts (Rev. 13:1, 11), which he himself distinguishes as protobeast (θηρίον α) and deuterobeast (θηρίον β), or the false prophet. See Revelation 13:12 and 16:13.

identified with the general populace of earth. Perhaps John is saying that he will have a rather nonspectacular grassroots beginning from among the common people, although this is certainly obscure and cannot be pressed.[15] This coming corresponds with the statements regarding his original being as perceived by those who saw him (Rev. 17:8, 11—"was"). He is then said to experience something that can be described as being "slain" and as a "fatal wound" (Rev. 13:3). At this point it seems as though it is more a system or coalition of kingdoms that is in view than an individual.[16] For a short period, at least, this slaying effectively removes the beast and his influence from the scene of power politics and it is said that he "is not" (Rev. 17:8, 11). Following this apparent demise he is pictured as having a miraculous healing (Rev. 13:3, 12), which is described as a coming to life (13:14). This return to life is "out of the abyss" (Rev. 11:7; 17:8)[17] and seems to be a sort of quasi resurrection. The ὡς [as if] in Revelation 13:3 suggests an "apparent" death; so this may well be an "apparent" return to life. Finally, he has a parousia[18] that will lead to the wonder and worship of the earth-dwellers (Rev. 13:3-4; 17:8). It is very obvious that this brief history of the beast's ascendency to power has remarkable paral-

[15]If there is any validity to the above suggestion, the coming of deuterobeast from the earth (ἐκ τῆς γῆς) may be intended to be linked with the earth-dwellers (οἱ κατοικοῦντες ἐπὶ τῆς γῆς), with whom are his major responsibilities (Rev. 13:8, 14-17).

[16]The head that is slain is one of seven kings. Revelation 13:3 thus may be a reference to the temporary destruction of some vital part of the beast's power structure.

[17]The term ἄβυσσος (abyss) is variously used in the New Testament for the place of the dead (Rom. 10:7) and for the abode of demonic spirits (Luke 8:31; Rev. 9:1-11), where Satan will be confined during the millennial Kingdom (Rev. 20:1-3). "The abyss" of Revelation 11:7 and 17:8 seems to be the place of the dead.

[18]In Revelation 17:8 John uses the verb form παρέσται (is to come), and Paul uses the related term παρουσία (coming) in 2 Thessalonians 2:9. It is most striking that this second coming of the man of lawlessness (protobeast) is said to be energized by Satan ("with all power and signs and false wonders" [ἐν πάσῃ δυνάμει καὶ σημείοις καὶ τέρασιν ψεύδους] [2 Thess. 2:9]). The same three Greek words for miracles are also used of our Lord's ministry (Acts 2:22; Heb. 2:4), but the works of 2 Thessalonians 2:9 are described as being ψεύδους (false). Ψεύδους is probably not to be understood as indicating a denial of the miraculous character of the works; rather, it describes the character of the works, which is counterfeit. By way of contrast, see Acts 2:22, which says that Jesus' miracles were works "which God performed through Him."

lels to the birth, death, resurrection, and second coming of Jesus Christ. It is even followed through by the establishing of a kingdom (Rev. 17:12-13) and an attempt to put down righteousness (17:14), although this will be abortive, since the pseudo-king will be conquered by the King of kings.[19]

The whole process described above, as well as all that will be given below, is traced to the dragon (Satan [Rev. 12:9]), who gives the beast "his power and his throne and great authority" (Rev. 13:2).

b. The description John gives of protobeast is one of the most significant aspects of this whole segment of the book. Instead of the romanticized concept held by the earth-dwellers, who are awestruck by his wonder-working, we have God's sober assessment through the seer. Protobeast is portrayed as a grotesque and wild beast[20] whose voracious appetite is not satisfied until everything in God's creation has been prostituted to satanic ends.

He is first described as having seven heads, which are the political lineage whence he comes (Rev. 13:1; 17:3, 9-10), and ten horns, each crowned with a diadem, which are ten petty rulers who yield their allegiance to him (13:1; 17:12-13). On the beast's heads there are blasphemous names, and a collation of the data given throughout the Apocalypse on the rulers of the earth during this period will show the aptness of this description (see, e.g., Rev. 6:15-17; 17:2; 18:3; 19:19).

All this description up to this point strongly suggests that the beast is not only a man but also a personified political force that eventually becomes a world government. It is a common thing to describe a government in terms of its leader or to see a government as the embodiment of an individual. The remaining data of Revelation 13—for example, the functioning of deuterobeast "in the presence of the beast" and the erection of his image (v. 14), as well as the personal nature of his judgment (Rev. 19:20; 20:10)—show, however, that the beast concept is not adequately explained on a governmental level alone.[21]

[19]In light of all these *similarities* to the life and ministry of Jesus Christ, which are too many to be coincidental, there seems to be little question that one of the ways that protobeast (Antichrist) opposes Christ is through *counterfeiting.*

[20]In Revelation 13:2 protobeast is actually described as a composite of three ferocious wild animals (cf. Dan. 7:1-8).

[21]Paul's description and title "man of lawlessness" indicate the same thing (2 Thess. 2:3-10).

c. Up until this point, the beast has been under at least nominal control of the harlot, but at about the middle of the Tribulation he, together with the ten kings who have submitted their power and authority to him, will turn on her and begin to ravage her (Rev. 17:16).[22] As was so often true in the Old Testament, so in this case: God's purposes in the affairs of men will be served by the godless (Rev. 17:17; cf. Psalm 76:10).

Having thus removed the one last obstacle to his absolute control of the kingdoms of earth, the beast will establish the first truly worldwide dictatorship. It is said that "*the whole earth*" will be amazed at him (Rev. 13:3); that *all* the earth-dwellers will worship him and the dragon (vv. 4, 8); that authority will be given him over *every* tribe, people, tongue, and nation (v. 7); and that *all* must have his permission to buy and sell (vv. 16-17).[23]

d. The reign of the beast will involve both political and religious domination. Since the harlot had earlier imposed a state religion on her subjects, the way was paved to extend this state religion to the whole world. Satan's desire to be "like the Most High" (Isa. 14:14) leaves no

[22]The forty-two months referred to in Revelation 13:5, during which the beast will exercise authority, must refer to the last three and one-half years of the Tribulation, since early in the Tribulation the harlot will master the beast (Rev. 17:3). Revelation 17:16 is probably to be understood as a capsulized statement of what may take a period of time to accomplish. The *divine* consummation of Babylon's judgment is finally realized near the end of the Tribulation (Rev. 16:19).

[23]This worldwide control will be unstable and short-lived. (See Dan. 11:36-45, which probably describes the beast and his period of ascendancy. Daniel indicates that during this time, which John tells us is only forty-two months in length [Rev. 13:5], this ruler will rise to the greatest heights and then descend to the lowest depths.) The instability and short life of the beast's worldwide control may be because of the brutal and oppressive nature of his rule. It should be noted that Revelation 16:12-16 and 19:19 give a somewhat different picture. In those passages the double strands of divine providence and human willfulness are intertwined. The armies of earth are said to be gathered at the bidding of Satan, the beast, and the false prophet (Rev. 16:13-14, 16); yet behind the scenes God's purposes in judgment are being accomplished in His own way and time (Rev. 19:17-21). Apparently, the armies of earth are bound in some way to serve the beast, who issues a call, at Satan's bidding, for them to assemble in Israel. They see this gathering as an occasion to throw off the oppressive hand of the beast and turn on him instead of as a time to come submissively and unitedly to his call. When it is apparent that an even greater enemy, the Lord Jesus Christ Himself, is coming on the scene with the armies of heaven, the armies of earth unite once again with the beast against their common foe.

room for other rulers or religious systems, even when they are basically evil themselves (see 2 Thess. 2:4). Consequently, the beast will overthrow even the fiendish Babylonian system so as to bring to the fore Satan's master plan for a religio-political world government. This will be effected on behalf of protobeast by deuterobeast.

This individual is also called a wild beast (the actual designation in Rev. 13:11 is ἄλλο θηρίον [another beast], hence the designation θηρίον β; while in Rev. 13:12 the leading figure in this government is called τοῦ πρώτου θηρίου [the first beast], hence the designation θηρίον α), since he, too, evidences the brutelike qualities of a possessed person. As such, he apparently gives the outward impression of harmless gentleness (he has "horns like a lamb" [Rev. 13:11]) but speaks with satanic authority ("he spoke as a dragon" [Rev. 13:11]). Deuterobeast's other title is "false prophet" (Rev. 16:13; 19:20; cf. Matt. 24:24), which further indicates his relationship to protobeast as well as gives an indication of the nature (ψευδο [false]) of his ministry.

He is a sort of prime minister to protobeast, for just as θηρίον α governs on the basis of authority granted by Satan (Rev. 13:2, 4), so θηρίον β functions by authority delegated to him by θηρίον α (13:12). His duties lie in two realms: the religious and the economic. It is in the first of these realms that he functions as a prophet, since his duty is to convince the earth-dwellers to worship the beast, and Satan in turn (Rev. 13:12, 3, 8). The credibility of his prophetic ministry is enhanced by the performance of great signs (13:13; 19:20; cf. Matt. 24:24), which lead to the deception of the earth-dwellers until they erect an image of protobeast (Rev. 13:14; cf. Dan. 9:27; 11:31; 12:11; Matt. 24:15; see also 1 Macc. 1:54; 6:7). His control of the people is strengthened by yet another miracle when he is enabled (whether by Satan or by protobeast is not clear, since the agent of ἐδόθη [there was given] in Rev. 13:15 is not specified) to give a semblance of life (πνεῦμα [breath]) to the image. The purpose of this miracle seemingly is to make of the image a sophisticated communications and surveillance system (Rev. 13:15).[24]

In addition to his religious role, deuterobeast also serves as minister of finance and trade. He administers a system of government control

[24]Modern examples of such a system may be seen in various propaganda and thought-control programs and in the secret police organizations of totalitarian states.

of buying and selling that touches every social stratum (Rev. 13:16)[25] and requires a sort of pledge of allegiance to protobeast. This emblem of submission is called a χάραγμα[26] and refers to a stamp, impression, or mark, perhaps something like a tatoo, since it will be placed on the right hand or forehead.[27] The mark will consist of protobeast's name, which is nowhere given, or the number of his name, which is 666 (Rev. 13:17-18).[28]

[25]At the time, this system of government control will seem perfectly logical, for food will be in short supply because of famine conditions and a lack of potable water as a result of the various judgments of God (see, e.g., Rev. 6:5-6; 8:6-11).

[26]All the New Testament occurrences of this term except one are in the Apocalypse (Acts 17:29; Rev. 13:16-17; 14:9, 11; 16:2; 19:20; 20:4). Moreover, every time χάραγμα is used in the Apocalypse it refers to the mark of the beast. Χάραγμα is derived from χαράσσω which means "to engrave." In Acts 17:29 χάραγμα refers to a graven image intended to be a representation of τὸ θεῖον (the Divine Nature). Josephus uses χάραγμα of God. It may be that there is some intended acknowledgment of the beast as divine by persons marked with a χάραγμα.

[27]William Barclay writes that this mark of the beast "could come from more than one ancient custom.

"(i) Sometimes domestic slaves were branded with the mark of their owner. . . . If the mark is connected with this, it means that those who worship the beast are the slaves, the property, of the beast.

"(ii) Sometimes soldiers branded themselves with the name of their general, if they were very devoted to him. . . . If the mark is connected with this, it means that those who worship the beast are the devoted followers of the beast.

"(iii) On every contract of buying or selling there was attached a *charagma,* a seal, and on the seal there was the name of the emperor and the date. . . . If the mark is connected with this, it will mean that those who worship the beast accept the law and the authority of the beast.

"(iv) All coinage had the head and the inscription of the emperor stamped upon it, to show that it was the property of the emperor. If the mark is connected with this, it will again mean that those who bear it are the property of the beast.

"(v) . . . When a man had burned his pinch of incense and had offered his worship to Caesar, . . . he was given a certificate to say that he had done so. That certificate preserved him from death by persecution and it gave him the right to trade and to buy and to sell. The mark of the beast may be the certificate of worship, which a Christian could only obtain at the cost of denying his faith and being false to his Lord" (William Barclay, *The Revelation of John,* 2:129-30).

[28]As a result of the exhortation in Revelation 13:18 to calculate, or figure out, the significance of the number of the beast, many fanciful and unfortunate attempts have been made to identify some historical personage by use of numerology. These identifications have ranged from Nero to Dr. Henry Kissinger. It is quite apparent that everyone who has played the risky game of numbers to date has not had the "understanding" to which John refers. The most sensible suggestion seems to be that built around the concept of six as the number of man (in light of man's creation on the sixth day). Thus

In addition to the furtherance of his authority and the exalting of his name given by deuterobeast, protobeast will engage directly in two other kinds of activity. He will enthrall the peoples of the earth with grand[29] and

---

666 would be man par excellence, which is perhaps the beast's own warped self-assessment. He is "The Man" so sublime as to be worthy of the worship of other men, lesser men. This suggestion comes nearest to coping with the one clue John gave as to the significance of the number—namely, that it is ἀριθμὸς ἀνθρώπου (man's number). The problem with this view is that it would require his name to be ἄνθρωπος (man) or ὁ ἄνθρωπος (the man), which total 1310 and 1380 respectively (on the basis of simple addition of the Greek numerical equivalents of each letter). (See also A. Deissmann, *Light from the Ancient East: The New Testament Illustrated by Recently Discovered Texts of the Graeco-Roman World,* pp. 276-78.)

The deification of man, a distortion of the biblical teaching of man's being made in the image of God (Gen. 1:26-31; 5:1-2), is ever *the* great sin of mankind. Paul refers to it as "the lie" (τῷ ψεύδει, author's translation) and defines it as the act of worshiping and serving the creature rather than the Creator (Rom. 1:25). In 2 Thessalonians 2:11 he further states that having rejected "the truth" that saves (2 Thess. 2:10), the people of the end times will believe "the lie" (τῷ ψεύδει, author's translation) of the man of lawlessness. They will embrace the satanic world scheme to replace the Creator with the creature and will accept Satan's world order in place of the plan of God. (There are in the Old Testament at least two remarkable precursors of the final man of lawlessness. One is the king of Assyria [Isa. 10:12-14], whom Professor Zvi Adar of the Hebrew University characterizes as the incarnation of the spirit of paganism. The king of Assyria's sin, which involved great power, which in turn bred pride and a false sense of wisdom, originated because he failed to perceive the proper place of man in God's world. The other noteworthy precursor of the final man of lawlessness is Antiochus Epiphanes, who is described prophetically in Daniel 8:21-25 and 11:36-39. His sin had the same ingredients and stemmed from the same roots.)

Leon Morris suggests a variation on the idea suggested in the first paragraph of this footnote: "We should understand the expression ["man's number"] purely in terms of the symbolism of numbers. If we take the sum of the values represented by the letters of the name *Iēsous,* the Greek name 'Jesus,' it comes to 888. Each digit is one more than seven, the perfect number. But 666 yields the opposite phenomenon, for each digit falls short. The number may be meant to indicate not an individual, but a persistent falling short. All the more is this likely to be correct if we translate 'it is the number of man' rather than 'a man.' John will then be saying that unregenerate man is persistently evil" (Leon Morris, *The Revelation of St. John: An Introduction and Commentary,* p. 174).

[29]The NASB gives "arrogant" and the RSV "haughty" as translations for μεγάλα. While those words may reveal the intended sense, it seems that the idea they express is comprehended in βλασφημίας (blasphemies). Perhaps "majestic" more nearly conveys the idea of μεγάλα, suggesting the hypnotic effect that protobeast's words will have on his listeners. (This effect is most graphically illustrated by Hitler's ability to entrance the German masses in the 1930s.)

blasphemous words, swaying them to worship himself, forsake the God of reality, and turn on God's people (Rev. 13:5-7; Dan. 7:8, 20, 23). These blasphemies will be directed toward God and all the glorified saints (Rev. 13:6), and as a consequence will involve a discrediting of all they taught and stood for as set forth in Scripture. Rather than intense persecution or isolated acts of martyrdom, he will engage in a premeditated plan of mass extermination of all living saints (Rev. 13:7) that will parallel Satan's genocidal attempt to destroy Israel (Rev. 12:13-17).

Thus Satan's all-consuming passion (see Matt. 4:8-9; Luke 4:5-7) will seemingly have been realized. His messiah will have risen to the apex of power by means of a fascination[30] induced by satanically enabled wonder-working; by spellbinding oratory; by revival of the cult of emperor worship; and by the invoking of economic sanctions. Here, finally, will be the realization of man's long-sought-for utopia,[31] but it will turn out to be a satanic nightmare.

[30]The word "fascination" is used here in its original sense of "enchantment by strange power or terror," as the power of fascination a snake has over a bird. Otto's comments are illuminating when, in speaking of fascination in a religious sense, he says that the thing that fascinates is "something that allures with a potent charm, and the creature, who trembles before it, utterly cowed and cast down, has always at the same time the impulse to turn to it, nay even to make it somehow his own." Continuing his discussion of the *mysterium tremendum,* of which he believes fascination is a part, he notes that the person who experiences the mystery "feels a something that captivates and transports him with a strange ravishment, rising often enough to the pitch of dizzy intoxication; it is the Dionysiac-element in the numen" (R. Otto, *The Idea of the Holy: An Inquiry into the Non-rational Factor in the Idea of the Divine and Its Relation to the Rational,* p. 31). It is quite clear that he uses "fascination" in a positive sense as he develops his thought (his term is "beatific" [pp. 35-36]). While there is no question that religion in general, and even certain manifestations of religious experience loosely identified as Christian, do evidence this phenomenon, it is alien to biblical Christianity and Judaism. Rather than a positive thing, it appears to me to be indicative of the demonic element in all false religions.

[31]*Utopia* is from the Greek word ἀτοπία, which means "no place." Hence it was applied to certain idealistic and visionary schemes for a perfect society that in reality exists "no place." While ἀτοπία does not occur in the New Testament, ἄτοπος, a related word meaning "out of place," does. In Acts 28:6 ἄτοπος refers to the expected result of the bite of a venomous snake and means "strange," "unusual," or "untoward"; and in Luke 23:41, Acts 25:5, and 2 Thessalonians 3:2 it means "wrong," "improper," or "unrighteous," indicating something that is morally amiss. In both usages something noxious is in view; so the kingdom of the beast is more an ἄτοπος than an ἀτοπία.

B. The Nations and the Return of Christ.

The primary truth emphasized in the relationship between Christ's return and the nations is that of judgment. By His coming they are overthrown and ushered into judgment (see below). These two items are stated in Revelation 19:11, which summarizes the description of the second coming of Jesus Christ to the earth as it is described in the verses following verse 11. He will judge all men and make war with the nations in righteousness (cf. Rev. 19:17-21).[32] It is most revealing to notice that in Revelation 17:14, where the vantage point is that of the beast and his ten-kingdom coalition, it is said that *they* wage war with the Lamb.[33] As sovereign Judge-King He fights them. As the suffering sacrifice for sin who has conquered death (i.e., as the Lamb), He is fought by them. The outcome of the battle is summarized in five words: "the Lamb will overcome them" (Rev. 17:14). While He will be accompanied by (μετὰ, [with]) the armies of heaven (Rev. 17:14; 19:14),[34] the reason (ὅτι [because]) given for their overthrow is that He is King of kings and Lord of lords. This Lamb whom they attack has the right to the throne of the world, not by default, as intended by Satan (Matt. 4:8-9; Luke 4:5-7), but by virtue of the fact that He is the Son of God, who alone has the right of eternal dominion (1 Tim. 6:13-16) and who became incarnate in the royal line of David (Luke 1:31-32; 2:4-5, 11) to atone for sin (Phil. 2:8-11) and render Satan powerless (Heb. 2:5-15).

Those who accompany the Lamb and share in His victory are designated as the "called and chosen and faithful" (Rev. 17:14). These three adjectives give a general description of the saints,[35] denoting them as

[32]There has been much discussion in recent years about the concept of a "just war" and even about the possibility of a "just war." Here, finally and without any question, will be a just war.

[33]It should be noted that in contrast to the believer, who is to pray for the coming of God's Kingdom (Matt. 6:10; Luke 11:2) and love Christ's appearing (2 Tim. 4:8), the nations are enraged at His coming (Rev. 11:18).

[34]Revelation 19:19 suggests that Christ's army will be involved in some active way in the battle, for the beast and his followers make war against the Lord *and* His army.

[35]It is clear from the word order and from the context that this is a nontheological statement. If a theological sense were intended, the order would have been "chosen, called, and faithful" (cf. Rom. 8:29-30). An example of the kind of literary form we have here is, "You are my true love first, last, and always"; logic would invert the second and third items. But it is not a philosophy of faithfulness that is being presented

addressees and recipients of God's good news (cf. 1 Cor. 1:23-24), as personally dear to God (Col. 3:12; 1 Pet. 1:1-2, by the association of election and foreknowledge[36]), and as reliable stewards of His grace (cf. 1 Cor. 4:1-2).

C. The Judgment of the Nations.

Other than the material to be considered below, the main passage dealing with the judgment of the nations is found in Matthew 25:31-46. There the focus of the judgment is upon individuals and has both positive (reward) as well as negative (punishment) aspects. The determinative factor will be a person's treatment of the Jewish people (Jesus is speaking and refers to "these brothers of Mine" [Matt. 25:40]) during

---

in Revelation 17:14. Rather, the emphasis is upon a kind of person, a quality of character.

[36]The concept of God's "knowing" people in the Old Testament and "foreknowing" them in the New conveys the idea of His setting special love upon them. The word *foreknowledge* has two basic usages in the New Testament. "In Acts 26:5 and 2 Peter 3:17, when used of men the verbal form means 'to know beforehand.' The substantival form is only used in one other passage, Acts 2:23, where it clearly involves prior choice. The one article *tēi* links both counsel and foreknowledge together in one thought and both are modified by *horismenēi,* 'determined' or 'fixed.' Peter's use of the verb form in 1:20 readily shows that he has more than mere prescience in view. Further, an examination of passages such as Romans 8:29; 11:2 makes it clear that God is not described as knowing what men will do but of knowing men. This emphasis upon the *whom* rather than the what *points to the fact that the thing which differentiates these men from others lies in the act of knowing rather than outside in the man.* This use of 'know' is also seen in the simplex form *ginōskō* in the New Testament, as well as in *yadha* in the Old Testament (see Genesis 18:19; Exodus 2:25; Psalm 1:6; 144:3; Jeremiah 1:5; Hosea 13:5; Amos 3:2; Matthew 7:23; 1 Corinthians 8:3; Galatians 4:9; 2 Timothy 2:19; 1 John 3:1). The meaning is thus 'to take special note of' or it is almost 'synonymous with "love," to set regard upon, to know with peculiar interest, delight, affection and action' (see Murray, *Romans,* I, 317). When the prefix *pro* is added, it thus comes to mean 'preceding (previous) special affection' or 'forelove,' 'sovereign distinguishing love' (Murray, p. 318). The standard by which God operates, that which moves Him in His choice of men, is love. (Cf. Paul's statement in Ephesians 1:5, *en agape proorisas.*) The difference between election and foreknowledge, then, is that election places the emphasis upon will, while foreknowledge has affection in mind. (In addition to Murray's excellent discussion [pp. 315–320] of Rom. 8:29, see also Stifler, *The Epistle to the Romans,* pp. 147–149.)" (W. Robert Cook, *Systematic Theology in Outline Form,* 2:6–7).

this time of extreme anti-Semitism, when identification with the Jewish people will jeopardize one's own well-being. On the other hand, in John's writing the focus is upon the two governmental systems of the end-times and is entirely negative.

1. *The judgment on Babylon, the great harlot.* The significance of this judgment may be gauged in part, at least, by the amount of attention John gives it. He dwells upon it in more than two chapters (Rev. 14:8; 16:17-21; 17:1-18; 18:1-24; 19:1-4), a total of fifty-two verses.

a. The judge is identified in Revelation 16:19 as God, and He is pictured as giving the harlot a cup of poisoned wine to drink (cf. Jer. 51:39).

b. His scourging will be through both nature and individuals. He will use the phenomena of nature in the form of earthquake and hailstones (Rev. 16:18-21), and He will use the beast and his followers against the harlot (Rev. 17:16).

c. The extent and thoroughness of the judgment are emphasized again and again in the prophecy. The harlot will be made naked and desolate, and she will be consumed with fire (Rev. 17:16; 18:8-9, 18); she will become the dwelling place of demons, unclean spirits, and other sordid creatures (18:2); she will be repaid for her sins in double measure (18:6); she will be given torment and plagues of pestilence (death), mourning, and famine (18:7-8); and she will be thrown down with violence and "in no wise be found any longer" (18:21, author's translation; cf. Isa. 13:19-22).[37]

d. The response of heaven to the angelic invitation to rejoice at the harlot's overthrow is a fourfold "hallelujah" (Rev. 18:20; 19:1-6). What a sharp contrast to the laments of the earth-dwellers over her fall (18:9-19). They selfishly mourn their losses, while the heavenly multitude extol the salvation, glory, power, truth, and justice of God.

2. *The judgment on the beasts.*

a. In the judgment of the beasts, the judge is again God, but in the

[37]The statement is very emphatic, employing the Greek double negative and ἔτι (any longer).

person of the returning monarch, Jesus Christ (Rev. 19:11). He is pictured as treading the "wine press of the fierce wrath[38] of God, the Almighty" (Rev. 19:15; cf. Psalm 75:8). The designation ὁ παντοκράτωρ (the Almighty) is used of both Father and Son repeatedly in the Apocalypse (1:8; 4:8; 11:17; 15:3; 16:7, 14; 19:6, 15; 21:22). With the exception of Revelation 21:22, where the Lord God, the Almighty, is viewed as the focal point of worship in the New Jerusalem, each use by John relates to God's coming to judge or reign or both. As is its English translation, παντοκράτωρ is a compound word composed of πᾶν (everything) and κρατέω (to take possession of, take hold of, hold fast). Thus we have the word-picture of "Him who has possession of and holds fast everything." It is most fitting that God should be seen in His omnipotence as the judge of the earth and the ruler of all things.[39]

b. The instrument and basis for the returning judge's action is the sharp sword that comes from His mouth. This seems to be a reference to His spoken words and is an idiom common to both the Old Testament (Isa. 11:3-4; Hos. 6:5) and the New Testament (John 12:48; Heb. 4:12) to refer to the judging power of God's word. It is no arbitrary standard by which the beasts will be measured and found lacking; it is the long-settled pronouncements of a changeless and righteous God.

c. The judgment in this case will involve the destruction of the armies of the earth (Rev. 19:17-18, 21). This will include the grisly "great supper of God," at which carnivorous birds will devour the flesh of the men and the animals slain in the battle, leaving nothing but a vast pile of bones as a mute testimony to the sinfulness of sin and the certainty of divine judgment thereon. Finally, the leaders themselves, the beast and false prophet, will be seized and thrown as living

[38]"Fierce wrath" is the translation of τοῦ θυμοῦ τῆς ὀργῆς, which literally reads "the intense wrath of the anger of God." The same expression is used of God's attitude toward Babylon (Rev. 16:19).

[39]The term παντοκράτωρ was also used frequently by the translators of the LXX. A few times it was used to translate the Hebrew term *Yahweh Sabaoth* (*i.e.,* God of hosts [e.g., Amos 3:13; 4:13]), but most frequently it was used to translate the Hebrew term *Shaddai* (*i.e.,* the Almighty [e.g., Job 5:17]). Today there is wide disagreement among scholars as to the proper meaning of the word παντοκράτωρ, but the translators of the LXX understood it to mean "omnipotent." See also earlier discussion on p. 54, footnote 28.

beings[40] into the lake of fire (Rev. 19:20; cf. Matt. 25:41). Thus, with every sense functioning[41] they will experience their punishment in a continuous way. That this experience will not be abated by their annihilation is seen from Revelation 20:10, which portrays a scene that takes place one thousand years later; in that scene they are still being tormented, and it will continue so "day and night forever and ever."

D. The Nations and the Kingdom of God.

Because that aspect of the Kingdom of God called the Millennium is sometimes referred to as the Messianic Kingdom, there is the danger of overlooking the fact that Jesus Christ is not only Israel's Messiah-King but also "KING OF THE NATIONS" (Rev. 15:3; Psalm 22:28). The song of Moses and of the Lamb sung by the glorified saints indicates that a day is coming when the nations will worship the Lord because of His righteous acts, which will have been revealed at that time (Rev. 15:3-4; cf. Psalm 86:9-10; Mal. 1:11).

While the doctrine of the Kingdom of God is progressively developed throughout Scripture, and while the Kingdom may be viewed as being manifested in stages and various forms, it must not be so compartmentalized as to shut off the intended interrelationship between the stages.[42] This interrelationship is seen in Revelation 11:15 as regards the future Messianic Kingdom and its relationship to the final, eternal form of the Kingdom. In this one brief logion of the voices from heaven, two aspects of the Kingdom of God are telescoped into a summary statement. The beginning of the future manifestation of the Kingdom of God in its *Messianic* form is noted by the words "has become" (ἐγένετο, an aorist indicative noting an act), while the words "will reign forever and ever" move us to its future *eternal* form (cf. Exod. 15:18; Dan. 2:44; 7:13-14). Notice that the reign Messiah begins during the Millennium

[40]The word is ζῶντες [living], not ζωός [alive]. Thus the emphasis is upon ongoing life rather than the static fact of being alive. Ζῶντες is in the emphatic position in the clause.

[41]While only two senses are specifically suggested in Revelation 19:20, namely touch (in the burning of the fire) and smell (from the burning sulphur), the fact that the two creatures are living suggests that they will hear the roar of the flames, see the raging inferno, and taste the agony of unquenched thirst.

[42]See pp. 89-90 and 234-41 for further discussion of the doctrine of the Kingdom.

is viewed as continuing into eternity. As John shows in Revelation 20-21, many events will transpire between the end of the thousand years and the coming of the New Jerusalem; but though the form of the Kingdom changes, the reign is seen as continuing on without a lapse.

1. *The Messianic form of the Kingdom of God.* As the heavenly choir of Revelation 11:15 indicates, the time is coming when "the kingdom of the world"[43] will become the Father's and Messiah's Kingdom (cf. Zech. 14:9). The foundation for this event was laid during the first advent, when the ruler of this world was judged (John 12:31; 16:11). From the beginning of the Messianic Kingdom, Messiah "will rule them [τὰ ἔθνη] with a rod of iron" (Rev. 19:15) as "KING OF KINGS, AND LORD OF LORDS" (19:16). This suggests that the nations as now contemplated are believing rather than unbelieving, since at this time all the ungodly among the nations will be slain (Rev. 19:17-18, 21).[44]

2. *The eternal form of the Kingdom of God.* The place of the various nations in God's eternal Kingdom is given in Revelation 7:9-17 and in Revelation 21:24-27. The multitude described in Revelation 7 is composed of Tribulation martyrs (v. 14) from "every nation" of earth (v. 9). They will continually serve God,[45] and He will care for their every need (Rev. 7:15-17).[46]

[43]It is not without significance that "kingdom" is singular here (in contrast, for example, to Matt. 4:8 and Luke 4:5). "The kingdom of the world" may refer to the satanic κόσμος as viewed under his sole authority, to the "one world" of protobeast (note the "every" and "all" of Rev. 13:7-8), or to the coalescing of the two, with the latter being the earthly manifestation of the former.

[44]This is corroborated by Matthew 25:31-46, where a division of the saved and lost among the Gentiles of the future is made. V. 34 shows that the millennial Kingdom is as much the saved Gentiles' as it is Israel's (although in a different way and for a different reason), since it was prepared for them from eternity past. Also, their being designated as "the righteous" in v. 46 and their possession of eternal life show that their entrance to the Kingdom is as believers.

[45]The term used here is λατρεύω, which is consistently used in the New Testament to indicate the idea of worshiping and serving combined. That meaning is reinforced in Revelation 7:15-17, for the service is said to be in God's sanctuary (ναός). In light of the statement in Revelation 21:22 that the Lord God and the Lamb are the sanctuary of the New Jerusalem, it becomes apparent that using λατρεύω is simply another way of saying that all the multitude's service will be a form of worship of God.

[46]The picture is a very tender one, for the gentle Lamb is viewed as a shepherd who not merely provides shelter, but a place of belonging; not only food and drink, but the removal of anxiety related to the struggle to supply life's basic needs; not only everlast-

Further indication of the interaction of the nations and the kings of earth[47] with the New Jerusalem is given in Revelation 21:24-27. They will walk (i.e., carry on the daily affairs of life) by the light of the glory of God and the Lamb. These kings will bring the glory and honor of the nations into the city as tokens of submission and praise to the Lamb on a continual basis. This commerce in things of the Spirit is a stark and refreshing contrast to the crass materialism and sensuality of the merchants of Babylon (see Rev. 18:9-19).

---

ing life, but all the resources needed to sustain it; not only comfort, but the removal of every occasion for sorrow and regret.

[47]In light of the "bad press" continually given to the kings of earth and the earth-dwellers up to this point in the Revelation, it is interesting to note how carefully John explains the difference between these kings and previous kings of the earth. These kings have their names recorded on the Lamb's book of life (the New Jerusalem's roster of citizens), since they are *not* numbered among the unclean, abominable, and lying.

XV

The Future of the Individual

A. The Earth-dwellers.

Among the various groups with which John deals in opening up our understanding of the future, there is one designated as "those who dwell on the earth." At first glance it may seem that this is simply a way of distinguishing these individuals from those who live in heaven, but a more careful examination of the use of the designation will reveal that something else altogether is in view. Those described as earth-dwellers have earth as their abode in a peculiar sense—namely, in the sense that they have affirmed earth as over against heaven as the focal point and ultimate goal of their existence. In contrast to the believer, whose "citizenship is in heaven," from which he "eagerly wait[s] for a Savior, the Lord Jesus Christ" (Phil. 3:20), these individuals see the earth as encompassing the center and circumference of their life.

As such, these people have an hour of testing designed for them (Rev. 3:10) that is without parallel in the history of the world.[1] They will be busy attempting to destroy the people of God, because all that the saints stand for is a contradiction of the way of life of the earth-dwellers (Rev. 6:10). During this period they will endure the three woes, or the fifth through the seventh trumpet judgments, which will include torment by demonic hordes, the destruction of one-third of the world's population, and the announcement of the coming of the Kingdom of Christ, which will be preceded by the outpouring of the plagues from the seven bowls of God's wrath (Rev. 8:13; cf. 9:1-21; 11:14-19; 15:1, 5-8; 16:1—18:24).

[1]See pp. 171-72.

The earth-dwellers will also be tormented by God's two especially commissioned witnesses during the first half of the Tribulation (Rev. 11:10). The very fact that the ministry of these two men is viewed by the earth-dwellers as torment when they are in actuality described as "witnesses" who "prophesy" (Rev. 11:3) shows how thoroughly the earth-dwellers are sold out to sin. The most revealing statement of all made about them is found in Revelation 17:8 (cf. 13:8).[2] There it is seen that they are not numbered among the redeemed, since their name is not written in the book of life; and, in fact, they were never included in God's elective purposes from the beginning. As difficult as the theology may seem to be, this is apparently an example of "vessels of wrath prepared for destruction"—vessels God has purposed to endure in order that He might show His wrath and make His power known (Rom. 9:22). The earth-dwellers are those who remain "dead in . . . trespasses and sins," who continually walk "according to the course of this world, according to the prince of the power of the air, of the spirit that is now working in the sons of disobedience," and who are "by nature children of wrath" (Eph. 2:1-3).[3]

1. *The satanic world kingdom.* In chapter 14 the world powers of the end-times were discussed as systems. At this point a brief consideration of the individuals enmeshed in those systems is in order.

a. The precursor of Satan's final kingdom effort is Babylon, the great harlot. John records that the earth-dwellers will be intoxicated with the wine of her immorality (Rev. 18:3). The picture given in the extended description that follows in Revelation 18 seems to be more of a people whose senses have been conditioned to approve the evil and reject the good than of a group whose senses have been dulled with drink. People from all walks of life and every stratum of society will be involved, from the most innocent and ordinary to the most sophis-

[2]In light of the plural ὧν (whose), the phrase "those . . . whose name has not been written" (Rev. 17:8) clearly refers to the earth-dwellers. In 13:8 it seems that the antecedent of οὗ (whose) is αὐτόν, that is, the beast, rather than the earth-dwellers, although most translations make the earth-dwellers the antecedent. Many manuscripts do read ὧν rather than οὗ, and some (e.g., p47) read τὰ ὀνόματα (names) as well.

[3]It is interesting to note that the phrase "those who dwell on the earth" is not used again after the description of judgment given in Revelation 17-18, perhaps because none of them will be left in the earth following Christ's return.

ticated and powerful (Rev. 18:9, 11, 15, 17, 22-25).

During this period and related to this system there will be a group of God's people living on the earth (Rev. 18:4). They are viewed as being in danger of participating in Babylon's sin and being contaminated by her evil; so they are urged to come out of her (cf. Isa. 52:11; Jer. 51:6, 9, 45; 2 Cor. 6:17).

b. The earth-dwellers who originally pledged allegiance to the harlot will turn to follow the beast when he overthrows her empire. At that time they will manifest their perverted, inhuman sense of values in another way by not allowing the bodies of the two slain witnesses to be buried. Rather, the bodies will be left in full view of the populace and will become the occasion for the earth-dwellers' making extensive celebration over the two witnesses' deaths (Rev. 11:7-10).

Furthermore, the earth-dwellers will wonder at and worship the beast, making him their god as well as their king (Rev. 13:3-4, 8, 12; 17:8).[4] One outward evidence of this obeisance will be their erection of an image of the beast at the instigation of the false prophet (Rev. 13:14), and the other will be the receiving of his mark, which will enable them to buy and sell (Rev. 13:16-17). Both of these acts are designed to bring the earth-dwellers into greater dependence upon the beast, for on the one hand they are shut up to him for the meeting of man's basic spiritual need (Rev. 13:15), the need to worship, and on the other hand they are shut up to him for the meeting of man's basic material need (Rev. 13:17), the need for food and clothing. Because of this unquestioning acceptance of the beast as god and king, the earth-dwellers will experience God's wrath both immediately (Rev. 16:10-11) and eternally (Rev. 14:9-10). The temporal experience of wrath will be so intense that they will chew their tongues from the pain and instead of repenting will blaspheme God all the more (Rev. 16:10-11; cf. 6:15-17; 9:20-21; 10: 8-9).[5]

[4]Revelation 14:9-12 shows that only unbelievers will engage in this practice and that believers cannot engage in it.

[5]Here is another good example of the Bible's rejection of any evolutionary philosophy. At the least, this picture shows no improvement of the human race over mankind immediately following the Fall. More accurately, this picture shows man to be worse: it parallels the situation in Noah's day, when God exterminated all but Noah's family.

As is true in the record of the harlot's rule, so here as well there is indication of the presence of believers during this time (Rev. 13:9-10). They are reminded that although the outward circumstances are more extreme than at any other time in human history, God's plan will be certainly accomplished. Things are not out of control. This knowledge provides a basis for steadfastness and a source of strength for faith. They will have nothing else to hold to; so they must trust in Him, even if captivity and martyrdom are the immediate consequence. Revelation 14:12 shows that this is not merely stiff-upper-lip stoicism or blind faith in a nameless, faceless Providence, but that their perseverance and faith are grounded in God's Word and in the person of Jesus. Even masterful self-control and noble purpose will eventually be frustrated if they are not focused on the proper objects.

2. *Physical death.* The key verse for any consideration of physical death in John's thinking is Revelation 1:18. Jesus Christ is said to be the living one who became dead, under normal circumstances nothing particularly worthy of note but in this case a seeming anomaly. As Peter points out, He is the very "Author" (ἀρχηγὸν) of life (Acts 3:15, marg.);[6] and as John has indicated, He is "living" water (as well as the "water of life") and "living bread" (as well as the "bread of life") (John 4:10-14; 7:37-38; Rev. 22:17; John 6:35, 48, 51). How can the one who is the essence of life submit to death? This is a part of the mystery of the gospel. But the statement continues to point out that although He genuinely experienced death He is alive again and forevermore. Thus while the anomaly is resolved the mystery remains. The impossible has taken place, and the one who accomplished it is now master of death and hades, removing their threat from the believer (Rev. 1:17-18) and assuring their claim on the unbeliever (cf. Rev. 6:8, where it is said that "authority was given" to death and hades, with the unnamed agent of the passive verb unquestionably being the Lamb [6:1]).

In the Apocalypse, information regarding the death of the earth-dwellers centers on John's description of the seal, trumpet, and bowl

[6]Notice that Peter develops the same tension in Acts 3:15 as John does here. The author of life is put to death and God raises Him back to life. Thus the tension is broken and the apparent contradiction resolved.

judgments and the coming again of Christ to the earth. (The final disposition of the dead will be dealt with on pp. 225-26.)

To begin with, death and hades are given authority to slay one-fourth of earth's population by various means (Rev. 6:8). Those who are not killed will seek death rather than life lived under God's scrutiny,[7] and they will seek death rather than the most frightening wrath of all: "the wrath of the Lamb" (Rev. 6:16). That which would bring to wrath the long-suffering Savior (1 Pet. 2:22-23), who forgave his executioners as He was dying (Luke 23:34), must be something very extreme. Later, as the trumpet judgments begin to unfold, many will die from the poisoned water supply (Rev. 8:11); others will seek death as a way of release from torment and it will elude them (Rev. 9:6); one-third of the remaining population of earth will die (Rev. 9: 15, 18); and those left alive will willfully continue in their demonism, idolatry, murder, sorcery (or drug traffic), immorality, and theft (Rev. 9:20-21). Finally, at the return of Christ those who have remained alive will either be killed in the last great battle (Rev. 19:21) or be sentenced to eternal torment (Rev. 14:9-11; cf. Matt. 25:41-46).[8] Thus, at its outset the millennial Kingdom will be populated by believers only.

3. *Resurrection.* In John 5:28-29 the apostle sets forth the basic truth regarding the doctrine of resurrection. He speaks of the time of resurrection as an hour, but he does not pinpoint an exact time. As in verse 25, which speaks of the spiritually dead coming to life rather than the physically dead, so here he uses the expression "an hour is coming." The difference is that in verse 25 he adds "and now is," showing that the "hour" is a general period of time.[9] During this period of time all will hear the Son of Man's call to life or judgment. The discriminating factor will be good deeds as over against worthless (φαῦλα [evil]) deeds (cf. Dan. 12:2; Acts 24:15), which factor John indicates elsewhere is an external indicator of a man's either having

[7]The day will come when this insane desire for separation from God will be granted. See 2 Thessalonians 1:9-10.

[8]The relationship between death and judgment will be developed below, pp. 220-26.

[9]The fact that the time of resurrection is usually identified with the end times has led some persons to the erroneous conclusion that all men will be resurrected at one time. Other portions of Scripture, as well as Revelation 20:4-6, show that although all men will be resurrected, various groups will be raised separately.

been declared righteous by God or being of the devil (1 John 3:7-8).[10]

Further distinction between these two aspects of resurrection is given in Revelation 20:4-6, where it is seen that a period of one thousand years separates the two. The "rest of the dead" (Rev. 20:5), that is, those not involved in the first resurrection, will be raised after the Millennium and just prior to the Great White Throne Judgment (Rev. 20:12-13). At that time the sea, the death, and the hades will give up the dead who are in them.[11] The sea is viewed here as a vast watery grave and death as the dread fourth horseman (Rev. 6:8), who is attended by hades, the interim abode of the departed spirits of the wicked.[12] Thus the resurrection of "the wicked" (Acts 24:15) will be completed and the stage set for their final judgment.

4. *Judgment.* In his writings, John deals both with what might be called intermediate judgment and with what might be called final judgment.

a. The first category may be designated as Tribulation judgment and is generally called the great day of the wrath of God and the Lamb (Rev. 6:17). A description of this phase of judgment is given in broad strokes in Revelation 14:15-20 through the use of the figure of reaping and treading the grapes of earth in the wine press of God's wrath (cf. Isa. 63:3-6; Joel 3:13).

This aspect of end-time judgment is developed in several unfolding stages, beginning with the opening of the seven-sealed book (Rev. 6:1). Out of that act comes all that follows. The first four seals to be opened, the famed "four horsemen of the Apocalypse," seem to be personifica-

[10]See pp. 135-36 for further discussion of this passage.

[11]While it sounds awkward to English-speaking people to use the definite article with "death" and "hades," it seems that the passage requires the use of "the." "Sea," "death," and "hades," and especially the latter two, are personified here (see v. 14), as they are very clearly in Revelation 6:8. Death and hades are grouped together as a combination concept distinct from the sea even though the repeated use of the definite article in the Greek marks each off as a distinct entity. The sea is one major place of burial, and the land, represented by hades, over which death reigns, is the other.

[12]"Hades" is variously used in the New Testament for a number of closely related concepts. It is seen as the opposite of heaven (Matt. 11:23; Luke 10:15); as the equivalent of Sheol, that is, the grave (Acts 2:27, 31); as the general interim abode of the departed spirits of the Old Testament period (Luke 16:23); and as the particular interim abode of the departed spirits of the wicked (Rev. 1:18; 6:8).

tions of all the judgments that are later announced by the seven trumpets and poured from the seven bowls of wrath. The first horseman is the most difficult to identify and has been variously named. Because of his similarities with the returning king (cf. 19:11), some have labeled him as Jesus Christ.[13] Others, due to the similarities coupled with apparently marked differences, have identified him as Antichrist. A third, and preferable view, sees the horseman as merely representative of a concept—perhaps something like bloodless conquest in which persuasive leadership sways the populace through ideological rather than martial means.[14] This is supported by the arrowless bow and by the white horse, which is the mark of a victorious monarch.[15] That this is a personified concept rather than a specific person is strengthened by the close relationship the first rider has with the other three, who are clearly not individuals. Also, there seems to be an intended progression from ideological conquest that gives a false sense of security to armed conflict to famine, which is often the aftermath of war, to death (cf. 1 Thess. 5:3; Jer. 6:14; 8:11; Ezek. 13:10; Luke 21:34-35). This period of

[13]There are more differences than similarities between the two horsemen, however, making identification of the horseman of Revelation 6:2 with Christ impossible. The only similarity is the white horse. As far as differences are concerned, this rider carries a bow (τόξον), whereas Christ has a sword (ῥομφαία); the rider of Revelation 6:2 wears a crown (στέφανος), whereas Christ wears many diadems (διαδήματα πολλά). It also seems very unlikely that the Lamb (Rev. 6:1) would announce His own coming in this way (R. H. Charles, *A Critical and Exegetical Commentary on the Revelation of St. John,* 1:164).

[14]Charles sees the order of the seal judgments as being based on the "Little Apocalypse" (Matt. 24:6-8 ff.; Mark 13:7-8 ff.; Luke 21:9-11 ff.), and there is no doubt that there is remarkable correspondence between the passages in the synoptics and the material given in Revelation 6. On the basis of these similarities he labels the first horseman as "war" and the second as "international strife," a distinction which is rather elusive (Charles, 1:158 ff.). But Charles misreads the gospel records, which say "And you will be hearing of wars and rumors of wars" (μελλήσετε δὲ ἀκούειν πολέμους καὶ ἀκοὰς πολέμων[Matt. 24:6]), "And when you hear of wars and rumors of wars" (ὅταν δὲ ἀκούσητε πολέμους καὶ ἀκοὰς πολέμων [Mark 13:7]), and "And when you hear of wars and disturbances" (ὅταν δὲ ἀκούσητε πολέμους καὶ ἀκαταστασίας [Luke 21:9]). "Hearing of wars and rumors of wars" is a vastly different thing from wars themselves. A part of the concept portrayed by the first horsemen will be the allaying of fears that arise from such rumors.

[15]That the white horse was commonly used in contemporary literature as a symbol of victory is well documented by Charles (1:162). He cites several sources, including Herodotus, Virgil, and Dio Cassius.

false peace will be short-lived (cf. Dan. 9:27) and will soon give way to the other phenomena that will mark the rest of the period. Each of these items—war, famine, and death—is repeated with increasing intensity in the following judgment series until less than 50 percent of the original population is left alive.[16]

The second horseman, who is undoubtedly war personified, takes from the earth the peace brought by the first horseman (Rev. 6:4). This inaugurates a series of wars of major magnitude, including one war in which a massive army from Mesopotamia kills one-third of the earth's population (Rev. 9:13-19). The wars come to a climax in the proverbial Battle of Armageddon, which is in reality an uprising of the powers of Satan and man in coalition against God (Rev. 16:12-16; 19:17-21).

The man seated on the black horse is a personification of famine. Minimum rations of the basic staples for life are seen to be unreasonably priced,[17] while oil and wine, always more available to the wealthy class because of their great expense, will likewise remain at their high prices.[18] This condition is exacerbated by the first four trumpet judgments, wherein one-third of the earth's vegetation, including food crops, is destroyed (Rev. 8:7); one-third of the sea life, which is a vital food source for much of the world, dies; one-third of the shipping, bringing among other things foodstuffs, is destroyed (Rev. 8:8-9); one-

[16]Revelation 6:8 accounts for one-fourth of the people and 9:18 for another one-third. When those who die from other miscellaneous causes are added, much less than 50 percent of the population is left.

[17]A χοῖνιξ (quart), an amount in fact less than a quart, would provide a bare subsistence diet for a family. It is priced at a δηνάριον (denarius), which was a working man's entire day's wage.

[18]The sense of μὴ ἀδικήσης in Revelation 6:6 seems to be "do not tamper with" the price of oil and wine; that is, leave them at their customarily high prices. Since grain, oil, and wine constitute the basic foodstuffs of a large portion of earth's population even today, it is quite apparent that as famine conditions intensify, the rich will gain an ever increasing monopoly over them. That monopoly will in turn lead to an effective stranglehold on the masses. Thus the stage will be set for the situation described in retrospect in Revelation 18:11-13. The wealthy merchants of earth will cater to the opulent, wantonly luxurious tastes of the rich (almost all the items listed as part of their cargo are luxury items, which only the very wealthy could afford in such times). This will serve to exaggerate the gulf between rich and poor as the rich get richer and the poor poorer. Also, this monopoly will lay the groundwork for the ultimate rationing system later established by the beast as he controls and manipulates *all* buying and selling (Rev. 13:16-17).

third of the fresh-water supply is poisoned, bringing great limitations to both drinking water and irrigation water (Rev. 8:10-11); and celestial light and energy sources are diminished by one-third, shortening the productive period of the day (Rev. 8:12). The famine will reach crisis proportions as a result of the bowl judgments, for everything in the sea will die (Rev. 16:3), all the sources of fresh water will be contaminated (Rev. 16:4-7), men will be scorched with the intense heat of the sun and be without water to slake their thirst (Rev. 16:8-9), and, in sharp contrast to the above, the beast's kingdom will be brought into an oppressive darkness that will cut off the whole process of photosynthesis, thus effectually destroying all food-producing plant life (Rev. 16: 10-11).

Famine and war lead to death, and the fourth horseman is so named (Rev. 6:5). Death sometimes mocks men as well as claims them. This is seen in the trumpet judgments, as men are smitten with a demonic plague that brings torment short of death (Rev. 9:1-11) upon all who are not protected with the seal of God (9:4; cf. Ezek. 9:4; Rev. 7:3), and it is seen in the bowl judgments, as beast worshipers are stricken with loathsome and malignant sores (Rev. 16:2) and pelted with hailstones of such an intensity that they are designated as a plague (Rev. 16:21).

In addition to these judgmental phenomena, there will be two other manifestations of God's wrath. He will send two witnesses among the people during the early months of the Tribulation with a prophetic message of judgment (Rev. 11:5-6). Their ministry will parallel the judgments described above, in broad terms at least; it will include destruction by fire and by drought, contamination of fresh water supplies, and plague (judgments similar to those brought by the red, black, and pale green horsemen, respectively).

Because of the nature of their ministry, the two witnesses will be clothed in the garb of mourning (Rev. 11:3). They are described metaphorically as "the two olive trees and the two lampstands that stand before the Lord of the earth" (Rev. 11:4; cf. Zech. 4:1-14). The figures are enigmatic, but perhaps are intended to convey the image of witness that is anointed by the Lord (Zech. 4:14).[19]

[19]Some commentators have tried to identify these two witnesses with Old Testament prophets such as Moses (see, e.g., Exod. 7:17-20; cf. Rev. 11:6) and Elijah (see, e.g., 1 Kings 17:1; 2 Kings 1:10; cf. Rev. 11:5-6) because of the similar miraculous deeds

When the period of their witness is completed (cf. Rev. 11:3, 7) the two witnesses will be slain by the beast.[20] Even then, however, their ministry will not be ended, for God will raise them from death and they will ascend bodily in the sight of all into heaven. This will cause great fear to fall upon the inhabitants of Jerusalem[21] and will be the occasion of a great earthquake (Rev. 11:11-13). As a result, one-tenth of the city will be destroyed and seven thousand of its inhabitants killed, while the remainder of the population will be terrified[22] and give "glory to the God of heaven." This latter response is most notable since it is the only example John records of a positive response to judgment during the entire Tribulation period. This marks these people as being in some way different from other earth-dwellers.[23]

Earthquakes are the other manifestation of God's wrath referred to above. As a part of both the seal and bowl judgments there will be seismic and celestial disturbances (Rev. 6:12-17; 16:17-21). They will include extraordinary solar, lunar, and astral phenomena, and world-wide topographical changes, including the submerging of islands, the leveling of mountains, and the destruction of cities. Not only will these judgments provide an effective demonstration of God's holiness as He punishes sin in its grossest and most developed forms, but they will also prepare the earth demographically and geographically for the coming Kingdom (Isa. 40:1-5). Jerusalem's warfare will be ended and her iniq-

---

performed. Such identification is very tenuous and is unnecessary in light of the fact that the witnesses are purposely left unnamed by John.

[20]This notable action will probably be one of the factors in the beast's rise to power. He will defy those who up to this point have been both despised (Rev. 11:8-10) and invincible (11:5-6) without any apparent harm to himself. He will thus strengthen the people's confidence in himself (cf. Rev. 13:7).

[21]While the city is not called Jerusalem in the context, the fact that it is identified as the place "where also their Lord was crucified" (Rev. 11:8) leaves no question about the matter. Although Jerusalem is not called "Egypt" elsewhere in Scripture, it is referred to as "Sodom" (Isa. 1:10).

[22]Note that the resurrection of the witnesses causes φόβος μέγας (great fear), whereas the earthquake makes the remainder ἔμφοβοι (terrified).

[23]Perhaps the difference lies in the fact that they are Jews (an inference arising from the fact that they are citizens of Jerusalem) and thus believers in the "God of heaven" (Rev. 11:13). It may be this response that triggers Satan's last major attempt to exterminate the Jewish race (cf. Rev. 12:13-17).

uity pardoned. The valleys will be filled and the mountains leveled. The glory of the Lord will be revealed for all to see.

b. The second category of judgment with which John deals is eternal punishment. Jesus Christ will be the judge on this occasion, for the Father has given all authority to execute judgment to Him, "because He is the Son of Man" (John 5:22, 27). As God's Son (John 5:22) He will surely judge justly, since He possesses all the perfections of deity; and as the Son of Man (John 5:27) He will judge with understanding of the human situation, having been a man among men (cf. Acts 17:31). The message of judgment is strangely enough designated as an "eternal gospel" (Rev. 14:6-7). It will take place between the end of the Millennium and the establishing of the new heaven, the new earth, and the New Jerusalem (Rev. 20:7, 11; 21:1-2), and it will take place at a location where a "great white throne" will be established (Rev. 20:11; cf. Dan. 7:9-10). Those involved will be the dead, without social distinction (Rev. 20:12), who have been characterized by all kinds of sin (Rev. 21:8; 22:15), but more specifically those who have not believed that Jesus is the God of reality (John 8:24; cf. 3:18, 36).

The standard used in this judgment is twofold. First, these people will be judged from the heavenly "books, according to their deeds" (Rev. 20:12-13).[24] God will use man's own standard and still find these people wanting. In addition, they will be judged from the "book of life," and since their names will not be recorded therein they will be condemned. In this case the standard is divine, since this book is the Lamb's; and the absence of a name in this family record will indicate that the individual was never born into His family (Rev. 21:27).

Finally, the nature of the punishment is designated. It will involve torment with fire and brimstone in the sight of the holy angels and the Lamb (Rev. 14:10),[25] and it will never cease (Rev. 14:11).[26] This will be

[24]This standard is often cited in Scripture as a basis for punishment. See, e.g., Psalm 28:4; Proverbs 24:12; Isaiah 59:18; Jeremiah 17:10; Romans 2:4-8; 2 Corinthians 11:15.

[25]This statement should be compared with 2 Thessalonians 1:9, which says that the punishment will be "away from the presence of the Lord." In the one case it is said that the punishment will be under His supervision, while in the other it is seen that the punishment will involve separation from the source of all benevolence.

[26]The everlasting nature of the punishment is emphasized by the double statement "forever and ever" (i.e., with no end) and "day and night" (i.e., without relief).

in "the lake of fire," which is designated "the second death" (Rev. 20:14-15). Believers "die" only once, and their "death" in reality is only a sleep (cf. 1 Thess. 4:14), for they will experience an awakening in the first resurrection. On the other hand, unbelievers will die twice: once when their bodies and souls are separated in physical death and again when their bodies and souls are reunited to be separated from God forever.

B. The Saints.

John uses a number of designations to identify the believers in the end times: "My people," "His bond-servants," "those who fear God," but one of the most frequently and generally used terms is "the saints." It is used to refer to God's people in connection with their prayers and God's answer (Rev. 5:8; 8:3-4; 18:20), in connection with their perseverance and faith (13:10; 14:12), in connection with their martyrdom at the hands of the harlot and the beast (13:7; 16:6; 17:6; 18:24), in connection with their service for God and the consequent reward (11:18; 19:8), and in connection with the final postmillennial rebellion of Satan and his followers as they make one last desperate effort to destroy the people and Kingdom of God and establish Satan's kingdom in its place (Rev. 20:9).

There does seem to be some evidence, albeit limited (and it would therefore be unwise to press it too far), that the term "the saints" is used on occasion to refer to one particular group within the larger body of God's people.[27] In Revelation 11:18 they are distinguished from "the

[27]Such distinctions are not without parallel in other New Testament literature. See Hebrews 12:22-24. On the other hand, it will be noted that in the following material no distinction is made between Old Testament believers and believers of the church age. Contrary to some dispensational teaching that makes a firm distinction between Israel as God's earthly people and the church as God's heavenly people, which distinction is to be maintained throughout eternity, the biblical evidence seems to show a progressive blurring of such distinctions as history moves toward its climax. Beginning with the time of the rapture and resurrection of the saints, these groupings, which during the outworking of God's historical purposes are legitimate to a certain degree, become less and less important. It should be observed that most passages dealing with the rapture and resurrection of the saints in the New Testament relate to individuals rather than to entities such as Israel or the church. Beginning with the Millennium and

prophets" (see also 18:24) and "those who fear Thy name," and in Revelation 17:6 they are distinguished from the "witnesses of Jesus." When the last reference is compared with Revelation 12:17, a hint as to the distinction may be found. In 12:17 it is clear that within Israel there are at this time Messianic (that is, believing) Jews. Perhaps in the few instances in which distinctions among believers are made, "the saints" are non-Jewish believers, while the other groups are Jewish believers.

1. *Physical death.* As with the earth-dwellers, so with the saints the key verse in the matter of physical death is Revelation 1:18 (see pp. 218-19). The glorified Christ has passed through death ahead of His own and transformed its character entirely for them. All that follows must be understood with that in mind.

All the information given by John regarding the death of the saints during the Tribulation involves martyrdom. In Revelation 6:11-13 and 7:13-17 (cf. 11:7) he describes the Tribulation martyrs in heaven. They will be slain because of the Word of God and their testimony of Jesus arising therefrom (Rev. 6:9; 20:4). This scene is apparently prior to their resurrection, because they are not yet embodied (Rev. 6:9). One of their concerns is that their deaths be avenged by God (Rev. 6:10), and they are counseled to wait for the answer to their prayer until the number of martyrs is complete (Rev. 6:11; cf. 14:13), which indicates that even martyrdom is a part of the perfect plan of God. These Tribulation martyrs are clothed with white robes (Rev. 6:11; 7:9, 13; cf. 19:14), suggesting that they have already received their reward for faithful service (Rev. 19:8; see below). The other primary concern of these martyred believers will be to serve God day and night, and as they do they will experience the pastoral care of the Lamb (Rev. 7:15-17; see pp. 213-14).

---

continuing on into the eternal Kingdom of God there is an interpenetration of time and eternity, heaven and earth. During the Millennium, saints with glorified bodies will relate to the people of earth. In the final form of the Kingdom, as set forth in Revelation 21:1 ff., such an interpenetration is clearly set forth (see especially vv. 1-7, 9-10) as the heavenly city comes down out of heaven to, or at least proximate to, earth. Thus it would appear that sharp distinctions between groups of saints in eternity is not biblically warranted and tends to lead to an unnecessary and potentially divisive elitism.

Although those who refuse to worship the beast or receive his mark (Rev. 13:7, 15; 20:4) and those who do not compromise themselves with the harlot (Rev. 17:6; 18:24) will be martyred, it should not be concluded that no believers will be left in the earth. Despite the desperate situation and the seeming impossibility of escape, some will live through those days (see Rev. 12:13-17; cf. Matt. 24:22; 25:31-34; Mark 13:13) and become the nucleus to populate the earth at the outset of the Millennium.

2. *Resurrection.* In contrast to the resurrection of unbelievers, whose resurrection is unto judgment and mere existence, the saints will be raised to "life" (John 5:21, 28-29). The secret to resurrection to life is stated by Jesus in John 11:23-27. It is relationship to Jesus Christ.[28] The saint, even though he dies, will live, for he is identified with Christ, who has conquered death. Thus, there is a sense in which the believer's physical death is different from that of the unbeliever (John 11:25), because the believer's death is only a step from life to life. There is also a sense in which one who has eternal life will "never" (οὐ μή, emphatic negation, and εἰς τὸν αἰῶνα [forever]) experience eternal death (John 11:26), because the powers of death cannot encroach upon the life of God possessed by the believer (cf. John 8:51).

The certainty of the believer's resurrection to life is underscored repeatedly by Jesus in His bread of life discourse (John 6:38-40, 44, 54). God has forged a chain with unbreakable links; it states that all those given by the Father to the Son will be drawn to Him, will believe in Him, will receive eternal life as a consequence, and will be raised by the Son.

While John only deals with the posttribulational phase of the resurrection of the just, he does intimate that it will have more than one phase. The Tribulation martyrs will "come to life," that is, their physi-

[28]Jesus' statement is that He *is* the resurrection and the life, not merely that He *gives* them. It is the one who believes in Him who will "live even if he dies" and who will "never die." "This transcends the Pharisaic view of a remote resurrection at the end time. It means that the moment a man puts his trust in Jesus he begins to experience that life of the age to come which cannot be touched by death" (Leon Morris, *The Gospel According to John: The English Text with Introduction, Exposition, and Notes,* p. 550).

cal life will be restored, just prior to the beginning of the millennial Kingdom (Rev. 20:4)[29] so that they will be in a form in which they can assist Christ with the governmental process during this period. The statement of verse 4 is expanded in verse 6 as John indicates that all who have part in the first resurrection will be priests of God and will reign with Christ. While this is not a direct statement, it does show that others than Tribulation martyrs are involved in the first resurrection. The times of these other phases of this resurrection are not given here.[30] References to pre-Tribulation saints as a kingly priesthood (1 Pet. 2:5, 9; Rev. 1:6; 5:10) strongly reinforce the intimation that others than Tribulation martyrs will be involved in the first resurrection.

3. *Christ's return.* The doctrine of the second coming of Jesus Christ has two facets, although they are more implicit than explicit in Johannine teaching.

a. In John 14:2-3 Jesus' promise to come for believers in this age is seen to follow His present activity of preparing many abiding places, which together make up one place called by Jesus "My Father's house" (cf. Rev. 21:3). The word μοναὶ (dwelling places) puts emphasis upon the permanence of these dwellings,[31] while the plural number shows that individual provision will be made for all the Father's children. It must not be overlooked, however, that they are all together in one place. Thus the picture is of each child having a suite of rooms in the Father's house. All will be with the Father, enjoying His hospitality and sharing

[29]Daniel 12:1-2 shows that Old Testament Jewish saints will also be raised at this time, while Isaiah 26:19 may suggest that Old Testament saints in general will be raised.

[30]In 1 Corinthians 15:23-24 it is seen that the first resurrection has three phases, while a comparison of 1 Thessalonians 4:16 with Revelation 20:4 shows that the second phase is further divisible into two subphases. The first phase is "Christ the first fruits" of all resurrection. The second phase is "those who are Christ's at His coming," the saints of all ages. Since His παρουσία (coming) has two stages (the rapture of the church [1 Thess. 4:15-17] and the coming to earth to establish the Kingdom [Matt. 24:27, 37-39; 2 Thess. 2:8]), there will be two stages to this phase of the first resurrection, one associated with His coming in the air for the church (1 Thess. 4:16-17) and the other associated with His coming with the saints to the earth (Rev. 19:14) to reign (Rev. 20:4). The final phase (τάγμα [order, *or* company] [1 Cor. 15:23]) will be at the close of the Millennium and will be "the end" resurrection when any saints who die during the Messianic Kingdom will be raised to inhabit the New Jerusalem (1 Cor. 15:24).

[31]The translation "mansions" (KJV) is misleading in light of the modern connotation of the word. Morris suggests "permanent residences" as a translation (p. 638).

His love. Jesus also says, "I am coming again" (John 14:3, author's translation). Where a future verb form is expected He uses a present tense to indicate the certainty of His return,[32] and by adding "again" he suggests another time (not "times") than the first. He continues the promise with "I will receive you" (author's translation), and in changing to the future tense He reinforces the force of the present tense of ἔρχομαι (I am coming) by contrast. Again the personal element is introduced with "to Myself." Although He has prepared a place, we are not seen as going to the place as much as going to the person. The aim of His return is that we may both be His and be where He is.[33]

Our going to be with Him at His rcturn facilitates the believer's experience of the heavenly vision (1 John 3:2-3; cf. John 17:24). Although our future as God's children is not fully manifest, we do know that "when He appears, we shall be like Him" (1 John 3:2).[34] "Be like" carries the idea of "resemble" (cf. Phil. 3:21), while the final clause of verse 2 gives the reason for the resemblance. The purpose Christ has in mind in having us with Himself is that we may behold His glory (John 17:24), and in order for us to see Him as He is in His glory our conformation to His image must be complete (cf. Rom. 8:29; Col. 3:4).

[32]Westcott is most certainly wrong in seeing the present tense as signifying continual comings (B.F. Westcott, *The Gospel According to St. John: The Authorized Version with Introduction and Notes,* p. 201). As Blass and Debrunner note, "In confident assertions regarding the future, a vivid realistic present may be used for the future" (F. Blass and A. Debrunner, *A Greek Grammar of the New Testament and Other Early Christian Literature,* p. 168). Similarly, N. Turner writes, "Concerning the *Futuristic* use of the *Present,* Moulton suggested that these presents differed from the future tense 'mainly in the tone of assurance which is imparted'; they are confident assertions intended to arrest attention with a vivid and realistic tone or else with imminent fulfilment in mind. . . . It is oracular sometimes in class[ical] Greek (e.g. Hdt 8, 140) and so it is not surprising that it is used so much in the NT of the Coming One, with the verb ἔρχομαι" (J. H. Moulton, *A Grammar of New Testament Greek,* 3:63).

[33]The use of ὅπου (where) shows that this is not a reference to such a coming as Pentecost. Other commentators associate this passage with the idea of Christ's coming for His own when we die, but then we go to Him. In John 14:23 Jesus uses the same verb in the future tense to refer to a time when believers will be indwelt by Father and Son and also uses μόνη (abode) for the only other time in the New Testament. A comparison of the two passages shows that 14:23 refers to the Godhead coming *to* the believer, whereas 14:3 speaks of Christ coming *for* him. John 14:23 is fulfilled in this age and John 14:3 in the age to come.

[34]"When" captures the sense here better than "if," for the uncertainty implied in ἐάν relates to the time, not the fact.

In turn, everyone who has this hope[35] of seeing Him as He is purifies himself. That is, by keeping this heavenly vision in mind one is led to the action of continuous self-purification.

At the very close of the Apocalypse, after completing his description of the end-times, John addresses himself once more to believers of this age in their own spiritual milieu by way of a divine charge (Rev. 22:6-21). The charge is divided into three parts by the repetition of the words, "I am coming quickly" (Rev. 22:7, 12, 20) as a sort of refrain. Thus the book closes with the promise of the joyful anticipation of His coming ringing in our ears. The eager response of John should likewise be ours: "Come, Lord Jesus."

b. The second facet of His coming is set forth in Revelation 1:7.[36] It is noted that on this occasion His coming will be public knowledge, since all will see Him, although the precise moment of His return will not be known until the moment He arrives (Rev. 16:15). In light of Revelation 3:10-11,[37] which precedes Revelation 19:11 ff. by seven years, it seems that this coming is a posttribulational event, whereas the event described in John 14:2-3 and 1 John 3:2-3, is pretribulational. The statement found in Revelation 16:15 is parenthetical within the bowl judgments; so it, too, relates to the coming to earth of Revelation 19. All believers, whether church saints or Tribulation saints, are to be ready for His return with a house that is in order.

4. *Judgment.* In the New Testament, the believer's judgment is referred to as the βῆμα (judgment seat) of God (see Rom. 14:10) and of Christ (see 2 Cor. 5:10). The term simply refers to a raised platform reached by steps.[38] It was originally used as a place for the deliverance of orations in Athens and was frequently used of the tribunal of a Roman magistrate.[39] The tribunal was the court of justice where the tribune, an official of ancient Rome whose duty it was to protect the

[35]This is not merely hope in Him but hope ἐπ' αὐτῷ (set upon Him [1 John 3:3, author's translation]). Biblical hope relates to a person, not a place or an event. Also, it involves a certainty ("we shall see Him" [1 John 3:2]), not a wistful longing.

[36]See pp. 190-92 for discussion of this passage.

[37]See pp. 168-72 for discussion of this passage.

[38]As, for example, the platform (on which the altar stood) in front of the nave in basilica style churches of the Byzantine period.

[39]G. Abbott-Smith, *A Manual Greek Lexicon of the New Testament,* p. 80. A New Testament example of this is found in John 19:13.

plebians from the patricians, defended the people. Without using the term itself, John develops this concept both negatively and positively as it relates to the believer's reward in the end-times.

Jesus the Savior will likewise be the judge of believers (John 5:22, 27; see p. 225), and His general aim in judgment is that they might be with Him to behold His glory (John 17:24).

a. In order that the believer may move appropriately toward that moment, John gives several means that will lead to desirable ends at that day. By abiding in Christ, the Christian will have confidence[40] when He appears and will not shrink from Him in shame (1 John 2:28; cf. Rev. 16:15). Abiding in Him (and He in us) perfects love with us, and the end is as above: "confidence in the day of judgment" (1 John 4:17). The reason is that our standing is the same as His, since we are in Him. The third means urged upon us is that we "watch" ourselves (2 John 8; cf. 1 John 3:3), that the effects of our service may not be lost.[41]

b. Rather than describe this time as a *βῆμα*, John calls it the "marriage of the Lamb" (Rev. 19:7). Revelation 19:8 makes it clear that the figure is intended to signify the time of reward for the Lamb's bride as He provides for her special wedding garments (cf. Isa. 61:10). The term "bride" is intended to encompass all the glorified saints from the beginning of God's redemptive purposes until that moment.[42] It cannot be limited here to church saints, which interpretation leads to the anomaly of allowing the metaphor rather than the context to be the determinative hermeneutical factor. While cultural factors need to be considered in interpreting the Scriptures, they should never be given precedence over the literary context. Revelation 21:9-10 identifies the bride, the wife of the Lamb, as the New Jerusalem, while in 21:2-3 the New Jerusalem is seen to be the tabernacle of God among men. When this passage is compared with Revelation 13:6, it is seen that the taber-

[40]*Παρρησία* originally meant "freedom of speech" and then came to mean "boldness" or "confidence," as here, denoting the "absence of fear which accompanies freedom of speech" (Abbott-Smith, p. 347).

[41]The writer to the Hebrews seems to be referring to the same concept when he says, "Pursue . . . the sanctification without which no one will see the Lord" (Heb. 12:14).

[42]In addition to the reasons for this conclusion given above, it should be noted that the term "bride" is not used of the church, as claimed by many dispensationalists, although the figure of Ephesians 5:22-33 is certainly a bride-figure. Here in Revelation, however, the term encompasses a larger group.

nacle of God is the equivalent of the glorified saints ("those who dwell in heaven").[43] The striking thing about verse 8, however, is that the wedding garment that is given to the bride, which by its description is intended to be a garment of honor, is made of the saint's own deeds of righteousness (cf. 2 Cor. 5:10). Today we are weaving the clothing we will wear for eternity. The beatitude of Revelation 16:15 takes on greater significance in light of this event. There is a very pragmatic reason why one should be alert and care for his garments now: namely, in order to avoid the shame of moral nakedness then.

A second beatitude of reward is found in this same context (Rev. 19:9). It is addressed to all who are invited to the Lamb's marriage supper (cf. Luke 14:15). This could very well be the same group as is encompassed by the term "bride"; but if the significance of the figure is pressed, one would say that this second beatitude may be addressed to the saints who, although they have access to the New Jerusalem, are apparently citizens of the new earth and may be designated as non-glorified (Rev. 21:24-27). Obviously, to be involved in the wedding or the dinner of celebration is a distinct honor and mark of the Lamb's approval.

The final beatitude of reward is addressed to the ones who wash their robes (and make them "white in the blood of the Lamb" [Rev. 7:14]). As such they will have right to the tree of life, with its various benefits (Gen. 2:9; 3:22-24; Rev. 22:2; cf. Ezek. 47:12), and access to the city (Rev. 21:27).

Several specific references to reward are also made by John. The sounding of the seventh trumpet, which in a sense is the beginning of the end (cf. Rev. 10:5-7), will signal that the time for giving reward has come (Rev. 11:18).[44] Three groups are named as recipients of reward,

[43]Furthermore, to assume that because there is reference to a "bride" in Revelation 19:7 it ipso facto means "church" is purely gratuitous. It does not follow that because John the Baptist employed a marital figure to describe *his* relationship to Christ or because Paul likens the believer's relationship to Christ to that of husband and wife that John's statements in the Apocalypse refer to the same thing. Some link between these various passages, which does not seem to exist, must be supplied before such a correspondence can be established.

[44]Revelation 22:12 seems to contradict this by associating reward with Christ's return, which idea the order of Revelation 19:7-11 seems to support. This apparent contradiction may be resolved by recognizing that Revelation 22:12 probably refers to the judgment of those yet living on earth when Christ comes again.

but exact identification in each case is uncertain. "Thy bond-servants the prophets" is no doubt a reference to those who have been God's special spokesmen, and there does not seem to be any reason to restrict them to any particular period of history. They will probably include Old Testament (Amos 3:7; Zech. 1:6), New Testament (1 Cor. 14:1, 3, 5), and Tribulation (Rev. 11:3) prophets. As suggested above, "the saints" often refers to believers in general, but in this context it may well have Gentile believers in view. The third group, "those who fear Thy name," may be Jewish Christians, since *godly* Jews throughout history have considered themselves the people of The Name.[45]

The substance of the reward is described in Revelation 21:1-7. It is stated (v. 7) that the "overcomer" will inherit certain things, and the items enumerated in the context include a dwelling place with God, tearless eyes, deathless years, the absence of sorrow and pain, spiritual satisfaction without cost, and a sort of miscellaneous category that encompasses everything stated and unstated: all things made new.

Finally, there is a sense in which reward may be diminished or even lost (2 John 8). By a failure to "watch" oneself, that is, by careless living and ministry, one may lose what he has accomplished and not receive his full reward. While "each man's praise will come to him from God" (1 Cor. 4:5), some will receive less praise than others.[46]

5. *The Kingdom of God.* The idea that the Kingdom of God may take very concrete and tangible form rather than be a romanticized, spiritual never-never land has been attacked in various ways. Some scholars,

[45]On the basis of a misinterpretation of Leviticus 24:16 the Jews have superstitiously refused to speak God's memorial name, *Yahweh,* from some time well before the Christian era. Consequently, they developed many surrogates such as *heaven* (e.g., 1 Macc. 3:18-19; 4:40; Matthew 3:2, "kingdom of heaven" for "kingdom of God"); or *Adonai,* which they say when reading the tetragrammaton in the Bible; or *Ha Shem* (The Name), by which they often refer to God in public conversation even in modern Hebrew. See the brief discussion in J. Bright (*A History of Israel,* p. 450). Also note that the cardinal theological proposition of Judaism is found in the Shema, "Hear, O Israel! The LORD [Yahweh] is our God, the LORD [Yahweh] is one!" (Deut. 6:4).

[46]Paul develops the same concept of differences of reward in 1 Corinthians 3:12-15. Note well that this is not to be confused with the partial rapture theory that bases one's participation in the rapture of the church on a legalistic formula. The rapture is not to be confused with the believer's reward. 1 Corinthians 15:51 and 1 Thessalonians 4:13-17 indicate that all believers of this age will be raptured.

wanting to completely internalize the concept and see it as an exclusively mystical experience, rely strongly on Luke 17:21, where the Lord says, "the kingdom of God is within you" (KJV).[47] This is to ignore the many passages that indicate a future earthly form of the Kingdom with real-life circumstances in many ways parallel to what we experience today (with some notable differences, such as an absolutely righteous ruler—see below). Other interpreters, convinced that all God's promises to Israel have been transferred to and are being fulfilled in the church, see the church as the only form of the Kingdom this side of eternity.[48] In this way, the Kingdom can be fulfilled "spiritually" without there having to be an earthly millennial Kingdom.

The theological reasoning that leads one to such conclusions as these is deeply rooted in certain presuppositions that have developed into extensive theological systems. It is not the purpose of this study to deal with these questions, but one issue that this kind of thinking assumes must be addressed. It seems to be a common assumption of those who hold some form of the viewpoints briefly described above that the Kingdom of God cannot be "spiritual" in taking an earthly, or Messianic, form. There seems to be a holdover from the ancient Greek philosophy that views the mind (spirit) as a good and pure thing and matter (things material) as evil. The most basic and damaging objection to this line of thinking is theological. From the beginning to the end of the Bible, God is set forth as the creator of all things, including the earth. He is the one who has joined the material and the immaterial in the high point of His original creative work: man. By the same token, He will demonstrate righteousness in the earth in a yet future form of the Kingdom of God on earth.

This is neither to deny that there is an intangible and internal aspect of the Kingdom of God nor to deny that the church is a part of His Kingdom. It is to deny the validity of the thinking that rejects a future earthly form of the Kingdom on purely dogmatic grounds that are

[47]The Greek text actually reads *ἡ βασιλεία τοῦ θεοῦ ἐντὸς ὑμῶν ἐστιν*, and the *ἐντός* may better be translated "in your midst" (NASB) or "among you."

[48]Another variation of the view that Israel has forfeited all rights to God's covenant promises sees the Kingdom as a purely heavenly thing, with the throne of David being equated with the throne of God in heaven.

based on an arbitrary allegorical hermeneutic.

In all likelihood, the Kingdom-of-God concept first surfaced in a tangible way out of Israel's covenant relationship with God.[49] The implications of the covenant relationship are certainly not limited to God's relationships with the nation Israel. In the New Testament the idea of God's people, whether conceived of in a national or in a personal sense, being within the sphere of His sovereignty is extended to all who have a covenant relationship with Him, whether it be through the old or new covenant. While the spheres of sovereignty vary (with Israel in the past and future, it is national; with the individual believers today, it is personal; with all submissive intelligences in the future, it will be eternal), they involve an extension of the rule of God, who is spirit, over the realm of man. Thus, in one sense at least, every manifestation of the Kingdom of God is spiritual.

Another item of introduction should be considered before we examine the two future forms of the Kingdom of God separately. This has to do with the relationship between the Messianic, or millennial, form of the Kingdom and its eternal form. While the Messianic Kingdom certainly looks back into history, in the sense that it is intimately linked with God's covenant promises to Israel in the Old Testament, for it is their ultimate fulfillment, it also looks forward to the consummation of all things in the eternal Kingdom of God. The Millennium is stage one, the preparatory stage, of the two-stage future manifestation of the Kingdom. It cannot be denied that there is a transition from one stage to the other as Satan is finally defeated, the lost are judged, and the present heaven and earth are supplanted by the new heaven and earth, but the continuity of the bliss of the saints continues without major interruption. This seems to be supported by Isaiah 65, where in an obviously millennial passage the new heaven and earth are mentioned.

A final matter involves the chronological relationship between the

[49]"The fact that the covenant follows the pattern of a suzerainty treaty is of profound theological significance. Through solemn oath the Israelite tribes accepted the overlordship of the all-powerful God who had delivered them and, as his vassals, engaged to live under his rule in sacred truce with one another in obedience to his stipulations.... .

. . . The covenant was Israel's acceptance of the overlordship of Yahweh. And it is just here that that notion of the rule of God over his people, the Kingdom of God, so central to the thought of both Testaments, had its start" (Bright, p. 149).

Millennium and the New Jerusalem. Should the New Jerusalem be viewed as coterminus with the Millennium as well as with eternity? Some scholars[50] have held that the New Jerusalem comes down and hovers between heaven and earth during the Millennium, thus providing a residence for the glorified saints, who will be reigning with Christ. It will then depart during the Great White Throne Judgment and will reappear and descend to the new earth in the eternal Kingdom. This explanation is based on an interpretation of Revelation 21 that claims that verses 1-8 relate to eternity while verses 9 ff. relate to the Millennium.[51] This, however, seems to be more eisegetical than exegetical.[52] The text makes much more sense if it is allowed its expected progression from old earth to New Jerusalem and new earth. Thus, the chronology that will be assumed below sees the New Jerusalem as following the Millennium and not being even temporarily parallel with it.

[50]E.g., J. Dwight Pentecost, *Things to Come;* John F. Walvoord, *The Millennial Kingdom.*

[51]Charles C. Ryrie, *Biblical Theology of the New Testament,* p. 362.

[52]The only apparent reasons for the unusual chronology suggested by Pentecost, Ryrie, and Walvoord seem to be theological. On the one hand, they assume that the presence of the bride (Rev. 21:9) is to be equated with the presence of the church, which their system will not allow in the Millennium. Consequently, they must move this into the future. If there is any reference to the millennial period, for which their system also calls, it must be later in Revelation 21, where there is no reference to the bride. As shown on p. 232 and in footnote 43, p. 233, however, the equation of the bride and the church is purely gratuitous. On the other hand, Pentecost, Ryrie, and Walvoord assume that glorified beings cannot live together with nonglorified beings; and since resurrected saints will reign with Christ during the Millennium, they will therefore need an abode somewhere other than earth. They then deduce that the New Jerusalem must be in existence during the Millennium, so that the glorified beings can live separately from the nonglorified beings, rather than allow the text to speak for itself on the basis of a normal application of the canons of hermeneutics. From this point it is but a short step to finding all kinds of items in Revelation 21 to support their idea. Such an approach, however, is to do theology backwards. Furthermore, the proposed problem does not really demand this kind of solution. The intermingling of glorified and nonglorified beings is not without precedent in the New Testament. Following His resurrection our Lord mingled with men prior to His ascension without causing any major problems. He did have a glorified body, since it was not bound by the normal conventions and limitations of our space-time existence. Furthermore, both the glorified Christ and glorified saints will meet with nonglorified beings all during the Millennium, and if any contact at all is sustained between the two groups an argument for a special abode loses its urgency.

a. The aspect of the future Kingdom of God that is Messianic, or millennial, is given limited but significant attention by John. The place is "the earth" (Rev. 5:10), the ruler will be Christ (Rev. 20:4), and the duration of the Kingdom in this form will be one thousand years (Rev. 20:4, 6).[53] The moral setting is given in Revelation 20:1-3 as the binding of Satan is described. Since the beast and false prophet, together with their adherents, have already been judged (Rev. 19:17-21), nearly as idyllic an earthly setting from a moral standpoint as can be attained short of a complete replacement of one order with another is provided, as is also true of the final stage of the Kingdom (Rev. 21:1—22:5).[54] In addition to those who actually live on the earth during this period, there will be another large group of individuals associated with Christ in the millennial government. They are identified both internationally, as coming from among all peoples of the earth (Rev. 5:9), and interdispensationally, as coming from every period of God's administration of history (Rev. 20:6 indicates that all those who are raised in the first resurrection will be involved; cf. 1:6; 20:4).[55] To be thus involved with Christ one must meet two qualifications: he must be redeemed by the blood of the Lamb (Rev. 5:9) and be raised from the dead (Rev. 20:4, 6).[56] These redeemed and resurrected saints will perform a dual function as prince-priests (Rev. 5:10, 20:6; cf. 1:6). Although John nowhere spells out the details of these roles, the title "priest" and the action "reign" suggest some kind of worship activity that has administrative responsibilities attached to it.

b. The final and eternal form of the Kingdom of God is given much more extensive attention by the apostle. First of all, he gives much detail

[53]The fact that the thousand-year figure is repeated five times in the course of six verses (20:2-7) points to the strong suggestion that it is no mere symbolic number; rather, it refers to a literal millennium.

[54]This of course is exactly the picture given by the Old Testament prophets in such passages as Isaiah 2:4; 9:4-7; 11:1-9; 14:3-6; 35:1-10; 54:13; 55:12; 65:20; and Zechariah 8:11-12.

[55]See pp. 228-29 for discussion of the first resurrection. Also note that as resurrected saints these individuals are beyond the reach of death and the second death and are thus suited for longevity of service.

[56]The primary point here seems to be that of glorification, which for most believers will come through resurrection but for some will come through rapture while they are yet living (see 1 Cor. 15:51-57).

about the place and its setting.[57] The primary figure he uses to describe this future Kingdom is that of a city (Rev. 21:2) named New Jerusalem, because it is of the new order rather than the old (contrast with Rev. 11:8) and yet has continuity of significance with old Jerusalem, which also is the city of our God; which is "holy," in contrast to most cities, which are centers of wickedness; which is "out of heaven" rather than of the earth (cf. Heb. 12:22); which is "from God" rather than being the product of man's handiwork (cf. Heb. 11:10); and which is radiant as a bride on her wedding day, in contrast to the filthy, blighted, depressed, and often morally decadent cities of man (cf. Heb. 10:16; John 14:3). This city is related to a new heaven and a new earth, which have replaced the present heaven and earth, and so it is in a pristine setting (Rev. 21:1; cf. 20:11).

The second major figure used to describe this final phase of the Kingdom is that of a bride (Rev. 21:9-11*a*). This seems to give emphasis to the moral makeup of the Kingdom, since she is described as having the "glory of God." As a bride, the Lamb's wife, she is the tabernacle of God, composed of all the glorified saints (Rev. 21:2-3).

John next takes these two figures and combines them as he describes a city bedecked as a bride. Her beauty and size are set forth in Revelation 21:11*b*-21. She will be 1,500 miles square and high;[58] she will be walled with perpetually open gates, which provide unbroken access (cf. 21:25); and she will have a twelvefold foundation named for the apostles. The beauty of the city is likened to various precious and semiprecious stones and metals, with the overall visual impact being that it is made of gold so pure that it is transparent as glass. She will be crowned with a radiant tiara formed by the glory of God, which lightens the city (Rev. 21:23; cf. 21:25; 22:5; Isa. 60:19-20). Her center of worship will not be a building but the persons of God and the Lamb (Rev. 21:22).

[57]It must be borne in mind that in this material John is describing something that is beyond the experience of the unglorified saints who read his statements. Furthermore, what he saw in his vision was sublime, but the only analogies he could use were from the experience of his readers and himself. Consequently, he repeatedly uses similies, as is indicated by the repeated use of ὡς (as) and ὅμοιος (like) in Revelation 21:1—22:5.

[58]If one were to place such a city on the present earth where Jerusalem is located, it would stretch north to the Black Sea, west to Greece, south to Ethiopia, and east to Iran. It would be nearly three hundred times higher than Mount Everest.

Her needs for both physical and spiritual sustenance will be met with an endless supply of drink (Rev. 22:1), food (22:2; cf. Ezek. 47:12), and health care (22:2). There will be no crime, evildoing, or curse in the city (Rev. 21:27; 22:3*a;* cf. Zech. 14:11), and the center of authority will be identified with the center of worship (Rev. 22:3; cf. 21:22).

Finally, the citizens of the Kingdom and their activities are noted. The repetition in Revelation 21:3 of statements indicating God's presence in the midst of His own people[59] gives great emphasis to the intimate relationship He will maintain with them. They will be His tabernacle, the place of His abode (cf. Rev. 13:6; 7:15; John 1:14; contrast with 2 Chron. 6:18). They will be His people (cf. Lev. 26:11-12; Ezek. 37:27), and God *Himself* shall be with them. He will give tender, personal attention to their needs by drying every tear (Rev. 21:4; cf. 7:17), abolishing death (cf. Isa. 25:8), and removing every occasion for sorrow and regret. They are reminded that God's promises to them are validated (γέγοναν [they are done] [Rev. 21:6])[60] by His own character, which is trustworthy and veracious (Rev. 21:5*b;* cf. 22:6), complete —τὸ Ἄλφα καὶ τὸ Ὦ (the Alpha and the Omega) (Rev. 21:6*b*), and eternal (Rev. 21:6*c;* cf. 22:13, which adds "the first and the last," indicating His exclusiveness and uniqueness in light of Isa. 44:6). These promises, which He guarantees on His own recognizance, include complete satisfaction as a gift (Rev. 21:6*d;* cf. 7:16), an eternal inheritance (Rev. 21:7*a*), and a reciprocal Father-son relationship that defies comprehension (Rev. 21:7*b*). While false class distinctions will be nonexistent in the heavenly city,[61] a sharp distinction between believer and unbeliever will be maintained. Only those whose names are recorded in the Lamb's book of life will be citizens of or even entrants into the

[59]Both σκηνή (tabernacle) and σκηνόω (dwell) are used in the verse; μετά (among) is repeated three times; and the possessive genitive of αὐτός (them, they) in reference to God's people occurs three times if the longer reading, which includes αὐτῶν θεός (their God) at the end, is allowed.

[60]The Nestle text reads γέγοναν. The Textus Receptus has γέγονεν (it is done).

[61]This is supported by the fact that all these promises are addressed to the saints without discrimination or qualification. Even the figurative description of the city confirms the lack of false class distinctions, for only one street is included in the city (Rev. 21:21), allowing for all to live on "Main Street." Other distinctions of a divinely determined and thus legitimate nature will be maintained, however, as may be seen in Hebrews 12:22-24 and the several rewards passages (see pp. 232-34).

city (Rev. 21:27; cf. 21:8; 20:12, 15; 13:8; 17:8).[62]

Contrary to popular opinion, the inhabitants of the New Jerusalem will not be inactive retirees who while away their days by flitting from cloud to cloud. Instead, they are described as δοῦλοι: bondservants submissive to their Master's will. Their service will take the form of worship[63] and reigning under the ultimate sovereignty of God and the Lamb (cf. Rev. 22:3, 5). While the statement "and they shall reign forever and ever" may simply be another way of saying "and they shall live like kings," in light of the purposiveness of all the other programs of God it would seem that there is more involved. We are not told over whom or what we shall reign; but it must be remembered that in addition to the Holy City with its millions, there will be the new heaven and new earth to be administered.

[62]While a verse like Revelation 21:8 may at first glance appear to be an intrusion into an otherwise positive description, the note struck here is not discordant at all. It provides the counterpoint to the theme of glory that is being developed, a black backdrop for the jewel being described (cf. 21:11). Thus the elective love of God is given depth and significance (rather than being seen as one-dimensional, bland, and capricious, as some persons would by their universalism understand it).

[63]The verb in Revelation 22:3*c* is λατρεύω (serve). It is always used in the New Testament of divine service.

XVI

The Future and Spirit Beings

Generally speaking, angelology is given rather short shrift in most theologies. In one sense this is understandable, since the general subject of angels is relatively unimportant in the whole gamut of theology. On the other hand, since the Scriptures portray the epitome of moral evil as being personally embodied in an angel, and since much of God's providential governing of the world is related to angels, the subject should probably receive more attention than it does.

John has a good deal to say about angels, both fallen[1] and unfallen, and nearly all of it relates to the eschaton. Much of the information about angels has been dealt with in earlier sections treating the world-system and the future of Israel and the nations. Consequently, certain items that would normally occur in a full treatment of Johannine angelology and satanology will not be repeated in this chapter.

A. Satan and His Angels.

1. *His counterfeit kingdom.* Satan's desire to build a kingdom similar to, and with a view to the supplanting of, God's Kingdom is repeatedly taught in the Bible. The various spheres of his sovereignty include the demon world, the world-system (*κόσμος*), of which all the unbelieving are a part, and the as yet future manifestations in

[1]In this study, I am taking the view that demons and fallen angels are identical beings, with the difference in terminology (*δαιμόνιον* [demon—e.g., Rev. 9:20] and *ἄγγελος* [angel—cf. Rev. 12:7]; see also *πνεύματα ἀκάθαρτα* [unclean spirits—Rev. 16:13]) simply pointing to different functions or characteristics of the same creatures.

Babylon (the great harlot) and in the kingdom of the beast.

a. As Satan's kingdom comes more into the open in the end-times, it will become apparent that even here he is attempting to imitate God in a twisted and repulsive way. God is a Godhead; and while Satan cannot duplicate this, he does attempt to imitate it. Sometimes this attempt at counterfeit has been referred to as the unholy trinity,[2] in light of Revelation 16:13, where the dragon (Satan), the beast, and the false prophet are associated as a troika who generate a trio of unclean spirits. Roles played by each of these members of the troika also lend credence to comparison with the Trinity, for Satan is repeatedly viewed as the central god-figure, the beast is to be identified as Antichrist, and the false prophet directs all attention to the beast and the dragon (Rev. 13:2, 4, 11–15).

Since the second and third persons of this troika have been considered in chapter 14, the prime focus of attention at this point will be given to Satan. In Revelation 9:11 he is designated as the angel of the abyss, the one who is king over the demonic hordes described in verses 1-10. As he functions in this capacity, his name in Hebrew is "Abaddon" (Destruction) and in Greek "Apollyon" (Destroyer), which names fit perfectly with the activity of the demon-locusts over which he reigns.[3] Many times throughout the Apocalypse Satan is called a dragon (e.g. 12:3, 7, 9; 13:2, 4; 20:2),[4] which name likewise serves to

[2]Some persons object to the use of the word *trinity* in regard to Satan and his associates because of its usage in Christian doctrine. Actually, however, the term may well be more appropriate for describing the unholy trio than it is for describing the true Godhead. A better term for the Godhead is *the Triunity,* because *triunity* suggests oneness in addition to threeness. On the other hand, the word *trinity*—in a secular sense—merely describes threeness without any necessary suggestion of oneness. *Trinity,* then, could be used to underscore the *threeness* of the unholy alliance. Perhaps, though, because of the traditional association of *trinity* with the Godhead, some other term than *trinity* should be used to refer to the devil and his associates. *Trio* or *troika* would serve well.

[3]The picture that is painted in Revelation 9:1-10 is a most fearful one and fits well with other descriptions in Old Testament and apocryphal literature. Locusts are often viewed as a plague or are used to describe the irresistible onslaught of a powerful enemy. See, for example, Exodus 10:12-15; Joel 1:1—2:11, and Wisdom 16:9.

[4]The dragon figure is used frequently in the Old Testament and in other literature of the ancient Near East to describe the enemy of God (or the gods). See, for example, Isaiah 51:9 and the *Creation Epic* of the Akkadians, sometimes called the *Enuma Elish,*

underscore the ferocity of the evil one.[5] That this dragon is said to be fiery red (Rev. 12:3)[6] adds to the terrifying picture already painted. The dragon is very specifically identified in several unmistakable ways by John in Revelation 12:9. He is "the serpent of old,"[7] which is without question a reference to the Garden of Eden (Gen. 3:15); "the devil," whose business is to slander[8] God, His people, and His work (cf. Job 1:6—2:11; Zech. 3:1; Rev. 12:10); "Satan,"[9] who opposes God in all His work (e.g., John 13:27); and the deceiver of the whole inhabited earth (Rev. 20:3, 8, 10; cf. 13:14; 19:20).

b. Several characteristics of Satan's kingdom should be noted, for although it may on occasion have a veneer of respectability, John strips away that veneer. In addition to those characteristics alluded to above in connection with the person of Satan, his kingdom is anti-Christ (Rev. 12:14), antibeliever (12:10-17), anti-Semitic (12:13-16), bestial (13:2), demonic (9:14-15; 12:3-4, 7; 16:13-14), and blindly suicidal (20:7-8).[10]

2. *His judgment.* Four facets of Satan's judgment are touched on by John. In each case the sphere of his sovereignty is narrowed further until he is finally cut off from all influence on any of God's creation. First, his judgment at the cross, which becomes the basis for all the judgments that follow, is noted in John 12:31 and 16:11. At this point believers are removed from his "touch"[11] (1 John 5:18). Next, in the middle of the Tribulation he will be thrown down to the earth so that

---

in J. B. Pritchard, ed., *Ancient Near Eastern Texts Relating to the Old Testament,* pp. 60-72, 501-3.

[5]John frequently uses ὁ πονηρός (the evil one) to refer to Satan in his malignant wickedness (John 17:15; 1 John 2:13-14; 3:12; 5:18-19).

[6]The word is πυρρός, from πῦρ [fire], and is found only one other time in the New Testament (Rev. 6:4), where it describes the third horseman of Tribulation judgment and represents war.

[7]The word is ἀρχαῖος, which means "ancient" or "original."

[8]Διάβολος is derived from διαβάλλω, which means "to slander, defame."

[9]The Greek term is a transliteration through Aramaic of the Hebrew שָׂטָן. In all three languages the meaning is "the adversary."

[10]As John indicates elsewhere, sin dulls the senses until man's mind is blinded to the truth (1 John 2:11; cf. John 3:19-20; 2 Cor. 4:3-4). Consequently, rational activity in matters moral and spiritual is not possible for citizens of Satan's kingdom (John 8:47; 14:17; cf. 1 Cor. 2:14).

[11]The word is ἅπτω, which refers to a laying hold on with a view to hostile action.

he will no longer have access to God as the "accuser of our brethren" (Rev. 12:7-10). Now his sphere of influence is narrowed even more so that he will no longer have voice in heaven regarding erring saints (Rev. 12:10; cf. Job 1:6—2:11), and even the heavens and their inhabitants will then have occasion to rejoice over his expulsion (Rev. 12:12*a*). This limitation as to place and time will excite him to great wrath against the earth and sea,[12] and especially against believing Jews who are not protected in the divinely provided wilderness hideout (Rev. 12:12, 17). Third, he will be bound, shut up, and sealed in the abyss (Rev. 20:2-3), which will be his prison (20:7) for the duration of the Millennium. Now the noose is drawn tighter, and for a stated period of one thousand years he will not be able to cause the nations to wander (πλανάω). Finally, in the purposes of God he will be released from his imprisonment,[13] deceive (πλανάω) the nations once again, be summarily defeated, and be cast into the lake of fire and brimstone to be tormented day and night forever and ever (Rev. 20:7-10). Now, at last, his grandiose plans for being "like the Most High" (Isa. 14:14) will be totally overturned and his influence over man and angel will be completely revoked. His punishment will continue without interruption forever.[14]

B. Holy Angels.

1. *Agents of information and communication.* As the term *angel* (ἄγγελος [messenger], from ἀγγέλλω [to announce or report]) suggests, one of the chief functions of the angels of God is to convey special information from God to man. The key verse in John's writings in this regard is Revelation 1:1 (cf. 22:6, 16), where at the very beginning of

[12]At this point he will apparently be aware that he has only "a short time" [ὀλίγον καιρόν] left to fulfill his purposes.

[13]The verb λυθήσεται (will be released) is passive, suggesting God's control over the situation. Satan is permitted to have one final "fling" and thus becomes God's precipitant to separate the ungodly out from among the other inhabitants of earth at the close of the Millennium.

[14]Rather than detract from the glory of the eternal city of God, this fact will enhance it. Even though the lake of fire will be completely separated from the New Jerusalem, it will still be in the same universe as an eternal memorial of the sinfulness of sin and the holiness of God.

the book John informs us that the special information he was to record was brought to him by an angel. The verb used here, together with those used in Revelation 22:6 and 16, helps to illuminate this function. Σημαίνω (as in Rev. 1:1, communicated) means to give specific information; δείκνυμι (as in Rev. 22:6, show) means to show in the sense of exhibit; and μαρτυρέω (as in Rev. 22:16, testify) presupposes the possession of some evidence such as an eyewitness would have. In this particular case the angel not only gives data, but on several occasions he also enables John to see what he is to report (e.g., Rev. 1:10-11; 4:1; 7:1; 10:1; etc.), and on other occasions he gives personal testimony to the veracity of his report (e.g., Rev. 19:9*b*).

Most of the information the angels convey to John is prophetic (Rev. 10:1-11; 19:9-10), and sometimes they even provide an interpretation (Rev. 17:7 ff.). In other instances their ministry is more general in that it is addressed to all intelligences in the universe (Rev. 5:2-3). They are also involved in the effecting of answers to prayer (Rev. 8:3-5).

2. *Agents of judgment.* One of the more particular messenger-functions angels perform lies in the area of judgment, both by way of announcement (Rev. 6:1, 3, 5, 7; 8:2, 6-8, 10, 12, 13; 9:1, 13-14; 11:15; 14:6-11; 15:1, 6-8; 16:1-4, 8, 10, 12, 17; 17:1-18; 18:1-24; 19:17-18) and by way of execution (Rev. 12:7-9; 14:15, 17-19; 20:1-3). On one occasion, at least, they are also instrumental in staying judgment.[15]

3. *Agents of praise.* The Apocalypse is filled with the music of heaven. In the unit composed of Revelation 4-5 alone there are six songs, with several others spread throughout the book. Angels are involved in five of these six songs, and there is a discernible progression and crescendo from individual groups to the joining of two and three choirs until at the end of Revelation 5 the combined choirs of the universe are singing and an antiphonal "Amen" is being rendered by the four living creatures.

The first song, one of pure *adoration* (Rev. 4:6-9), is sung by the four

[15]It must be recognized that in every case they perform what they are bidden rather than independently undertake an action. This fact is indicated, for example, by the angel's rejection of John's impulse to worship him and by his assertion that he is a fellow servant (not δοῦλος [servant] but σύνδουλος [fellow servant]) with John (Rev. 19:9-10; 22:8-9).

living creatures (cf. Ezek. 1:5-10; 10:14).[16] It offers praise, honor, and thanks to God for His perfections of holiness, omnipotence, and eternality and thus is a worship hymn centered in God Himself. The second song, which is a companion to the first and is provoked by it, is not an angelic utterance but fits so integrally into this section that it must be mentioned. It, too, is a song of *adoration,* but it is sung by the twenty-four elders.[17] They ascribe glory, honor, and power to God for His works of creation and providence and thus provide a complement to the song of the living creatures—the latter being in praise of His person and this being in praise of His works.

The next song, which is designated as a new song (cf. Psalms 33:3; 40:3; 96:1-6; 98:1-3; 144:9; 149:1; Isa. 42:10; Rev. 14:3), is sung by these first two groups combined. It is addressed to the Lamb, and its topic is His worthiness to inaugurate the consummation of all things (Rev. 5:8-10). It takes the form of a hymn of *praise* for His works of redemption and sanctification.

In the fourth song, the living creatures and elders are joined by numberless angels (Rev. 5:11-12; cf. 1 Chron. 29:10-13) to sing a song of *honor* to the slain and resurrected Lamb, who is worthy to assume His sovereign rights as Lord of the universe. It involves the ascription to Him of power, riches, wisdom, might, honor, glory, and blessing.

The fifth and sixth songs are actually two parts of a grand cosmic chorale that includes a doxology, or song of *glory,* and an amen that is repeated as a refrain by a quartet from the larger choir (Rev. 5:13-14). The whole universe will reverberate with the combined voices of all created things as they sing blessing, honor, glory, and might to Him who sits upon the throne and to the Lamb.

[16]The passages in Ezekiel seem to support the idea that these creatures are cherubim and thus angelic.

[17]Their identification is very difficult, for no specific information is given regarding their origin. The only clues are the number twenty-four and their function as elders. As elders they are probably representative of some leadership function, and we know that both second-Temple Judaism (e.g., Acts 25:15) and the early church (e.g., 1 Tim. 5:17) designated their leaders as elders. Perhaps Revelation 21:12 and 14 give a clue regarding the number with the reference to the twelve tribes and the twelve apostles. If this line of thought is correct, the twenty-four elders are representative of the two major groups of the redeemed: Israel and the church.

The other three angelic choruses include another doxology (Rev. 7:11-12), which is sung by the angels, the four living creatures, and the twenty-four elders in worship of God. It is about those whom He redeemed from the great Tribulation, and it is preceded and concluded with an amen and includes seven elements of praise, as does the other song sung by this same group (see Rev. 5:11-12). In this case the order is changed and "thanksgiving" is substituted for "riches." Also, there is a song of judgment sung by the angel of the waters (Rev. 16:5-6); it affirms God's righteousness[18] in judging the way He did those who martyred the saints and prophets. The final song of the book (Rev. 19:1-7) is sung by the full choir of heaven and is said to sound like "the voice of a great multitude and as the sound of many waters and as the sound of mighty peals of thunder" (Rev. 19:6). It is a great hallelujah chorus praising God for His true and righteous judgments, His sovereign rule over the universe, and the coming marriage of the Lamb.

"Hallelujah! For the Lord our God, the Almighty, reigns" (Rev. 19:6).

Thus, in stark contrast to Satan and his angels, who will be tormented for eternity in the lake of fire, the angels of God, together with all the redeemed of the ages, will spend eternity praising Him who alone is worthy.

[18]It is interesting to note that on this occasion the angel refers to God both as δίκαιος (righteous) and as ὅσιος (righteously holy).

Epilogue

It should be quite evident from the preceding study that the scope of John's theology cannot be expanded. It begins in eternity past—"In the beginning was the Word"—; it immediately inserts itself into history—"And the Word became flesh, and dwelt among us"—; and, after extensive development, finally ushers us into eternity future—"And I saw a new heaven and a new earth."

But his primary concern is depth rather than breadth. In his gospel he gives extensive treatment to the theology of salvation; and, lest anyone miss the point, he declares, "but these have been written that you may believe that Jesus is the Christ, the Son of God; and that believing you may have life in His name" (John 20:31). From the divine standpoint, all that gives meaning to reality has its roots in eternity past (John 1:1-3); but from the human standpoint, that which gives meaning to life began with the incarnation (John 1:14) and the atonement (John 1:29).

While in his gospel John views salvation as an end, in 1 John it is also seen as a means. This concept is even anticipated in his statement of purpose for the gospel in the last clause of John 20:31: "and that believing you may have *life* in His name" (italics added). First John is the apostle's development of the theology of the Christian life. Here he has a threefold statement of purpose.[1] His desire is that this life may

[1]This threefold statement of purpose is seen in the three appearances of the verb γράφω (write) together with ἵνα (in order that).

involve complete joy (1 John 1:4), covered sin (1 John 2:1), and settled assurance (1 John 5:13).

But *life today* is no end in itself, either. Consequently, John devotes a third and climactic volume to the theology of future things (Rev. 1:1; 22:6). In the book of Revelation he develops the unfolding of the Kingdom of God in manifest form. The slain Lamb (the Savior) is unveiled as the lion of the tribe of Judah, the root of David (the sovereign) (Rev. 5:5-6); the priestly Lord of the churches (Rev. 1:20) is unveiled as the King of kings and Lord of lords (Rev. 19:16). This life is seen to be merely an interlude between the prehistorical glory of eternity past and the posthistorical glory of eternity future. It is a sort of temporal prelude to the symphony of eternity. The message that first began as a cryptic protevangelium in Genesis 3:15, was later introduced into history by a lone voice in the wilderness (John 1:23), and today is announced to the world by the church (Acts 1:8), will in that day be sung fortissimo to the universe (Rev. 19:6) by an innumerable multitude.

When every knee has bowed, every tongue confessed that Jesus Christ is Lord, every wrong has been righted, every sin judged, every hunger satisfied, every thirst quenched, every tear dried, every sorrow comforted, every heartache removed, every pain relieved, every weakness strengthened, every ignorance informed, every covenant fulfilled, every promise kept, doxology will become a way of life as paeans of praise spring spontaneously to the lips of all the creatures of God.

Hark how th' adoring hosts above
    With songs surround the throne!
Ten thousand thousands are their tongues;
    But all their hearts are one.
Worthy the Lamb that dy'd, they cry,
    To be exalted thus;
Worthy the Lamb, let us reply,
    For he was slain for us.
To Him be pow'r divine ascrib'd,
    And endless blessings paid;
Salvation, glory, joy, remain
    For ever on his head!

Thou hast redeem'd us with thy blood
    And set the pris'ners free;
Thou mad'st us kings and priests to God,
    And we shall reign with thee.
From ev'ry kindred, ev'ry tongue,
    Thou brought'st thy chosen race;
And distant lands and isles have shar'd
    The riches of thy grace.
Let all that dwell above the sky,
    Or on the earth below,
With fields and floods and ocean's shores,
    To thee their homage show.
To Him who sits upon the throne,
    The God whom we adore,
And to the Lamb that once was slain,
    Be glory evermore.[2]

[2]Paraphrase of Revelation 5:9-14 from *The Psalter and Church Hymnary,* pp. 375-76.

Bibliography

Abbott, E. A. *Johannine Grammar.* London: A. & C. Black, 1906.

Abbott-Smith, G. *A Manual Greek Lexicon of the New Testament.* New York: Scribner's, 1956.

Aland, K.; Black, M.; Metzger, B.; Wikgren, A., eds. *The Greek New Testament.* New York: A.B.S., 1966.

Aland, K.; Black, M.; Martini, C. M.; Metzger, B.; Wikgren, A., eds. *The Greek New Testament.* 3rd ed. New York: A.B.S., 1975.

Albright, W. F. *From the Stone Age to Christianity: Monotheism and the Historical Process.* 2nd ed., with a new intro. Garden City, N.Y.: Doubleday, 1957.

______. "Recent Discoveries in Palestine and the Gospel of St. John." In *The Background of the New Testament and Its Eschatology,* edited by W. D. Davies and D. Daube. Cambridge: University Press, 1956.

Alford, H. *The Greek Testament.* 4 vols. Boston: Lee & Shepard, 1872.

Arndt, W. F., and Gingrich, F. W. *A Greek-English Lexicon of the New Testament and Other Early Christian Literature.* Chicago: U. of Chicago, 1957.

Barclay, W. *The Gospel of John.* 2 vols. The Daily Study Bible. Philadelphia: Westminster, 1956.

______. *The Letters of John and Jude.* 2nd ed. The Daily Study Bible. Philadelphia: Westminster, 1960.

______. *The Revelation of John.* 2nd ed. 2 vols. The Daily Study Bible. Philadelphia: Westminster, 1960.

Barr, J. *Biblical Words for Time.* 2nd rev. ed. London: S. C. M., 1969.

Barrett, C. K. *The Gospel According to St. John.* London: S. P. C. K., 1962.

______. *The Gospel of John and Judaism.* Translated from the German by D. M. Smith. 1st Am. ed. Philadelphia: Fortress, 1975.

Berger, P.L., and Neuhaus, R.J., eds. *Against the World for the World: The Hartford Appeal and the Future of American Religion.* New York: Seabury, 1976.

Bernard, J. H. *A Critical and Exegetical Commentary on the Gospel According to St. John.* Edited by A. H. McNeile. 2 vols. The International Critical Commentary. 1928. Reprint. Edinburgh: T. & T. Clark, 1962 (vol. 1), 1963 (vol. 2).

Blass, F., and Debrunner, A. *A Greek Grammar of the New Testament and Other Early Christian Literature.* Chicago: U. of Chicago, 1961.

Blidstein, G. J. "Messiah in Rabbinic Thought." In *Encyclopaedia Judaica,* 16 vols. (New York: Macmillan, 1971-72), 11 (1971):1410-12.

Boice, J. M. *The Gospel of John: An Expositional Commentary.* Grand Rapids: Zondervan, 1975.

______. *Witness and Revelation in the Gospel of John.* Grand Rapids: Zondervan, 1970.

Bright, J. *A History of Israel.* Philadelphia: Westminster, 1952.

Brooke, A. E. *A Critical and Exegetical Commentary on the Johannine Epistles.* New York: Scribner's, 1912.

Brown, R. E. *The Gospel According to John.* 2 vols. Garden City, N. Y.: Doubleday, 1966, 1970.

______. "The Paraclete in the Fourth Gospel." *New Testament Studies* 13 (1966-67): 113-32.

Bruce, F. F. *The Epistles of John.* Old Tappan, N. J.: Revell, 1971.

Bullinger, E. W. *A Critical Lexicon and Concordance to the English and Greek Testament.* London: Longmans-Green, 1924.

Bultmann, R. *The Gospel of John: A Commentary.* Translated by G. R. Beasley-Murray. General eds. R. W. N. Hoare and J. K. Riches. Philadelphia: Westminster, 1971.

———. *The Johannine Epistles: A Commentary on the Johannine Epistles.* Edited by R. Funk. Translated by R. P. O'Hara with L. C. McGaughy and R. Funk. Philadelphia: Fortress, 1973.

———. *Theology of the New Testament.* 2 vols. New York: Scribner's, 1951 (vol. 1), 1955 (vol. 2).

Candlish, R. S. *A Commentary of 1 John.* Carlisle, Pa.: Banner of Truth, 1973.

Cassuto, U. *A Commentary on the Book of Genesis.* 2 vols. Translated by I. Abrahams. Jerusalem: Magnes Press, Hebrew U., 1961-64.

Chafer, L. S. *Systematic Theology.* 8 vols. Dallas: Dallas Seminary, 1947.

Charles, R. H. *A Critical and Exegetical Commentary on the Revelation of St. John.* 2 vols. The International Critical Commentary. 1920. Reprint. Edinburgh: T. & T. Clark, 1963 (vol. 1), 1959 (vol. 2).

Clark, G. H. *The Johannine Logos.* Philadelphia: Presby. & Ref., 1972.

Colwell, E. C. "A Definite Rule for the Use of the Article in the Greek New Testament." *Journal of Biblical Literature* 52(1933):12-21.

Cook, S. A.; Adcock, F. E.; and Charlesworth, M. P., eds. *The Cambridge Ancient History.* 12 vols. Cambridge: University Press, 1923-39.

Cook, W. R. *Systematic Theology in Outline Form.* 2 vols. Portland, Oreg.: Western Seminary, 1970.

Cremer, H. *Biblico-Theological Lexicon of New Testament Greek.* Edinburgh: T. & T. Clark, 1954.

Cribbs, F. L. "A Reassessment of the Date of Origin and the Destination of the Gospel of John." *Journal of Biblical Literature* 89(1954): 38-55.

Cullmann, O. *Christ and Time: The Primitive Christian Conception of Time and History.* Translated from the German by F. V. Filson. Philadelphia: Westminster, 1964.

———. *Early Christian Worship.* Translated by A. S. Todd and J. B. Torrance. Chicago: Regnery, 1953.

Dana, H. E., and Mantey, J. R. *A Manual Grammar of the Greek New Testament.* New York: Macmillan, 1955, 1957.

Deissmann, A. *Light from the Ancient East: The New Testament Illustrated by Recently Discovered Texts of the Graeco-Roman World.* Translated from 4th German ed. by L. R. M. Strachan. New York: Harper, n.d.

Didache. In *The Apostolic Fathers,* translated by Kirsopp Lake, 1: 303-33. 2 vols. The Loeb Classical Library. Cambridge: Harvard U., 1913.

Dodd, C. H. *The Interpretation of the Fourth Gospel.* Cambridge: University Press, 1953.

______. *The Johannine Epistles.* New York: Harper, 1946.

______. *More New Testament Studies.* Grand Rapids: Eerdmans, 1968.

Dods, M. "The Gospel According to John." In *The Expositor's Greek Testament,* edited by W. R. Nicoll, 1:653-872. 5 vols. Reprint. Grand Rapids: Eerdmans, 1970.

Dupont-Sommer, A. *The Essene Writings from Qumran.* Oxford: Blackwell, 1961.

Eichrodt, W. E. *Theology of the Old Testament.* 2 vols. London: S.C.M., 1961, 1967.

Ellis, E. E. *The World of St. John: The Gospel and the Epistles.* London: Lutterworth. New York: Abingdon, 1965.

Field, F. *Notes on the Translation of the New Testament.* Cambridge: Cambridge U., 1899.

Findlay, G. G. *Fellowship in the Life Eternal.* Grand Rapids: Eerdmans, 1955.

Flusser, D. "Second Temple Period." In *Encyclopaedia Judaica,* 16 vols. (New York: Macmillan, 1971-72), 11 (1971): 1408-10.

Gaebelein, A. C. *The Gospel of Matthew.* 2 vols. bound as one. New York: Our Hope, 1914.

Gillquist, P. E. *Love Is Now.* Foreword by S. Wirt. Grand Rapids: Zondervan, 1970.

Godet, F. *A Commentary on the Gospel of John.* 2 vols. New York: Funk & Wagnalls, 1885.

Grant, R. M. *A Historical Introduction to the New Testament.* 1st ed. New York: Harper & Row, 1963.

Gundry, R. H. *The Church and the Tribulation.* Grand Rapids: Zondervan, 1973.

Guthrie, D. *New Testament Introduction.* 3 vols. Chicago: Inter-Varsity. London: Tyndale, 1961-65.

Harrison, E. F. "The Gospel According to John." In *The Wycliffe Bible Commentary,* edited by C. F. Pfeiffer and E. F. Harrison. Chicago: Moody, 1962.

———. "A Key to the Understanding of First John," *Bibliotheca Sacra* 3 (1954):39-46.

———. "Worship." In *Baker's Dictionary of Theology,* edited by E. F. Harrison. Grand Rapids: Baker, 1960.

———, ed. *Baker's Dictionary of Theology.* Grand Rapids: Baker, 1960.

Harrison, R. K. *Introduction to the Old Testament: With a Complete Review of Old Testament Studies and a Special Supplement on the Apocrypha.* Grand Rapids: Eerdmans, 1969.

Hendriksen, W. *New Testament Commentary: Exposition of the Gospel According to John.* 2 vols. Grand Rapids: Baker, 1953.

———. *More Than Conquerers: An Interpretation of the Book of Revelation.* Grand Rapids: Baker, 1952.

Hodge, C. *Systematic Theology.* 3 vols. London: Nelson, 1871-73.

Hodges, Z. C. "Fellowship and Confession in 1 John 1:5-10." *Bibliotheca Sacra* 129 (1972):48-60.

Hort, F.J.A. *The Apocalypse of St. John I-III: The Greek Text with Introduction, Commentary, and Additional Notes.* 1908. Reprint. Minneapolis: James & Klock, 1976.

———. *The Epistle of St. James: The Greek Text with Introduction, Commentary as Far as Chapter IV, Verse V, and Additional Notes.* London: Macmillan, 1909.

Howard, J. G., Jr. "Interpersonal Communication: Biblical Insights on the Problem and the Solution." *Journal of Psychology and Theology* 3 (1975):243-57.

Howard, W. F. *Christianity According to St. John.* Philadelphia: Westminster, 1946.

Hunter, A. M. *The Gospel According to John.* Cambridge: University Press, 1965.

Jacobsen, T. *The Treasures of Darkness: A History of Mesopotamian Religion.* New Haven: Yale U., 1976.

Kaufmann, Y. *The Religion of Israel: From Its Beginnings to the Babylonian Exile.* Translated and abridged by M. Greenberg. Chicago: U. of Chicago, 1960.

Kent, H. A., Jr. "The Gospel According to Matthew." In *The Wycliffe Bible Commentary,* edited by C. F. Pfeiffer and E. F. Harrison. Chicago: Moody, 1962.

Kittel, G., and Friedrich, G., eds. *Theological Dictionary of the New Testament.* 9 vols. Grand Rapids: Eerdmans, 1964.

Kummel, W. G. *The Theology of the New Testament: According to Its Major Witnesses: Jesus—Paul—John.* Translated by J. E. Steely. Nashville: Abingdon, 1973.

Kysar, R. "Background of the Prologue of the Fourth Gospel: A Critique of Historical Methods." *Canadian Journal of Theology* 16 (1970):250-55.

———. *The Fourth Evangelist and His Gospel: An Examination of Contemporary Scholarship.* Minneapolis: Augsburg, 1975.

Ladd, G. E. *A Commentary on the Revelation of John.* Grand Rapids: Eerdmans, 1972.

———. *A Theology of the New Testament.* Grand Rapids: Eerdmans, 1974.

Law, R. *The Tests of Life: A Study of the First Epistle of St. John.* 2nd ed. Edinburgh: T. & T. Clark, 1909.

Lenski, R. C. H. *The Interpretation of St. John's Gospel.* Minneapolis: Augsburg, 1942, 1961.

———. *The Interpretations of I and II Epistles of Peter, the Three Epistles of John, and the Epistle of Jude.* Minneapolis: Augsburg, 1961.

Liddell, H. G., and Scott, R. *A Greek-English Lexicon.* New York: Harper, 1864.

Lightfoot, J. B. *Saint Paul's Epistle to the Galatians: A Revised Text with Introduction, Notes, and Dissertations.* 2nd ed. London and New York: Macmillan, 1866.

Longenecker, R. N. *The Christology of Early Jewish Christianity.* Studies in Biblical Theology, 2nd series, no. 17. Naperville, Ill.: Allenson, 1970.

McClain, A. J. *The Greatness of the Kingdom.* Grand Rapids: Zondervan, 1959.

Macdonald, A. B. *Christian Worship in the Primitive Church.* Edinburgh: T. & T. Clark, 1934.

Manson, W. *The Incarnate Glory: An Expository Study of the Gospel According to St. John.* London: Clarke, 1923.

Mayor, J. B. *The Epistle of St. James: The Greek Text with Introductory Notes, Comments, & Further Studies in the Epistle of St. James.* Grand Rapids: Zondervan, 1954.

Meyer, H. A. W. *Critical and Exegetical Handbook to the Gospel of John.* New York: Funk & Wagnalls, 1884.

Milligan, G. *St. Paul's Epistles to the Thessalonians: The Greek Text with Introduction and Notes.* Grand Rapids: Eerdmans, 1952.

Milligan, W. *The Revelation of St. John.* London: Macmillan, 1886.

Moffatt, J. "The Revelation of St. John the Divine." In *The Expositor's Greek Testament,* edited by W. R. Nicoll, 5:279-494. 5 vols. Grand Rapids: Eerdmans, 1970.

Moody, D. "God's Only Son: The Translation of John 3:16 in the Revised Standard Verson." *Journal of Biblical Literature* 72 (1953): 213-19.

Morgan, G. C. *The Gospel According to John.* Westford, N. J.: Revell, n.d.

Morris, L. *The Apostolic Preaching of the Cross.* Grand Rapids: Eerdmans, 1955.

———. *The Gospel According to John: The English Text with Introduction, Exposition, and Notes.* Grand Rapids: Eerdmans, 1971.

———. *The Revelation of St. John: An Introduction and Commentary.* The Tyndale New Testament Commentaries. Grand Rapids: Eerdmans, 1969.

———. *Studies in the Fourth Gospel.* Grand Rapids: Eerdmans, 1969.

Moule, C. F. D. *An Idiom Book of New Testament Greek.* Cambridge: University Press, 1953.

Moulton, J. H. *A Grammar of New Testament Greek.* 4 vols. Naperville, Ill.: Allenson, 1908-76. Vol. 1, *Prolegomena,* 3rd rev. ed., 1908. Vol. 2, *Accidence and Word Formation,* by W. F. Howard, 1929. Vol. 3, *Syntax,* by N. Turner, 1963. Vol. 4, *Style,* 1976.

Mowinckel, S. *Psalmenstudien.* 2 vols. Oslo: Kristiania, 1922.

Otto, R. *The Idea of the Holy: An Inquiry into the Non-rational Factor in the Idea of the Divine and Its Relation to the Rational.* Translated by J. W. Harvey. New York: Oxford U., 1958.

Pache, R. *The Person and Work of the Holy Spirit.* Translated by J. D. Emerson. Chicago: Moody, 1954.

Painter, J. *John, Witness and Theologian.* London: S. P. C. K., 1975.

Payne, J. B. *The Theology of the Older Testament.* Grand Rapids: Zondervan, 1962.

Pentecost, J. D. *Things to Come.* Findlay, Ohio: Dunham, 1958.

Peters, G. N. H. *The Theocratic Kingdom of Our Lord Jesus, the Christ: As Covenanted in the Old Testament and Presented in the New Testament.* 3 vols. Grand Rapids: Kregel, 1952.

Plummer, A. *The Epistles of John.* London: Cambridge U., 1911.

———. *The Gospel According to St. John: With Maps, Notes, and Introduction.* Cambridge: University Press, 1893.

Pollard, T. E. *Johannine Christology and the Early Church.* London: Cambridge U., 1970.

Pritchard, J. B., ed. *Ancient Near Eastern Texts Relating to the Old Testament.* 3rd ed. with supplement. Translators and annotators, W. F. Albright et al. Princeton: Princeton U., 1969.

The Psalter and Church Hymnary. Rev. ed. London: Oxford U., 1927.

Rainsford, M. *Our Lord Prays for His Own.* Chicago: Moody, 1952.

Ramsay, W. M. *The Letters to the Seven Churches of Asia and Their Place in the Plan of the Apocalypse.* Grand Rapids: Baker, 1963.

Ridderbos, H. N. *The Epistle of Paul to the Churches of Galatia.* The New International Commentary on the New Testament. Grand Rapids: Eerdmans, 1953.

Robertson, A. T. *The Divinity of Christ in the Gospel of John.* New York: Revell, 1916.

______. *Epochs in the Life of the Apostle John.* New York: Revell, 1935.

______. *Word Pictures in the New Testament.* 6 vols. New York: Richard R. Smith, 1930.

Robinson, J. A. T. *Honest to God.* Philadelphia: Westminster, 1963.

______. *Twelve New Testament Studies.* Naperville, Ill.: Allenson, 1962.

Ross, A. *The Epistles of James and John.* The New International Commentary on the New Testament. Grand Rapids: Eerdmans, 1954.

Rosscup, J. E. *Abiding in Christ: Studies in John 15.* Grand Rapids: Zondervan, 1973.

Ryrie, C. C. *The Basis of the Premillennial Faith.* New York: Loizeaux, 1958.

______. *Biblical Theology of the New Testament.* Chicago: Moody, 1959.

______. "The First Epistle of John." In *The Wycliffe Bible Commentary,* edited by C. F. Pfeiffer and E. F. Harrison. Chicago: Moody, 1962.

______. *The Holy Spirit.* Chicago: Moody, 1965.

Sauer, E. *The Triumph of the Crucified.* Grand Rapids: Eerdmans, 1932.

Scott, W. *Exposition of the Revelation of Jesus Christ.* 4th ed. Westwood, N. J.: Revell, n.d.

Scroggie, W. G. *A Guide to the Gospels.* London: Pickering & Inglis, 1952.

Seiss, J. A. *The Apocalypse: A Series of Special Lectures on the Revelation of Jesus Christ.* New York: Munson, 1865.

Shank, R. *Life in the Son: A Study in the Doctrine of Perseverance.* Springfield, Mo.: Westcott, 1960.

Smith, J. B. *A Commentary on the Book of Revelation.* Scottdale, Pa.: Herald, 1962.

Stagg, F. *New Testament Theology.* Nashville: Broadman, 1962.

Stauffer, E. *New Testament Theology.* New York: Macmillan, 1955.

Stevens, G. B. *The Johannine Theology: A Study of the Doctrinal Contents of the Gospel and Epistles of the Apostle John.* New York: Scribner's, 1894.

———. *The Theology of the New Testament.* New York: Scribner's, 1947.

Stone, M. "Judaism in the Time of Christ." Newsletter no. 1, 1973-74, of the American Schools of Oriental Research. Reprinted from the *Scientific American.*

Stott, J. R. W. *The Epistles of John: An Introduction and Commentary.* Grand Rapids: Eerdmans, 1964.

Strack, H. L., and Billerbeck, P. *Kommentar zum Neuen Testament aus Talmud und Midrasch.* Munchen: Beck, 1922-61.

Streeter, B. H. "The Rise of Christianity." In *The Cambridge Ancient History,* edited by S. A. Cook, F. E. Adcock, and M. P. Charlesworth, 11:253-93. 12 vols. Cambridge: University Press, 1923-39.

Swete, H. B. *The Apocalypse of St. John.* London, New York: Macmillan, 1906.

———. *The Last Discourse and Prayer of Our Lord: A Study of John.* London: Macmillan, 1914.

Tasker, R. V. G. *The Gospel According to St. John: An Introduction and Commentary.* Grand Rapids: Eerdmans, n.d.

Temple, W. *Readings in St. John's Gospel.* London: Macmillan, 1952.

Tenney, M. C. *Interpreting Revelation.* Grand Rapids: Eerdmans, 1957.

———. *John: The Gospel of Belief.* Grand Rapids: Eerdmans, 1948.

Thayer, J. H. *A Greek-English Lexicon of the New Testament.* 4th ed. 1901. Reprint. Grand Rapids: Baker, 1977.

Thiessen, H. C. *Introductory Lectures in Systematic Theology.* Grand Rapids: Eerdmans, 1949.

Thomas, W. H. G. *The Apostle John.* Grand Rapids: Eerdmans, 1961.

Trench, R. C. *Commentary on the Epistles to the Seven Churches in Asia: Revelation II, III.* 4th ed. rev. London: Kegan, Paul, Trench, 1886.

______. *Synonyms of the New Testament.* New York: Blakeman & Mason, 1859.

Turner, G. A. "The Date and Purpose of the Gospel by John." *Bulletin of the Evangelical Theological Society* 6 (1963):82-85.

Von Rad, G. *Old Testament Theology.* 2 vols. Translated by D. M. G. Stalker. New York: Harper, 1962.

Vos, G. *Biblical Theology, Old and New Testaments.* Grand Rapids: Eerdmans, 1954.

Walvoord, J. F. *The Holy Spirit.* Findlay, Ohio: Dunham, 1954.

______. *The Millennial Kingdom.* Findlay, Ohio: Dunham, 1959.

______. *The Revelation of Jesus Christ: A Commentary.* Chicago: Moody, 1966.

Weidner, R. F. *Biblical Theology of the New Testament.* New York: Revell, 1891.

Westcott, B. F. *The Epistles of St. John: The Greek Text with Notes and Essays.* Grand Rapids: Eerdmans, 1952.

______. *The Gospel According to St. John: The Authorized Version with Introduction and Notes.* Grand Rapids: Eerdmans, 1954.

Willmering, H. "The Epistles of St. John." In *A Catholic Commentary on Holy Scripture.* New York: Nelson, 1953.

Subject Index

Author Index

Scripture Index

Greek Word Index